Presented To:

_____

From:

_____

Date:

_____

GATEWAY

to the

SEER

REALM

DESTINY IMAGE BOOKS BY BARBIE L. BREATHITT

Hearing and Understanding the Voice of God

So You Want to Change the World?

GATEWAY

to the

SEER

REALM

Look Again *to* See
BEYOND *the* NATURAL

BARBIE L. BREATHITT

DESTINY IMAGE® PUBLISHERS, INC.

P.O. Box 310, Shippensburg, PA 17257-0310

"Promoting Inspired Lives."

This book and all other Destiny Image, Revival Press, MercyPlace, Fresh Bread, Destiny Image Fiction, and Treasure House books are available at Christian bookstores and distributors worldwide.

For a U.S. bookstore nearest you, call 1-800-722-6774.

For more information on foreign distributors, call 717-532-3040.

Reach us on the Internet: www.destinyimage.com.

ISBN 13 TP: 978-0-7684-0305-3

ISBN 13 Ebook: 978-0-7684-8781-7

For Worldwide Distribution, Printed in the U.S.A.

1 2 3 4 5 6 7 8 / 16 15 14 13 12

DEDICATION

I dedicate *Gateway to the Seer Realm* to my loving, godly mother, Nan B. Breathitt. She is the one who encouraged me to always seek God for His wisdom and views on life. She has been my example of a virtuous Proverbs 31 woman. She was a passionate wife whose marriage remained faithful and strong until God called home her beloved Douglas, who was also my best friend.

Mom has always been the unselfish, doting caregiver to those she meets. Through the years, she has opened her home to those in need and adopted them as her own. She always has the best interests of others at heart. As a mother, her wise instructions to her maturing children have been both kind and strong, bringing her family up in the nurture and admonition of the Lord. She and her life lessons guarded my back and kept me from error. My spiritual life would not be on this chosen path if not for her dedicated search for truth and her unfailing love for Jesus, for her family, and for me. As an intercessor, her fervent prayers are perpetually before the throne. Her spiritual gifts and insight have been passed on to both her natural and spiritual children.

Mom, I want to thank you for always being there for me. You taught me to keep looking until I could see life and others through God's eyes of love.

ENDORSEMENTS

Most prophetic training books focus on hearing God and speaking what you hear. Barbie's book is one of the few that actually deals with the ability to see in the spirit. It is packed full of foundational teaching and practical examples of how to develop the seer gift in your life.

Doug Addison
Author, *Personal Development God's Way*
www.dougaddison.com

Barbie Breathitt is as trustworthy and solid as they come. Her faithfulness to the Word of God and to the Holy Spirit has made her a trusted seer before God and among the Church Jesus is building. The hand of God on her life is all the endorsement she really needs. You would do well to both carefully read her words and then take them to heart.

Pastor Don Nori Sr.

Preparations for the great Jewish wedding in Heaven are in their final stages. This is why it is mandatory that you be supernaturally equipped to *only* do what you see the Father doing! Barbie Breathitt's new book will prepare you to walk into this last days anointing.

Sid Roth
Host, *It's Supernatural!* Television
http://www.sidroth.org/

Barbie Breathitt's book, *Gateway to the Seer Realm,* will truly stir you to faith and activation. The eyes of every believer can be opened to see as God sees. You will enjoy Barbie's practical and faith-building teaching and encouragement in this book.

Patricia King
www.xpmedia.com/

CONTENTS

FOREWORD BY JAMES W. GOLL 13

FOREWORD BY CHUCK PIERCE 15

INTRODUCTION..19

Chapter 1   THE WORD REVEALED 23

Chapter 2   THE SEER SEES 43

Chapter 3   VISUAL CONTACT WITH LIGHT 81

Chapter 4   SEERS ARE SHEPHERDS OF GOD'S GLORY........87

Chapter 5   THE PARABOLIC LIFE OF A SEER 105

Chapter 6   THE POWERFUL WEAPON OF PRAYER.............119

Chapter 7   NOTHING IS IMPOSSIBLE WITH GOD 139

Chapter 8   CALLED TO BE CHAMPIONS 153

Chapter 9   KNOWN BY GOD 167

Chapter 10 FRIENDS WITH ANGELS 191

Chapter 11 VISIONS 211

Chapter 12 GODLY WISDOM 237

Chapter 13 PROPHESY LIFE 251

Chapter 14 TRANCES 263

Chapter 15 THE ALL-SEEING HEALER 287

CONCLUDING CHALLENGE 327

FOREWORD
BY JAMES W. GOLL

IT'S TIME TO SEE MORE CLEARLY!

In different periods of time, in both Hebrew and Christian Church history, the Holy Spirit has highlighted a particular theme. It was never hidden in the heart of God, or in the Word of God, but it seems like it was hidden to the understanding of people. Then all of a sudden, a light comes on and people are illuminated with brilliant, amazing, history-changing revelation.

This is what happened when Martin Luther read from the book of Romans, *"...The just shall live by faith"* (Rom. 1:17 NKJV). Piercing revelation broke through the dark ages of the Church world, and the Great Reformation tumbled into existence. It grew into a mighty force that changed the face of Christianity from that point on. We still reap the fruit of that revelation today.

In recent years, the Holy Spirit has been blowing with a fresh wind of enlightenment on the entire dimension of prophetic life and ministry. It was never hidden in the heart of God or in the Word of God, but it was hidden to the hearts of people, waiting for hungry men and women to search out these almost forgotten ways. Even more specifically, the ways of dreams, visions, trances, ecstatic experiences, angelic visitation, interpretation of signs and wonders, and much more are exploding in this generation.

Perhaps I have been one of the pioneer prophetic writers, paving a way that many others are building upon. Such is the case with the life and ministry of Barbie Breathitt. She has gleaned from various forerunners, and the Holy Spirit has developed her into one of the clearest voices we have today in her own right. She is a clear vessel for the Lord.

Gateway to the Seer Realm is one of the most comprehensive books written to date on the various realms of revelation as it pertains to prophetically seeing in the Spirit. Barbie Breathitt combines unique storytelling, depth of scriptural understanding, and experiential truths with one of the highest level gifts of revelatory interpretation I have witnessed today.

Saying it is well written is an understatement. Saying it could be a modern classic is more likely the truth. Time will tell. At bare minimum, it is a great compliment and follow-up to the books on these related subjects that I have composed.

Frankly, I will read and reread this book. It stuns me in its breadth, its width, and the Spirit of wisdom and revelation that rests upon it. The teacher just got taught!

You hold in your hand something I ached for forty years ago. This is true fruit of the convergence of the ages. Well done! Well done!

James W. Goll
Encounters Network • Prayer Storm • Compassion Acts
Author of *The Seer, Dream Language, The Lost Art of Intercession, The Coming Israel Awakening,* and many more.

FOREWORD

BY CHUCK PIERCE

Many times, the Lord uses dreams and visions to speak to us. That is why I feel *Gateway to the Seer's Realm: Look Again to See Beyond the Natural,* by Barbie Breathitt, is so vital for this hour. We are actually in a ten-year season of seeing! There are few people as qualified as Barbie to take us on a journey of understanding the seer realm. She has not only written and taught on interpreting the direction God gives to each of us on a daily basis, but she is also one who sees in a supernatural way.

We are much more visual as a society in the world today. We now live in a *seeing* season. However, I sense that we are a people who miss much of what we should see. Therefore, I hear the Lord saying, *"Look again!"* He wants us to see *beyond*—to see in ways we have not seen! The Lord is saying:

> I am calling you from beyond! You have been held in a place that I am calling you from. I am beyond where you are now. *Come from where you are to beyond! Come from where you are to beyond! Come from where you are to beyond!* For I am marshaling My army, and I am calling you forth. I am causing you to be raised up. I am calling even the dry bones to come together this season. I am calling together and raising up this mighty army. You will go forth

in My name. You will see kingdoms brought down. You will see kingdoms raised up. This is the season and the hour when I am marshaling My army.

In the past I told you to look and look again. But in this season, I am telling you to look, look again, and look beyond. *Look, look again, and look beyond, because* **beyond** *is the fullness of the promise.* Beyond is the clustering that I have sent. Beyond is the positioning. Beyond is the alignment. Beyond is the release. So look, look again, and look beyond!

Go beyond the natural into the supernatural. This is the time to heal and go with signs and wonders following. Beyond is into eternity. *I am going to give you eyes to see the plans of eternity past, present, and future.* I will begin to make a whole picture from the past to the present and to the future.

From the beginning of creation, humanity was created to commune with God. Because God created us with a body, soul, and spirit, we were given a different value from the rest of creation. We were made as spiritual beings. Our human spirits allow us to exercise intelligence, perception, and determination and to make moral choices; and they enable us to exceed above and have dominion over any other creature in the earth realm. This intrinsic worth drives us to know our Creator as well as to know the hope of our calling and the reason we exist.

The spirit is the highest function of our being. It is through our spirits that we commune with the spiritual world. When we open our human spirits and allow the Holy Spirit to come and reside within us, we come into a holy union with our Creator. It is through our human spirits that the Holy Spirit gives us the revelation necessary to accomplish His will on the earth. Because this is an ongoing process, we should expect God to commune with us daily as we seek Him. He longs for us to draw near to Him so we can know His heart and His greatest desires for our lives.

Moses gave us a beautiful example of and reason for why we should be seeking God on a daily basis. In Exodus 29, Moses received revelation on the twice-daily offerings. The day was opened and closed with the gift of worship to and communion with God. Verse 42 says, *"This shall be a continual burnt offering throughout your generations at the door of the tabernacle of meeting before the Lord, **where I will meet you to speak with you"*** (NKJV). What a wonderful principle for us! If we will come before God on a daily basis, He will meet us, join with us, and speak to us.

In His infinite creativity, God can speak to us through any number of ways. He can speak to us as God the Father, as Jesus the Son, and as the Holy Spirit. God can also speak to us through the Word. That is why a Scripture can just seem to leap off the page and cause our day to change. Always remember that the Word of God is living and active (see Heb. 4:12). God can speak to us through other people, as well as His creation (see Rom. 1:20). He can speak to us through experiences and circumstances, through angels, and through His audible voice. And many times, He uses dreams and visions to speak to us.

As you read this incredible book, always remember: Things are becoming *seeable!* There is an opportunity for each of us to see differently! He is determined for us to see in ways we have never seen before. His *eye is* watching over us. Watch with *Him* as the storms of life come and go in this new season. Look deep into every circumstance that comes your way. Allow Him to reveal His plans and purposes through your dreams and visions. *God wants to give you clear vision to see beyond your present state.* Ask God to restore and refresh your vision for your future.

He is saying,

*Let Me touch your eyes and **look again!** You could not see at all. I then touched you. However, you are not seeing clearly. Let Me touch you again! Let Me lift your eyes and cause you to look up! Then, when you relook at the situation you are in, you will see clearly!*

I don't know of a better way to start this journey of seeing than by turning the page and reading what Barbie shares. *Gateway to the Seer Realm* will open a new gate into a realm of seeing spiritually. Go through this gate as you read this book!

Chuck D. Pierce
President, Global Spheres, Inc.
President, Glory of Zion International Ministries, Inc.

INTRODUCTION

The searing desert heat blistered my skin. I lay helplessly drained upon the parched sands. The sun baked my skull. The pain was unbearable. My heart was pounding out of my chest with rapid, wrenching convulsions. Thirst and the lack of water caused my blood to congeal and my veins to collapse. Life was ebbing away. Death was sure. My vision blurred as the cactus and briars formed a tangled cage around me. Dust lined the inside of my parched lips as a fly buzzed annoyingly around my sweat-caked hair.

My mind could no longer distinguish truth from fiction. Visions began to play before my senses. I could hear and feel the presence of life not seen. The ground began to shake, and the sound of pounding thunder muffled through the sand in my ears. An Acrida grasshopper flipped away as all motion and wildlife ceased their movement. I could feel the ground moving. The sound of pounding continued to gain force as it raced toward me. It was a stampede of running horses. Their nostrils flared and manes flew as their hooves pounded the ground with sounds of thunder.

A cloud of noise rumbled through the cloud of dust as the molten monsters crashed through the sparse vegetation, crushing all under their blazing hooves. Their heads were thrown high, and a sense of dire panic drove them in a frenzied flurry across the barren wasteland. I could hear their furious breathing and wretched power as the sheer force of their life burst over the sandy knoll by my head.

A large, rugged man clung to the reins of the team of eight monsters. He leaned into the rushing wind blowing over his rugged figure. He was strong and looked as powerful as the team raging before him. His face was brown and serious. His eyes were focused and determined, as if he was plowing toward his destiny with all the fury and exuberance of the muscled creatures before him.

He wore a mantle of fur. A leather belt crisscrossed his chest. Flames of fire burst from the back of the horses, engulfing the front of the chariot in which he stood. The power and energy of the sight was pure horror. I lay on the ground as if I was dead. My tongue stuck to the back of my teeth as my eyes followed this ensemble over the next hill. Onward they raced until finally they rose into a tornado of twisting wind and dust. The howling sound of the wind was deafening. I clasped my ears to protect them against the crushing pressure. The horses flew without wings and shot upward into the sky. The grizzly man simply stood in the chariot holding the reins and rose in unison with the furious team of horses.

The clouds parted like a rotten potato sack, and instantly the horses shot into the opening. The man followed close behind and emptied into the space between the skies. Then the clouds slammed shut with a brazen thud, and the man and wild horses were gone. The sound of silence deafened me as I listened for an echo of any indication that what my mind had seen was the same visionary encounter; my spirit screamed it was real.

Gawking into the sky, I looked and waited like a woman gone crazy. Finally my eyes drifted downward to the mountainous horizon in the distance. The sound of the desert did not return, but remained silent. No birds or bugs moved. The sand lay where it had lain for centuries. I crawled to my knees by pressing my weight on a rock. I planted my foot on the shifting sand. My eyes caught sight of a tiny glowing twig that had fallen from a burning branch. I could see the flame and smell the burning ember. Just a few feet from the smoldering bush lay a mantle. The mantle had fallen from the mysterious man in the chariot. I watched it land on the sand. I knew it was waiting to be picked up and received by me. *If I can just reach that mantle and take it up, my ordinary life will forever be changed,* I thought.

NATURAL OR SPIRITUAL VISION?

We live in a wonderful world full of colors, sights, and sounds. Carefree children run and play in lush green parks, letting their imaginations prepare them for the future. We see colorful birds and hear their diverse songs. Varied creatures chirp and warble in the bright sunshine, bringing pleasure to both our vision and hearing. How desperate we would be if we were to lose our wonderful senses. We use them every moment of our lives to experience the glorious world around us. Our sight and hearing are of inexpressible value. I would never want to give up or lose any one of my senses, and neither would you.

Now, imagine what life would be like if we were physically blind and deaf and void of any sense. Imagine a world without sight, a world where people are blinded by a dense cloud of darkness. Can you envision a world where a thick veil covered the eyes, making color non-existent? Visualize a dreary world that is bereft of color, vision, spiritual perception, or hope—a dark world without a bright future.

Thankfully, this awful vision is not factual. We can come back to reality. It's easy and natural to open our physical eyes and see the beauty that surrounds us.

The same can be said for our spiritual vision. It is possible to go through life without seeing the glorious world that is ever present, mysteriously tucked into the unseen crevices of the natural world. At times, we have difficulty finding our spiritual eyes and ears. It is as if we are spiritually dead. To truly see, we must have our spirits awakened; otherwise, we continue to live without hearing or seeing the spiritual world. Without waking our spirits, our senses are veiled, dulled to the presence of a world that exists in tandem with the physical world. Our senses are immature because we lack training. We need practice to discern between right and wrong, good and evil.

What would life be like without true spiritual vision? Many people already know. They are not aware of a spiritual kingdom because their senses have not been awakened to recognize its presence. It is possible to develop our spiritual eyes to see beyond the natural scope of our existence. We can remove the veils that blind. We can learn to look again. Our eyes can be opened to the vision that lies beyond the natural—opened to see into the realm of possibilities and beyond into the realm of impossibilities.

Now, imagine what life would be like if we were spiritually blind. Imagine a world without seers, a world where people are blinded by a dense spiritual cloud of darkness.

Chapter 1

THE WORD REVEALED

The prophet Elijah lived during a time when a lot of witch-craft, spiritual darkness, and sexual perversion existed. Jezebel ruled the nation through fear and intimidation. She gathered and groomed false prophets who prophesied her vision and desires. There was a famine for the hearing of the Word of the Lord. When the Word of the Lord is limited or rare, people go into exile and bondage because of their lack of true spiritual knowledge. Honorable men who have an ability to lead are lacking from the populace. People begin to throw off restraints and they reject the ways of God.

When those who see and hear revelation are lacking in leadership positions, evil people erupt unrestrained. God's laws are ignored and become of no effect, unleashing man's chaotic lawlessness rules. An evil vision brings poverty. True spiritual vision releases prosperity. It is in times like these that the Lord enabled the true prophets and seers of God to find clarity and vision from the Lord.

The Lord used Elijah to be an answer to that spiritual famine and to initiate a season of prophetic activity. Elijah's spiritual journey and training took him through many emotional transitions and geographic locations. The challenging things Elijah experienced enabled him to become a *voice*, not an echo or a sound.

At Elijah's first appearance in Scripture, he declared to King Ahab, *"As the Lord, the God of Israel lives, before whom I stand, surely there shall be neither dew nor rain these years, except by my word"* (1 Kings 17:1). Elijah knew that he stood before the Lord God Almighty as His prophetic voice to a nation. Yet Elijah had not developed enough of God's power, presence, or spiritual authority to totally defeat the paralyzing witchcraft that flowed through Jezebel and her false prophets. God devised a series of challenges to equip Elijah. These tests and trials developed his spiritual confidence to know that the mantle God had placed upon him was enough when his confidence remained secured upon God alone.

After Elijah confronted King Ahab, the Lord told Elijah to go east of the Jordan River and hide by the brook, Cherith. Elijah isolated himself with God at Cherith, a place of circumcision, testing, and the cutting away of the flesh. There he was delivered from fear and the reproach of his old life so that he could move by the spirit. In Cherith, Elijah learned to trust God for both his natural provision through the brook and his supernatural provision through the ravens who fed him.

However, the provision in Cherith lasted only for a season. Natural famine and drought bring both physical and spiritual change. They release poverty and death. Eventually the brook that Elijah depended on for natural provision dried up. As there was in Elijah's day, today there has been a famine for the hearing of the word of God. However, God is going to release the word of the Lord through the prophetic voice, just as He did with Elijah.

> *Then the word of the Lord came to him, saying, "Arise, go to Zarephath, which belongs to Sidon, and stay there; behold, I have commanded a widow there to provide for you." So he arose and went to Zarephath, and when he came to the gate of the city, behold, a widow was there gathering sticks; and he called to her and said, "Please*

get me a little water in a jar, that I may drink" (1 Kings 17:8-10).

Next Elijah entered through the gate of Zarephath. Gates represent authority and greater opportunity. Usually gates shut out the enemy and provide safety to those who dwell within. But these gates represented Elijah coming against the fiery gates of hell to gain new authority. *Zarephath* means "place of dying", "the place of refining and smelting metal,"[1] which is needed to form weapons and tools of warfare. He learned to take his authority over the enemy in Zarephath. The wicked Queen Jezebel's father, Ethbaal, ruled as priest and king in this area of Sidon.

God sent Elijah to Zarephath so that a poverty-stricken, pagan widow could provide for him during the famine. He found her gathering sticks for her last meal, which represented her desperation, simplicity, and childlike faith. Children were not allowed to carry fire. The children's fathers provided the fire once the sticks were gathered. Elijah as a Father of Israel came with the same heavenly fire to ignite her sticks as had consumed the sacrifice and altar on the mount. She prepared their meals from the little bit of oil and meal that never ran out because of God's prophetic touch. She gave her all when she trusted the word of the Lord in Elijah. God provided for her and delivered her household from starvation.

Elijah gained his fiery authority through intense warfare in Zarephath. When Elijah recognized who God was in him and who he was in God, the word of the Lord sent him to find and confront King Ahab, who represented Satan's rule.

On his way to locate Ahab, Elijah met Obadiah. Elijah commanded Obadiah to tell Ahab, "I am here!" (This was a much bolder, authoritative stance than Elijah's previous introduction of himself as one who stood before the Lord God of Israel.) Elijah told King Ahab to gather the prophets of Baal and the people of God and meet him on Mount Carmel (see 1 Kings 18:1-19). Elijah then called the people to repentance. The fire of God fell upon a rebuilt altar, consuming the water-soaked sacrifice, along with the wood, stones, and dust. Elijah then commanded the people to seize the prophets of Baal, and he executed them by sword at the Brook Kishon (see 1 Kings 18:20-40). However, although the bodies of the false prophets were destroyed, the spirit of Jezebel's witchcraft and control still reigned.

Part of becoming a seer is learning how to sense things in the spirit realm. Elijah heard the sound of rain in the realm of faith before the sound had manifested in the natural earthly realm. Elijah then said to Ahab, *"...There is the sound of abundance of rain"* (1 Kings 18:41 NKJV). Then Elijah ran to the top of Mount Carmel in an act of faith, where he prayerfully bowed down in a birthing position with his face between his knees. After praying, he commanded his servant seven times, *"Go up now, look toward the sea"* (1 Kings 18:43 NKJV). The seventh time, there was a cloud as small as a man's hand rising out of the sea. Elijah sent his servant to Ahab with this message: *"...Prepare your chariot and go down, so that the heavy shower does not stop you"* (1 Kings 18:44). Then the hand of the Lord came upon Elijah, empowering him to outrun Ahab's chariot.

Elijah was able to destroy the false prophetic vessels, but he could not defeat the spirit behind Jezebel without becoming God's prophetic voice in the world. Jezebel threatened his life, causing him and his servant to retreat to Beersheba, the place where Abraham dug seven wells. Elijah left his servant in Beersheba. He could not go into angelic territory accompanied by anyone. Elijah then journeyed into the wilderness by himself. There Elijah encountered an angel who told him to eat the heavenly food he had prepared for him. The angel appeared to Elijah twice. Each time the angel touched Elijah. The angel also fed Elijah angel's food to supernaturally empower him to do the impossible. The angel's word, touch, and food gave Elijah strength to travel forty days and nights to Mount Horeb (see 1 Kings 19:1-8). Horeb is also known as Sinai, the same place where Moses received the Ten Commandments.

Elijah went into a cave on the mount of God. The word of the Lord came to Elijah there, as a Theophany of Jesus, and asked, *"What are you doing here, Elijah?"* (1 Kings 19:9). Elijah responded,

> *I have been very zealous for the Lord, the God of hosts; for the sons of Israel have forsaken Your covenant, torn down Your altars and killed Your prophets with the sword. And I alone am left; and they seek my life, to take it away* (1 Kings 19:10).

We will meet the same word of the Lord, Jesus—who appeared also to Abraham and Isaac—in the cave, but we will only encounter the Father when we quietly stand on the Rock Jesus. Elijah waited on the rock for God's voice to speak. As he waited in silence, he saw the Lord pass by (see 1 Kings 19:11-13). When the Lord passes by, He is evaluating our progress for promotion. If we have been obedient to the word of the Lord, the Lord will increase the magnitude of the calling, authority, and sphere of influence we possess.

ELIJAH HEARD THE WHISPER

> *Then he came there to a cave and lodged there; and behold, the word of the Lord came to him, and He said to him, "What are you doing here, Elijah?" He said, "I have been very zealous for the Lord, the God of hosts; for the sons of Israel have forsaken Your covenant, torn down Your altars and killed Your prophets with the sword. And I alone am left; and they seek my life, to take it away." So He said, "Go forth and stand on the mountain before the*

Lord." And behold, the Lord was passing by! And a great and strong wind was rending the mountains and breaking in pieces the rocks before the Lord; but the Lord was not in the wind. And after the wind an earthquake, but the Lord was not in the earthquake. After the earthquake a fire, but the Lord was not in the fire; and after the fire a sound of a gentle blowing. When Elijah heard it, he wrapped his face in his mantle and went out and stood in the entrance of the cave... (1 Kings 19:9-13).

As we progress through life, we will experience at least four sounds. The winds of change will blow; our foundations will shake, crumble, and be rebuilt; the fire will fall to consume the chaff and ignite the glory; and after we learn to discern these sounds, the still small voice of the Lord will prevail.

In *hei*—(the still small voice[2] reveals the divine nature, creative power, grace and breath of God found in His names. *Hei* reveals the expanse of God's creation. The Hebrew symbol *hei* is depicted by an open window that allows a heavenly wind or breath to blow in a new prospective. As God's arms are extended to help man in times of need)—there is a silence. The still small voice speaks to our subconscious through a whisper that reveals truth. Think of the prophet Elijah. He experienced a whisper, the sound of a gentle blowing or breath, as compared to the great and strong wind that rent the rocks, shook the earth, and released lightning and fire.

Elijah had encountered the furious wrath of Jezebel. She was determined to murder Elijah just has he had slain four hundred and fifty of her prophets of Baal.

In fear for his life, Elijah had retreated to the safety of a dark cave. He felt as if he had failed God. Elijah prayed, "I have had enough, please take my life Lord, I am no better than my fathers." Twice the angel of the Lord came to touch, comfort, and feed a weary Elijah. When Elijah had consumed the heavenly food, he was empowered to travel forty days and nights to Mount Horeb.

Elijah was used to hearing God's voice manifest in one particular way. He had experienced many spectacular miracles. He saw the fire falling from heaven to consume the offering, water, and stones of the altar. But God wanted to empower and expand Elijah's ability to know Him in the diversity of His many manifold ways. God planned to anoint Elisha with twice the anointing that rested upon Elijah. So God had to expand Elijah's spiritual knowledge so he could impart it to the next generation of prophets and seers.

The word of the Lord came to instruct Elijah while he was discouraged in the cave. The voice of the Lord directed Elijah to move forward and to stand before the Lord as He passed by. The word of the Lord takes many forms; but it is always progressive, it is never stale or stagnant. The word of the Lord can come as a voice, as an angel, as the Lord Jesus, as the written or spoken word coming from someone in our realm of influence. Part of becoming a seer is learning to see, hear, and discern the different ways the word of the Lord comes to us.

The word of the Lord said, "Get out of this cave and go back the same way you came through the desert to Damascus. There you will anoint Hazael as king over Aram. Then anoint Jehu son of Nimshi as king over Israel. Next, anoint Elisha son of Shaphat from Abel Meholah. Train him to be the prophet who takes your place when your spiritual journey in life is fulfilled. Jehu will kill anyone who escapes Hazael's sword, and Elisha will kill anyone who escapes from Jehu's sword." Each valiant man God selected for this unified team had a specific anointing and role to play to bring down the reign of Jezebel.

The divine names of God carry hei; therefore, the Shekinah is present. The Shekinah is the glory of God, a visible

dwelling or manifestation of the presence of God in a luminous cloud that refers to the instances when God showed
Himself visibly—on Mount Sinai (see Exod. 24:9-18) and
in the Holy of Holies of the tabernacle and in Solomon's
Temple.[3] Hei is connected to neshemah, meaning "soul; the
breath of life that God breathed into the first man, Adam;
associated with the vitality of intelligence or (comprehen-
sion) or spiritual perception."[4] It connects and alludes to
shamah, which means "God is present here."

The Prophet Elijah lodged himself in a cave in Horeb
and complained to God, *"...I alone am left; and they seek my
life, to take it away"* (1 Kings 19:10). In response, the incarnate
Word of the Lord came to and then passed by Elijah. Before
we can see the Father, we must see both the written Word
and the living Word, Jesus.

I believe Elijah wrapped his head with his mantle before
he left the cave to meet with God to symbolize that God
was removing his negative mental strongholds of depression
and isolation. God healed Elijah's five natural and spiritual
senses, which are represented in the head. Then the Lord
revealed to Elijah His united team strategy. Elijah was to
anoint Hazael and Jehu as kings. Then Elijah was to anoint
Elisha as prophet in his place because he would be able to
carry a double portion of Elijah's anointing. This alignment
of kings and prophets would create the needed skills and
anointings to take the enemy, Jezebel, out of commission.

> *The Lord said to him, "Go, return on your way to the wil-
> derness of Damascus* [destruction], *and when you have
> arrived, you shall anoint Hazael king over Aram; and
> Jehu the son of Nimshi you shall anoint king over Israel;
> and Elisha the son of Shaphat of Abel-meholah you shall
> anoint as prophet in your place. It shall come about, the
> one who escapes from the sword of Hazael, Jehu shall put
> to death, and the one who escapes from the sword of Jehu,*

*Elisha shall put to death. Yet I will leave 7,000 in Israel,
all the knees that have not bowed to Baal and every mouth
that has not kissed him."*

*So he departed from there and found Elisha the son of
Shaphat, while he was plowing with twelve pairs of oxen
before him, and he with the twelfth* [twelve pair means
double or twenty-four oxen]. *And Elijah passed over to
him and threw his mantle on him.* (This was the same
mantle that had healed Elijah in the presence of
God.) *He left the oxen and ran after Elijah and said,
"Please let me kiss my father and my mother, then I will
follow you." And he said to him, "Go back again, for what
have I done to you?" So he returned from following him,
and took the pair of oxen and sacrificed them and boiled
their flesh with the implements of the oxen, and gave it to
the people and they ate. Then he arose and followed Elijah
and ministered to him* (1 Kings 19:15-21).

Elijah wanted to hear God's voice, so he was looking for
the lightening, thunder, and earthquakes. However, God
manifested Himself in the hei, in the breath, in a whisper
of the still small voice that came to Elijah. The unmovable
voice of God said, "This is the essence of who I AM." We can
know God in this way. God reveals Himself in the silence of a
whisper. So often we expect God to demonstrate Himself in
the audible voice or some undeniable demonstration of His
might and presence. Often, it is in the stillness within that
He begins to speak to us. In that breath of hei is the Shekinah. His presence abides there.

We are waiting on the weightiness of His *kabhodh* glory
to fall upon us. So God connects to our souls through His
Spirit, the same breath of life that God breathed into Adam.
We are able to comprehend His presence in that still voice.
Every living person on earth is wired to be able to hear the
still small voice of God. If God speaks to us or shows Himself

to us in other ways, that is just an added blessing. I want to know God in all of His different dimensions and manifestations. Like Moses, I long to know Him face to face—where He speaks to me plainly and not through a veil of mystery. As we continually hunger for Him, He will reveal more of Himself to us.

Before we become the voice of the Lord, we will experience the sounds of the rain, fire, wind, and earthquake in our lives. The rain will fall. The earth will quake and shake. The wind will blow, and the fire will fall and consume everything that keeps us from the presence of God.

Pentecost released a sound from Heaven like a mighty rushing wind. Fire settled on their heads. Peter gave voice to the presence of the Holy Spirit's latter rain. In life, we have many earth-shattering experiences, but they only change a few lives. When we hear His voice, we will release a revival wind of fire that will change the world just like the apostles did.

Elijah trained his servant, Elisha, to look and see, to listen and hear, and to prophesy the word of the Lord. Then it was time for Elijah to return to Heaven. God sent a heavenly chariot that carried Elijah out of time into the concealed revelation of nothingness or the spiritual expanse of Heaven's eternity. Elijah told Elisha, "...*If you see me* [not the chariot or horses] *when I am taken from you, it shall be so for you* [he would receive a double portion of Elijah's spirit]..." (2 Kings 2:10).

Elisha had to pass many tests and persevere in order to walk in Elijah's double mantle (see 2 Kings 2:1-18). Elijah asked Elisha to stay in Gilgal, the place of cutting, circumcision, and the rolling away of reproach, but he refused. When God removes our past failures and reproach, we must walk through the gates of authority into the new place with God. The failures in our lives do not disqualify us—they are the very things that qualify us for greatness in God.

Elijah moved on to Bethel, the place or house of God, the gates of Heaven. Bethel was a place where people went to seek counsel from God. Elisha followed Elijah to Bethel to learn how to obtain God's counsel. We must follow the leading of the Holy Spirit to the next place of testing to progress spiritually. We cannot remain complacent or stagnant; the river of God always flows.

The sons of the prophets then came to Elisha in Bethel and said, *"Do you know that the Lord will take away your master from over you today?"* (2 Kings 2:3). Elisha said in response, *"Yes, I know; be still!"* (2 Kings 2:3). Elijah told Elisha to remain in Bethel while he went on to Jericho. But Elisha said, *"...I will not leave you"* (2 Kings 2:4)

The sons of the prophets in Jericho, a place of fragrance and warfare, had also been shown that Elijah was going to be taken away from Elisha that day. Elijah and Elisha traveled on to Jordan, a place of flowing down or descending, where fifty men of the sons of the prophets stood opposite them at the Jordan River. Elijah took his mantle, folded it together, and struck the waters of the Jordan, which divided, allowing both prophets to cross over on dry ground.

> *When they had crossed over, Elijah said to Elisha, "Ask what I shall do for you before I am taken from you." And Elisha said, "Please, let a double portion of your spirit be upon me." He said, "You have asked a hard thing. Nevertheless, if you see me when I am taken from you, it shall be so for you; but if not, it shall not be so." As they were going along and talking, behold, there appeared a chariot of fire and horses of fire which separated the two of them. And Elijah went up by a whirlwind to heaven. Elisha saw it* [the whirlwind created by the chariot] *and cried out, "My father, my father, the chariots of Israel and its horsemen!" And he saw Elijah no more. Then he took hold of his own clothes and tore them in two pieces* (2 Kings 2:9-12).

Elijah did not hand his mantle to Elisha; Elisha had to pick it up after Elijah was taken into Heaven. The word mantle in Hebrew is addereth, which means a wide, large overgarment, robe or dress; a blue ephod of sheep skin that contained the glory. The root word is Adar which is also the word for the last month on the Hebrew calendar. The month of Adar is the best time to remove any personal barriers to holiness. It is a time to create the potential for the greatest joy. Adar is the final month of the year; it completes the year. Hence, it is a time of completion. The root meaning of adar is "glorious, splendid, marvelous, and mighty." As a noun, it is rendered as "a cloak or mantle."[5]

> *He also took up the mantle of Elijah that fell from him and returned and stood by the bank of the Jordan. He took the mantle of Elijah that fell from him and struck the waters and said, "Where is the Lord, the God of Elijah?" And when he also had struck the waters, they were divided here and there; and Elisha crossed over* (2 Kings 2:13-14).

Jewish traditions indicate that the mantle that fell from Elijah was a Talit or prayer shawl. The Talit of a prophet or master teacher would have dark purple-blue threads in the corner tassel. People believed that the purple thread contained miracle power. This is why the woman with the issue of blood wanted to touch the hem of Jesus' Talit or garment (see Mark 5:25-34). When she touched Him, Jesus felt power leave Him and said, *"Who touched my garments?"* (Mark 5:30). After she was healed, He told her, *"Your faith has made you well..."* (Mark 5:34)—not a purple thread.

Elijah's Talit, mantle, or Adar symbolized that Elisha had removed any barriers to his relationship with God. He was no longer the servant, but had now stepped into the place of the prophet he had served. The word *Adar,* in Hebrew, is spelled: *Aleph, Daleth, Resh.*[6] The *Aleph* represents God or a beginning, a link between Heaven and earth. The *Daleth* is a doorway to the four corners of the earth or God's creative works in the world. The *Resh* represents healing and wholeness.[7] Hence the word *Adar*, (fire-god) is the sixth month of the civil year when Purim is celebrated by Jews. It represents God opening a doorway to healing power, restoration, and wholeness. Adar was also celebrated in the twelfth month of the sacred year of the Jews as it was doubled every second year to make the lunar year agree with the solar year.

Elijah's mantle was a doorway to God's power. Clearly the *Aleph* in the word for mantle, *Adar*, suggests that it is God's eternal doorway, not Elijah's. That is why Elijah did not give his mantle to Elisha. Elijah told Elisha that if he saw him taken, he would have his desire to carry on the prophetic ministry with a double portion of his spirit.

The mantle is a symbol of joy and completion. Elijah left his mantle as a sign that he had completed his assignment. Elisha picked up Elijah's mantle, indicating the start of a new era of double; he was picking up where Elijah left off and beginning his own ministry as a prophet. Elijah's mantle was a symbol of an agreement of power and authority between Elijah and God. Elisha's picking up of Elijah's mantle symbolized that he was entering into a covenant agreement with God. When Elisha used Elijah's mantle to part the Jordan River, God established His agreement or promise with Elisha.

ELISHA SUCCEEDED ELIJAH

Everyone is at a different level of hearing and seeing in their spiritual understanding. Elisha had walked with, served, and been personally trained by Elijah for years. He had been tested and tried in every spiritual discipline. The sons of the prophets had been through training as well; yet they did not possess the level of seeing, knowing, or perceiving that Elisha had developed. Elisha saw the heavenly chariot of fire and the horses come to separate him from

Elijah. But Elisha kept his eyes focused on his goal, Elijah. Elisha didn't allow the spectacular heavenly display of Elijah's homecoming to divert his gaze from the anointing that rested on Elijah. When Elisha saw the chariots of God arrive, he cried out, *"My father, my father, the chariots of Israel and its horsemen!"* (2 Kings 2:12).

The sons of the prophets saw only the stormy whirlwind the chariot created. They were distracted by the sudden changes in the spiritual atmosphere. The sons of the prophets were left wondering if Elijah had been transported to Heaven or if he had been transported to another geographic location. They could see the spirit of Elijah rested on Elisha. Yet, to obtain peace of mind, they still requested that Elisha grant them permission to search the region for Elijah for three days. Elisha knew Elijah had been taken to Heaven. His focused eyes saw beyond the natural realms of sudden change into the invisible realm of the Spirit.

> *Now when the sons of the prophets who were at Jericho opposite him saw him, they said, "The spirit of Elijah rests on Elisha." And they came to meet him and bowed themselves to the ground before him. They said to him, "Behold now, there are with your servants fifty strong men, please let them go and search for your master; perhaps the Spirit of the Lord has taken him up and cast him on some mountain or into some valley." And he said, "You shall not send." But when they urged him until he was ashamed, he said, "Send." They sent therefore fifty men; and they searched three days but did not find him. They returned to him while he was staying at Jericho; and he said to them, "Did I not say to you, 'Do not go'?"* (2 Kings 2:15-18).

The names of both Elijah (The Lord Is My God, Spiritual Champion) and Elisha (God Will Save Me, Protected) carry the record of what they represent, but not necessarily how they saw—if they are thought to be seers. Elijah's name means "God is Jehovah" or "YHWH is my God." He, like all of us, functioned as the Father's recorder on earth.

In the case of God's servant Elijah, the chariot was a trans-dimensional carrier of God's servant. The chariot of God transported Elijah out of time into the eternal realm where Elijah had always existed in heavenly places. When the fullness of time arrived, God reached down to retrieve the recording of Himself that He had placed within Elijah. Elijah came to restore all things back to God. He was called to turn the hearts of the fathers back to the sons, to turn the sons' hearts back to the fathers, and to make ready a people for God, lest God curse the earth (see Mal. 4:6). Elijah's anointing was to restore righteousness and protect the earthly realm from being struck with a curse caused by sin.

Elisha's name means "God is salvation" or "My God is salvation." He functioned under a double portion of Elijah's spirit.

THE PROPHET ELISHA

Elisha's eyes saw beyond the veil of the natural into the supernatural realm where God's army of fiery angels and chariots reside. His eyes were not limited by situations or hard facts. He knew to look beyond the natural to see God's power and provision. He trusted more in the realm of faith than what seemed to appear in the natural.

This is God's plan and desire for each and every one of us. We are to look again with the eyes of love, not fear, to see beyond what is presenting itself in the natural. There is a higher supernatural realm of vision that offers safety and security and deliverance from dangers and difficulties.

When fear blinded Elisha's servant, the prophet's prayer was able to open the attendant's spiritually blind eyes to see the coexisting spiritual realms of angels (see 2 Kings 6:17).

Knowing that more are fighting for us than against us brings a peace beyond our present understanding.

Prayer delivers us from fear. Prayer opens our eyes to see God's ever-present answer, while at the same time a prophetic decree will blind our enemies and place them at our mercy (see 2 Kings 6:18). For God to trust us at this level, we must develop greater amounts of obedience and compassion. God wants to trust us with the lives of our enemies. God tests and tries us until He knows that we will not execute our own judgment or harm people in any way. We need to see everyone through the eyes of God's love. We will be tested on how we respond to our enemies until we learn to respond correctly in love.

When God delivers our enemies into our hands, we must return good for evil, blessings for curses, and loving-kindness for abuse (see Luke 6:35). The Lord is the only one who should ever move in judgment. He said, *"Vengeance is Mine…"* (Rom. 12:19). We have no right to be vengeful; it is God's place to vindicate us. We are called to love our enemies and to be kind to those who persecute, use, and abuse our kindness (see Matt. 5:44-45).

When an enemy strikes, forgive and turn the other cheek as Jesus did. We should lead our enemies to salvation so that their eyes will be opened to God's saving word, loving spirit, and grace. It is time to love like God loves, see like God sees, obey what God's Word says, and then do what God does. This is what happened with Elisha:

> *Now when the attendant of the man of God had risen early and gone out, behold, an army with horses and chariots was circling the city. And his servant panicked, "Alas, my master! What shall we do?" So Elisha answered, "Do not fear, for those who are with us are more than those who are with them." Then Elisha prayed and said, "O Lord, I pray, open his eyes, that he may see." And the Lord opened*

*the servant's eyes and he saw; and behold, the mountain
was full of horses and chariots of fire all around Elisha*
(2 Kings 6:15-17).

The army had come to do the prophet great harm, but
God protected Elisha. When Elisha's enemies came down
off the mountain to pursue him, Elisha prayed to the Lord
again. He asked God to strike his enemies with blindness,
which He did. This removed the enemy's power and control. They were forced into a vulnerable place, wandering
in darkness and confusion. The prophet placed his trust in
God. In their new, weakened state of total dependence and
humiliation, the enemy had to trust and blindly follow Elisha to Samaria. Elisha told them, *"This is not the way, nor is
this the city; follow me and I will bring you to the man whom you
seek"* (2 Kings 6:19). And Elisha brought them to Samaria.

Elisha's enemies had to walk through the process of
trusting the one they were sent to destroy. Once they arrived
at the promised location, in the midst of Samaria, Elisha
prayed once more that God would reopen their blind eyes.
Their vision was restored. New vision was given in the midst
of their enemies (see 2 Kings 6:20). We will also be given a
new higher spiritual vision in God when we learn to move in
love and compassion towards our enemies. Love is the gateway that opens our natural eyes to see by the spirit of God.

Like most of us who have been wounded by an enemy or
betrayed by a spouse or close friend, our first instinct—like
the king of Israel—is to harm, retaliate, or kill the enemy
who has been delivered into our hands. If we hate someone,
in God's eyes, it is the same as if we have murdered them.

*Then the king of Israel when he saw them, said to Eli-
sha, "My father, shall I kill them? Shall I kill them?" He
answered, "You shall not kill them. Would you kill those
you have taken captive with your sword and with your
bow?..."* (2 Kings 6:21-22).

Elisha told the king of Israel to respond according to the greatness of God's loving-kindness, to make his enemies the objects of compassion in the presence of all their captors. Elisha encouraged the king to feed the Arameans, to provide for and care for his enemies instead of killing them. So the king prepared a feast for the enemy soldiers, and they ate to their fill.

> *"...Set bread and water before them, that they may eat and drink and go to their master." So he prepared a great feast for them; and when they had eaten and drunk he sent them away, and they went to their master. And the marauding bands of Arameans did not come again into the land of Israel* (2 Kings 6:22-23).

Elisha's mercy kept his spiritual eyes open so he could triumph over judgment. When we walk in love, our spiritual vision and perceptions remain pure. Offering God's great grace to those who harm or persecute us will not only bless them but also lead us to victory. The King of Israel's enemies were delivered into his hands. The King was eager to execute judgment and destroy his enemies, but the prophet carefully redirected his focus to blessing and not destruction. Good will always triumph over evil. Love will also bring forth a better result than hate. Never greet your enemy in the same malignant spirit he has come against you with. Never return evil for evil, but learn to bless others instead of cursing. We are not of this world, so we cannot respond in the spirit of this world. God is love, so we must respond in the power of His might.

To obtain true spiritual vision, we must be willing to become meek, lay down our right to be right, and walk in a spirit of love.

ENDNOTES

1. *Nelson's Illustrated Bible Dictionary*, (Nashville: Thomas Nelson Inc., 1986), s.v. "Zarephath."

2. Barbie L. Breathitt, *When Will My Dreams Come True? Dream Interpretation Nuggets, Times and Seasons,* (Self-published, 2011).

3. *Nelson's Illustrated Bible Dictionary,* s.v. "Shekinah."

4. James Strong, *Strong's Exhaustive Concordance of the Bible,* (Nashville: Thomas Nelson Inc., 2010), Hebrew #5397.

5. Matthew Easton, *Easton's Bible Dictionary,* (New York: T. Nelson and Sons, 1823-1894), s.v. "Adar."

6. Dugan, *The Dugan Bible Dictionary,* (Jubilee Publishing Group, 1994), s.v. "Adar."

7. Ibid.

Chapter 2

THE SEER SEES

Seers are those who have developed their spirits to go beyond time, space, and seasons. Seers reveal His Story (history) or the reality of the past, the ever present now, and the spiritual realms of the future. It is time to see Jesus, the Beautiful One!

Seers are those who have spiritual eyes to see in the realm of the spirit. The Lord shows them things ahead of time through visitations and angelic messengers and in dreams, visions, and trances. Seers often receive strong visual and physical impressions. They become accustomed to hearing both the audible and the internal voice of the Lord. They see prophetic words formulated or written on people or transposed over objects in the open external. They observe internal pictures or visions, like watching a private screening of a movie. They see sentences appear in their spirits or in midair, like reading a ticker tape. It's like gazing into an ancient book of mysteries or reading a heavenly scroll or television prompter.

> *Then He said to me, "Son of man, eat what you find; eat this scroll, and go, speak to the house of Israel." So I opened my mouth, and He fed me this scroll. He said to me, "Son of man, feed your stomach and fill your body with this scroll which I am giving you." Then I ate it, and it was sweet as honey in my mouth (Ezek. 3:1-3).*

SEERS GIVE WITNESS OF GOD

Jesus is the greatest seer who ever lived. When Jesus walked the earth, He constantly communed with His heavenly Father in prayer. Prayer brings us into the vision realm so we can see the answers to our prayers materializing before they physically manifest. As we place our faith in the vision and believe, we are able to open a spiritual gateway for the answers to our prayer to come into existence. Because of Jesus' great love for His heavenly Father, He was able to see into the visionary realm. He was also able to see a coin in a fish's mouth that could pay the temple tax for Peter and Himself.

Matthew 17:24-27 tells the story of Jesus and His disciples going to Capernaum. Men were collecting a two-drachma temple tax from everyone. A man came to Peter and asked, *"Does your teacher not pay the two-drachma tax?"* (Matt. 17:24). Peter answered, "Yes" and went into the house; but Jesus intercepted Peter, saying, *"What do you think, Simon? From whom do the kings of the earth collect customs or poll-tax, from their sons or from strangers?"* (Matt. 17:25). When Peter answered, *"From strangers"* (Matt. 17:26), Jesus said: *Then the sons are exempt. However, so that we do not offend them, go to the sea and throw in a hook, and take the first fish that comes up; and when you open its mouth, you will find a shekel. Take that and give it to them for you and Me* (Matt. 17:26-27).

Can you imagine being able to look past the natural realm and see your answer or the source of your supply? We can! Jesus did, and He is our example. Jesus saw the shekel in the fish's mouth. Jesus told Peter to drop his hook in the water. He knew the first fish Peter caught would be the one that contained the coin to pay both of their taxes.

Jesus could be standing in the middle of a crowded city street or be seated in a home and still see a fish in the nearby sea with a coin in its mouth. When a need presented itself in any situation, because Jesus was a man of prayer, He was able to see the answer in the realm of the spirit. He developed His spiritual eyes to see beyond the natural realms and earthly situations.

Jesus looked beyond normal, expected barriers into Heaven and saw what the Father was doing. Then He followed God's actions, voice, and plans. Jesus did what He observed in Heaven. Jesus only did what He saw the Father doing (see John 5:19, John 4:48-53, John 5:6). Jesus could look past the natural earthly realms and see into Heaven's eternal realms. He brought and established the kingdom of Heaven on earth.

The important things of life, such as the eternal realm, are invisible to the natural eye. Although they are invisible, they still carry a tangible weight and presence. Only the eyes of the heart can see the spiritual realm of reality. When our eyes are tuned to see by love's light, everything begins to come into focus.

When we were children, we spoke, planned, reasoned, and thought like children. When we wanted something, we would cry, point at the object, scream, and throw temper tantrums to demand our way. When we mature, we put away our childish and immature ways of seeing and communicating (see 1 Cor. 13:11). We develop the fruit of the Spirit: love, joy, peace, patience, kindness, goodness, faithfulness, gentleness, and self-control (see Gal. 5:22). We no longer demand our selfish ways, but we become servants to God and to others.

The more we come to know God and His ways, the clearer our visionary sight becomes. The foggy mist that distorts our vision begins to clear and evaporate. When we don't know Him, our vision is dim, like having to watch life through the reflection of a smoky mirror. Our perception and understanding is limited, and we only know and see in part. The closer we draw to God to discern His presence and ways, the more fully we will know God and discover our desperate need for Him. God will manifest His goodness and power right before our eyes. Our vision will expand, and God's plan for our lives will come into focus and clarity.

When the brightness of the morning sun (Son) manifests in our lives; faith, hope, and love will also increase. God's great light will shine in our hearts. We will see it all very clearly then, just as God sees us. We will know Him intimately as He knows us! Spiritual maturity will bring us into completeness. There are three things that will lead us toward that consummation: steady trust in God, an unswerving hope, and an extravagant love—but most of all love!

The eyes of the Lord are searching for those with a servant's heart of love so that He can support and promote them: *"For the eyes of the Lord move to and fro throughout the earth that He may strongly support those whose heart is completely His..."* (2 Chron. 16:9).

We, just like Jesus, can do nothing in our own flesh, strength, or abilities. Our success comes by His great grace and favor shining upon us.

> *For by their own sword they did not possess the land, and their own arm did not save them, but Your right hand and Your arm and the light of Your presence, for You favored them* (Ps. 44:3).

As His bride, we need to rest our hand in the cleft of His strong arm and allow Jesus to gently lead or escort us every step of the way. Jesus was tempted in every area of life that we are tempted in, yet He didn't sin. Jesus was tested in the desert and overcame the wilderness walk. He knows the way out of lack and the desert trials. His Word is the illumination of His presence upon our path. His light guides our steps. The light of His presence enables us to rest in His embrace and to take the next step with a renewed confidence. Jesus was continually connected to what was occurring in heaven while He walked the earth.

The prophet Isaiah looked into Heaven while standing on the earth. He saw the Lord seated on a throne, lofty and exalted. The glory of God's robe filled the temple, and he saw the six-winged Seraphim that stood above Him. He heard the Seraphim calling out, *"Holy, Holy, Holy, is the Lord of host, the whole earth is full of His glory"* (Isa. 6:3). Isaiah observed the foundations of the thresholds tremble at the voice of him who called out. He saw the temple fill with the smoke of His glory. He called out, *"Woe is me, for I am ruined! Because I am a man of unclean lips...for my eyes have seen the King, the Lord of hosts"* (Isa. 6:5). Then Isaiah saw one of the seraphim fly with a burning coal in his hand to touch his lips. Thus, his iniquity and sin were forgiven (see Isa. 6:6-7).

Isaiah was a prophet, yet he was able to look into the realms of Heaven. We have the same gifts and abilities to look past the natural into the supernatural, to apprehend that which God wants to reveal and release. God wants His kingdom to manifest in and through us. Isaiah saw the Lord sitting on a throne wearing a robe that filled a heavenly temple. The six winged Seraph stood around Him calling to each other, "Holy, holy, holy, the Lord All-Powerful is God. His Glory fills the whole earth."

Isaiah heard a heavenly sound that was so loud that it caused the door frame to shake, and the Temple filled with a glorious smoke. Isaiah feared he would be destroyed for seeing a holy God when he lived among sinful man and had not been through a purification process. He didn't realize that it is God's desire that we all see Him high and lifted up. Jesus said, *"If I be lifted up I will draw all men unto me"* (see John 12:32). Jesus is seated at the right hand of the Father. As we lift our eyes toward heaven to gaze upon Jesus' beauty, we will obtain a heavenly perspective and see things the way God intended us to see them.

The seer is given an eternal picture from heaven, which is the recording issued by the Father—His wisdom, counsel, and actions. When Christ is openly revealed, we'll see Him—and in seeing Him, we'll become like Him. As we begin to see Him and become like Him, we can begin to reveal Him. Whatever we focus upon, we empower to change us. Whoever we spend time with we take on that person's form, image, ways, belief structure, and actions. If we spend quality time in the presence of the Lord, we will be transformed into His image. This is not limited to the speaking of prophecy, as a prophet would do; rather, the seer is a witness who sees and hears all created things—regardless of time, space, or matter—and gives testimony or evidence of God's existence.

We are called as God's witnesses. Facts are established by a witness of two. One witness is heaven and the other is earth. Both heaven and earth bear witness to the greatness of God (see Deut. 30:19). A witness gives testimony. Seers are witnesses of the events that occur in heaven; and they must possess the power of God to demonstrate them on earth.

SEERS GIVE EVIDENCE OF GOD

Seers are observers of the Father's recorded script or video that shows and tells of His powerful demonstrations in the invisible realm. They see what God is doing; they follow what He is doing; and they bring it forth into manifestation. Seers are witnesses to the power and glory of divine reality. They demonstrate God's presence so that people can see His loving-kindness manifested through the miraculous. Seers demonstrate God's presence in their everyday lives and in the marketplace in order to touch, heal, and deliver those with whom they come into contact. Through seers, we see God heal in a practical application. Whenever they see a need, they fill it with the presence of God.

Seers see into the depths of the Spirit, yet gaze beyond "nothingness" to give evidence of God. God did not create a world, set it in motion, and then step out of our existence.

God is still intricately connected and very much involved in creating dreams and hearing and answering prayers.

Seers carry the silence of God in the area of perspective and into spiritual perception. God brings a heightened sensitivity to our spiritual perceptions by aligning them with our natural senses. God wants us to be able to see Him, perceive Him, and know what He is doing so that we are able to release it. God mirrors Himself in and through us as He steps into our reality, out of the invisible realm and into the natural realm, transforming it into the supernatural.

Seers reflect revelation to the outside world from the dimensions of God Himself. God is so magnificent that we can only take a small sliver of Him and begin to reveal it. Every one of us has a part in revealing the greatness of God. We each have a part in demonstrating God's presence because we are one body. God is looking for a place to rest His head. He is the head. We are the body that the head comes to rest upon. When God finds His resting place on the shoulders of a body that operates in His authority, the body of Christ will rise up in powerful demonstration, following His lead.

Seers mirror God's actions to give them entrance or manifestation, thus God's presence is established on earth. Therefore, seers communicate as extensions of God's limitlessness and His expansion. Seers are used by God to bring into existence what God brings out, displays, or reveals through the breathing in and out of the ebb and flow of the Spirit's creativity.

SEERS INTERACT WITH THE SPIRIT REALM

Seers interact with the spiritual realms of heavenly creatures, beasts, lights, winds, and a host of heavenly beings and angelic messengers. Seers have developed an intimate relationship with the Lord Jesus, who is the only true gateway or door to the spiritual realm. When believers enter the realm of the supernatural through Jesus, their youthfulness and strength are renewed like that of the eagle (see Eph. 4:23, Ps. 103:5). The presence of the Living Word renews their minds. A literal physical and spiritual restoration process takes place in the presence of the anointing. They are given beauty for their ashes and words of restoration for the ashes of others (see Isa. 61:3).

But when nonbelievers or those moving in the occult try to peer into or enter the realm of the Spirit without going through Jesus, they become weak and sickly and they die prematurely. Jesus said, "My sheep hear My voice and another they will not follow" (see John 10:1-6). Jesus is the only way, the truth, and the sole gateway that leads to God, the Father, who alone grants eternal life.

SEERS PRIMARY FUNCTION

The Old Testament refers to seers with two words: *ra'ah* and *chozeh*. Both of these words indicate that the primary function of seers is to see the concealed realm, things that God shows them. Seers receive revelation knowledge through the invisible angelic realms of visions, trances, and dreams. Seers are called to relate to God through the intimacy of faith, hope, and love. An atmosphere of peaceful meditation allows seers to enter into the spiritual perception of visionary sight. They are able to gaze into the invisible realms of glory and behold the beauty of the Lord, and so are you! David said it this way:

> *One thing I have asked from the Lord, that I shall seek: That I may dwell in the house of the Lord all the days of my life, to behold the beauty of the Lord and to meditate in His temple* (Ps. 27:4).

Beholding Jesus or "meditating upon His Word," is the act that brings transformation to the heart and mind. For what we behold, we become (see Josh. 1:8, Rom. 12:2, and 2 Cor. 3:18). So let us gaze at the beautiful Son!

Ra'ah means "to look and see, as in a vision, to gaze, view, experience, look upon, behold, discern, or to perceive by the Spirit." *Chozeh* means "to behold a vision, stargazer, or to gaze into the realm of the Spirit with approval and agreement, a prophet that sees, a seer."

Seers receive revelation beforehand, as they wait upon the Lord's powerful, manifested presence. Their revelations come through their ability to rest in the mystical realm of visions, dreams, pictures, lights, angelic messengers, and trances rather than simply receiving auditory impressions as the prophet.

I regularly experience this type of revelatory phenomenon. For me, it takes quiet times of worship, extended peace and solitude, meditation on His Word, and a hushed reflection on the presence of the Lord. Once I am able to still my mind, my spirit begins to release love toward God. When I feel His love moving on me, I begin to soak in an atmosphere of panoramic visions. The revelations I have received for my books, messages, and articles come through these quality alone times, resting in the Holy Spirit's presence.

Holy Spirit guides me through the Scriptures to impart deeper insights, making connections with truth I haven't understood before. Holy Spirit reveals faces of individuals that will appear in audiences. In the quiet times of meditation, He shows me peoples' situations, along with words of wisdom and understanding that are able to deliver them. I see what they will be wearing, and I am given words of knowledge for their healing and miracles before I arrive at the event.

I have met people at conferences and felt an instant connection, as if we were already good friends. This is because of the spiritual interactions we have already had with each other in the realm of vision. I felt as if I had already been a guest in their homes and carried on many conversations with them; yet we had never met in real life, only in the spirit, through prayer.

For example, one particular time, while I was flying to a meeting, I focused on the Lord. I asked Him to speak to me about the upcoming meeting. As the plane was landing, I gazed out the little window to see a huge Illinois cornfield ready for harvesting. The movie, *Field of Dreams,* with Kevin Costner, instantly came to mind. I heard a voice quote the famous movie line, "If you build it, he will come."

As I watched the edge of the cornfield, I saw people begin to emerge from between the stalks outlining the length of the harvest field. The statement continued to ring in my ears, "If you build it, he will come."

Later that night, when the pastor was in my direct line of vision, the Holy Spirit reminded me of the quote. He said to tell him, "If he will build it, I will come." I publically shared the vision I received on the plane and the quote. With tear-filled eyes, the pastor said, "That very quote is on a plaque that sits on my desk. I was hesitant to launch a building program. I asked the Lord to speak a confirming word. Now I know it's His plan for me to proceed. Tonight I got my answer!"

Many people misquote the movie line thinking it says, "If you build it, they will come." We don't need the people to come to fill our churches; we need Jesus, we need Him (the Holy Spirit) to come. The presence of the Holy Spirit will draw the crowds and fill the house; nothing else will do.

The messages and visions we receive are not always so pleasant. For example, I have observed the angry faces of hostile people who met behind closed doors in other states. They secretly plotted people's destruction or demise. I knew they were motivated by the accuser of the brethren and a spirit of jealousy because they were threatened by other anointed people.

The evil intent of their hearts was to smear reputations by placing people's character in question. I was given each of their names, and their livid faces were shown to me. I was even shown the main leader, who was not even present in the room at the time. He thought he was concealed as he worked behind the scenes, pulling all the strings. I heard their harsh, caustic, accusatory conversations, and it grieved my heart. Some of the people they intended to destroy had faithfully served them.

Their actions were like those of the fearful and jealous King Saul, who felt threatened by God showing David favor. I heard their plots as they formulated slanderous campaigns. "We will watch their Websites, and when they receive an invitation to minister, we will make phone calls to place their character in question and to discredit them. We'll release slanderous emails to cripple their momentum. We will systematically eliminate their influence by casting a dark shadow over motives. We will use any and every means possible to destroy them." How heartbreaking! What do we do when the Lord allows us to see something that is so hurtful? The answer is to pray for the ones who are planning evil to repent from their wicked ways. Show them love so they can change.

The Word of God says to love our enemies and those who use or persecute us and those who say all manner of evil against us falsely (Matt. 5:11). If the Word of God says it, we are going to be tried and tested in that area by experiencing it in our lives. When the difficult trials come, how we respond determines our next anointing and the level of power we will possess in the coming years.

Sadly, some people have a poverty mentality of "us four and no more." They don't understand that it takes the whole body of Christ, working together in unity, to build the kingdom of God. There is plenty of work for all of us to do. We need each other. If we will build it (The kingdom of God!), He will come!

Jesus told His disciples not to hinder people from demonstrating the Gospel in this New Testament story.

> *John said to Him, "Teacher, we saw someone casting out demons in Your name, and we tried to prevent him because he was not following us." But Jesus said, "Do not hinder him, for there is no one who will perform a miracle in My name, and be able soon afterward to speak evil of Me. For he who is not against us is for us"* (Mark 9:38-40).

Luke 9 tells of the time when Jesus was preparing for His ascension back into Heaven. He was passing through Samaria on His way to Jerusalem. He sent messengers ahead to make hospitable arrangements for Him there. But Jesus was not received by the Samaritans because they knew He was on His way to Jerusalem. When Jesus was not welcomed with open arms by the Samaritans, James and John said, "Lord, do you want us to call down fire to consume them or a lightning bolt from heaven to destroy them?"

But when Jesus heard what was in their hearts, He turned to rebuke and correct the disciples. "No! You do not know what kind of spirit is operating through you. I did not come to destroy people's lives, but to save them! We are not to harm others; we will simply move on to another village where we are accepted" (see Luke 9:51-56).

An Old Testament example of a seer looking behind closed doors to hear an enemy's conversation took place in 2 Kings 6:8-23. The prophet Elisha received twice the anointing of Elijah because he received a double portion of Elijah's spirit. Elisha developed his seer's gift and his relationship with God so he was able to perform twice the miracles of Elijah. Elisha was able to listen to the secret battle plans of kings as they spoke in their private bedchambers. Elisha would report the secret counsel of foreign kings to the King of Israel.

> *Now the king of Aram was warring against Israel; and he counseled with his servants saying, "In such and such a place shall be my camp." The man of God sent word to the king of Israel saying, "Beware that you do not pass this place, for the Arameans are coming down there." The king of Israel sent to the place about which the man of God had told him; thus he warned him, so that he guarded himself there, more than once or twice. Now the heart of the king of Aram was enraged over this thing; and he called his servants and said to them, "Will you tell me which of us is for the king of Israel?" One of his servants said, "No, my lord, O king; but Elisha, the prophet who is in Israel, tells the king of Israel the words that you speak in your bedroom." So he said, "Go and see where he is, that I may send and take him." And it was told him, saying, "Behold, he is in Dothan." He sent horses and chariots and a great army there, and they came by night and surrounded the city* (2 Kings 6:8-23).

God enabled the prophet Elisha to see into the king's bedchambers to spy and overhear his battle plans and strategies. When Elisha learned the enemy's plans he informed the king of Israel. The enemy king was outraged, but God protected His messenger from harm even though a great army of horses and chariots were sent out against Elisha. When we walk in God's light nothing that is concealed in darkness can remain.

THE EMMAUS ROAD

We are called to demonstrate the power of God. When the two disciples walked the Emmaus (warm wells) road, they encountered Jesus. The two men saw Jesus, they walked and talked with Jesus, yet they did not recognize Him as the resurrected Lord (see Luke 24:17). Jesus had taken on a new, glorious form as He often does.

Jesus comes in a form we are not familiar with and it offends our mind. Jesus is the Son of God and son of man, the Word, the Lamb and the Lion, the Advocate, Friend, Defender, Provider, Lord and Savior of the world, and so much more. God is Spirit, so He communicates to us through the spirit of truth. The Bible tells us that where two or more are gathered "I AM there in their midst" (see Matt. 18:20). The disciples felt that they knew this man who walked and talked with them. Jesus asked, "What are you discussing?" They answered Him:

> *"But also some women among us amazed us. When they were at the tomb early in the morning, and did not find His body, they came, saying that they had also seen a vision of angels who said that He was alive. Some of those who were with us went to the tomb and found it just exactly as the women also had said; but Him they did not see."*
>
> *And He said to them, "O foolish men and slow of heart to believe in all that the prophets have spoken! Was it not necessary for the Christ to suffer these things and to enter into His glory?"*
>
> *Then beginning with Moses and with all the prophets, He explained to them the things concerning Himself in all the Scriptures (Luke 24:22-27).*

Their understanding was quickened by His spiritual words of wisdom. They listened as Jesus, the resurrected Son of God, the master teacher, taught about Jesus the prophet and seer. Their spiritual ears bore witness to His greatness, but their eyes did not recognize Him in the natural because He came in a different form. Jesus had entered into His glory!

> *And they approached the village where they were going, and He acted as though He were going farther. But they*

urged Him, saying, "Stay with us, for it is getting toward evening, and the day is now nearly over." So He went in to stay with them (Luke 24:28-29).

Jesus always desires to take us farther down the road than we are willing to walk with Him. We set the limits on the heights, depths, or distances Jesus can take us. But in His mercy and great grace, He is willing to recline and rest with us. He will bless us and commune with us until we are ready to take the next step. We are destined to know Him from glory to glory.

Jesus continued to commune with the men as they rested around the dinner table. Jesus remained with the men until their eyes were opened to see Him for who He is and to discern truth.

When He had reclined at the table with them, He took the bread and blessed it, and breaking it, He began giving it to them. Then their eyes were opened and they recognized Him; and He vanished from their sight (Luke 24:30-31).

The disciple's eyes were opened to recognize Jesus when He broke the communion bread. Jesus came to share a meal with the disciples to release the promises of the words He had spoken on the Road to Emmaus. Prophetic promises are released in the Covenant meal of Communion if we are able to rightly discern His body.

The bread represented His body that had been broken for the salvation of the world. God healed Jesus' broken body. Jesus walked and talked in resurrection power. When the disciples recognized Jesus in His resurrected state, He vanished from their sight. When our dim eyes are opened to see at one level or dimension, Jesus will start the process of enabling us to see Him on an ever-increasing level of clarity. Once Jesus vanished from their presence,

They said to one another, "Were not our hearts burning within us while He was speaking to us on the road, while

He was explaining the Scriptures to us?" And they got up that very hour and returned to Jerusalem, and found gathered together the eleven and those who were with them, saying, "The Lord has really risen and has appeared to Simon." They began to relate their experiences on the road and how He was recognized by them in the breaking of the bread (Luke 24:32-35).

When we discover who Jesus is at one level, He will empower us to know Him in a deeper and more profound way. Our hearts are ignited to burn with a passionate love. The living, resurrected Word will manifest in flesh once again.

Jesus was the firstborn of many brethren. God knew Jesus was the prototype, the first of many sons and daughters to come. God had a divine plan from before time began. God knew us before He brought the world into existence. He chose us and made us right with Him. After we are saved, He gives us His glory. God fashions the lives of those who love Him to reflect Jesus' image on earth. Every one of us mirrors a diverse form and reflects a different aspect of Jesus. God orchestrates everything to bring forth His love and purpose in our life. God is faithful to establish us on a solid foundation, to build us until we are transformed into His image. We see who we are destined to become in glory when we see Jesus (see Rom. 8:28-30).

As we mature in Christ we take on His form. We look more like the God we love. None of us look the same as we did ten years ago. If we are not continually changing then we are stagnant. Each new move of God is known for its uniqueness. What is the form that God will take during our day and time? We read about the God of the Bible. We know how He appeared in the different moves of the past. But how will He appear in our time? What are the different ways He can come? Are there ways that we have not seen or experienced yet? Will we accept the new move of God or judge it? Will we discern it by the spirit?

God wants to open our eyes to see so that we can know Him in a new way. God said, "Behold I make all things new. I do a new thing, do you not perceive it?" (see Isa. 42:9). Since He is God, He can come anyway He desires!

God is asking, do you not perceive the new thing or the new ways in which I am coming? So often we do not understand or perceive the ways of God. God comes in a unique and special way through every person; but we don't recognize the various forms and expression of God when they are resident in man. *Perception* talks about the realm of the spirit where our senses are activated to perceive Him walk down the road past the natural into the supernatural. As God releases the seven spirits of God (see Rev. 4:5), the reverential fear of the Lord will return.

Saul also encountered Jesus on a barren road called Damascus (destruction), *And he said, "Who are You, Lord?" And He said, "I am Jesus whom you are persecuting,* (Acts 9:5). In his zeal, he had gained letters from the high priest to bind, threaten, and murder the Lord's disciples. As Saul approached Damascus, a blinding light suddenly flashed around him. Saul fell to the ground, where the voice of God confronted him. "Saul, Saul, why are you persecuting Me?"

Saul responded, "Who are You, Lord?"

And He said, "I am Jesus, whom you are persecuting; stand up on your feet, go to Damascus, and you will be given directions there." The men who were with Saul were mute. They heard the heavenly voice that spoke to Saul, but their eyes were not given vision to see anyone. Saul arose from the ground. His eyes were open, yet he was blind and saw nothing. Saul remained in Damascus fasting and praying for three days without sight.

The Lord worked to bring Saul into the kingdom by speaking to Ananias in a vision. "Get up and go to Straight

Street, where Saul is praying. I have shown him your face in a vision. He has seen you laying hands on him to restore his sight. Tell him he is my chosen vessel to bear My name before the Gentiles and kings. I have shown him visions of how much he must suffer for My name sake." (See Acts 9:1-16.)

> *So Ananias departed and entered the house, and after laying his hands on him said, "Brother Saul, the Lord Jesus, who appeared to you on the road by which you were coming, has sent me so that you may regain your sight and be filled with the Holy Spirit." And immediately there fell from his eyes something like scales, and he regained his sight, and he got up and was baptized; and he took food and was strengthened* (Acts 9:17-19).

In this amazing Bible passage, we see multiple examples of the supernatural realm demonstrated. The Bible brings spiritual illumination to the believer through the vision realm, prayer, healing, and prophecy. Saul underwent a spiritual transformation to become the apostle Paul. This process of deprogramming Saul began on the road to Damascus (destruction). But the process continued over the next fourteen years—two complete cycles of seven to bring him into perfection. Saul lived in wilderness isolation, learning to overcome a religious spirit that was zealous to destroy the people of God. The Holy Spirit taught Paul to hear the voice of the Lord and to understand the vision realm.

His natural vision was lost in order for him to gain his spiritual vision. The eyes usually are the instruments from where our brain or mind's eye receives pictures. Even so, if you close your eyes, you will be able to envision, or see, the face of someone you love or with whom you are well acquainted. While Saul was not able to see with his physical eyes, God showed him a mental picture of a stranger, the face of Ananias. Natural vision is often the enemy of the unlimited supernatural realm of vision. The scales that blind our natural sight must be removed. Our spiritual sight must be healed so we can gaze past our own carnal understanding into the infinite dimensions of Christ. Spiritual sight will allow us to obtain the light of revelation.

REVELATION IS LIGHT

Revelation is light, which shows the revealed things of God. Illumination is reflection or the response to God's revelation. The function of seers is to assist in or facilitate what they see in the invisible realm by bringing it forth from God to communicate it to people.

The Hebrew word *or* means light. *Or* is the brilliance that comes when a soul is enlightened by God's revelation. The light of God shines in us. It also shines on us. When the light of God is on us, the favor of God will open double doors for us and follow us through those doors as a rearguard. The Bible says, *"Surely goodness and mercy will follow me all the days of my life"* (Ps. 23:6 NKJV). The blessings of God come and overtake us. When the light of God is on us, the *or* is present to release favor. It is the brilliance of God's light that shines out of our souls. When favor rests upon us, we will be chosen out of a crowd of people and God's light will cause us to rise to the top. For example, out of all the hundreds of virgins who were prepared to meet the King, only Esther was chosen to replace Vashti as queen (see Esther 2:17).

In a metaphorical sense, *or* signifies the light of life reigning over death. All of us experience walking through the dark valley of the shadow of death at times. We are crucified with Christ; nevertheless, we live. Eternal life is released in us when salvation comes to us. So we have life and that life is more abundant than those who have not received eternal life. We should always be increasing in God. *"For You have delivered my soul from death, indeed my feet from stumbling, so that I may walk before God in the light of the living"* (Ps. 56:13).

As believers we are assured of a joyful, blessed life in God's light even though we may stumble in times of great darkness (see Ps. 23:4). *"Do not rejoice over me, O my enemy. Though I fall I will rise; though I dwell in darkness, the Lord is a light for me"* (Mic. 7:8). God's light will shine through us even during the dark night of our soul. He promises that His word will be a lamp to keep our feet from stumbling and a light that shines ever brighter on our path. We are called to let the light of the Lord shine through us so men can see God's work manifesting in our life.

WALK IN THE LIGHT OF GOD'S FAVOR

We are called to walk in the light, the *or*, before the presence of kings and world leaders. The light of God rested upon Esther so she gained the king's favor. He extended his scepter to Esther, telling her, "Ask what ever you will and it will be granted to you up to half my kingdom" (see Esther 5:3). God's light, or outshining, will cause us to find favor. Moses' face shone with the *or*—the presence of God (see Exod. 34:29-30). Peter had the outshining of God's presence in his life, and the sick were healed and demons were cast out when he walked by people on the streets (see Acts 5:15). God promises us that His presence will be a light to our paths. *"In the light of a king's face is life, and his favor is like a cloud with the spring rain"* (Prov. 16:15). When we make God happy He gives favor to great men so they can in turn extend great grace to us.

The apostle Paul was brought before many kings, and he was able to present the gospel (see Acts 23–28). The Bible tells us not to worry about what to say at those times, but that God will give us the words to say (see Matt. 10:19). His sheep hear His voice, and another they will not follow (see John 10:3-4). We don't have to be worried about what to say or how to testify. We will know what to say because the Spirit of God will speak to and through us. We testify of the goodness of

God in the land of the living. Seers are especially adapted to bring glory to God in many different ways.

Seers are those who have trained their whole body, mind, and spirit to hear the joyful sounds and expressions of God. They walk in the light of God's countenance. When we know God we will also know His sound and see His light.

> *How blessed are the people who know the joyful sound! O Lord, they walk in the light of Your countenance* (Ps. 89:15).

When we discern the sound of the Lord's coming, we will be awakened from a spiritual slumber and the light of His countenance will shine upon our face.

> *For the Lord has poured over you a spirit of deep sleep, He has shut your eyes, the prophets; and He has covered your heads, the seers* (Isa. 29:10).

When God's face is turned toward us, we begin to reflect it. Second Corinthians 3:15-18 says that every time our faces are turned toward the Lord, another veil is removed:

> *But to this day whenever Moses is read, a veil lies over their heart; but whenever a person turns to the Lord, the veil is taken away. Now the Lord is the Spirit, and where the Spirit of the Lord is, there is liberty. But we all, with unveiled face, beholding as in a mirror the glory of the Lord, are being transformed into the same image from glory to glory, just as from the Lord, the Spirit.*

When the veils are removed, people can see God's light and glory. We are also able to see God more clearly in another dimension each time another veil is removed. We see Him in a way we have never seen Him before. His countenance lights us up even more.

As believers, we are assured a joyful, blessed life in God's light. Psalm 23:4 says, *"Even if I walk through the valley of the shadow of death, I fear no evil, for You are with me; Your rod and*

Your staff, they comfort me." God's light shines, even when we experience the valleys in life. His light is before us on the path so we can take the next step. God's light is not a flood light, but a lamp that is sufficient to show the next step. The more we love with a pure heart the more we shine.

The Bible teaches that if we will purify our hearts and cleanse our hands, we can worship in the spirit of unity and truth to release the glory. Love, joy, peace, thanksgiving, hate, jealousy, bitterness, and unforgiveness are not just attitudes; they are powerful forces that appear in the realm of the spirit as colored wavelengths of light vibrations and substances.

> *Or do you not know that your body is a temple of the Holy Spirit who is in you, whom you have from God, and that you are not your own? For you have been bought with a price: therefore glorify God in your body* (1 Cor. 6:19-20).

There are many different types of language, including body language. Human languages are very elementary compared to the more complex and symbolic spiritual language of Heaven. God communicates to us through His written Word; through our hearing or reading of the rhema word of God; through pictures in trances, dreams, and visions; through feeling impressions in our physical bodies; and through intuitive knowing. Our understanding of the ways of God increases when we are made aware of the different eternal ways God communicates to us. Spiritual language and communication contacts our heart first. Intellectual communication travels through our minds first and then contacts our heart. God is always communicating His love to our heart. God is love. God is also white light.

SPIRITUAL MEANINGS OF LIGHT

God's white light contains all the visible and invisible spectrums of color. The three corners of the triangular prism can represent the white light of the Trinity reflecting the seven beautiful colors in the rainbow. The colors that are visible and those that are invisible to the natural eyes communicate a brilliant message to those who have eyes to see.

Our dreams and visions are full of variations of these seven different rainbow colors. Dreams are often like the colorful vapors of a rainbow. Dreams quickly come and go and are easily forgotten if not recorded within five minutes. Spiritual images are a gift from God to be treasured. Each experience comes in its own individually wrapped package. Dreams and visions are a wonderful vehicle for bringing a peaceful resolve to the problem areas of life.

These various shades of colored light enable us to understand whether our souls or spirits or a balance of both are ruling our lives. By observing the intensity, hue, value, and tint of colors that appear, we can determine whether the dream or vision is coming from the spirit or the soulish realm.

If the white light of God is filling our lives, then the dominant colors appearing in our dreams will likely be: red, symbolizing the Spirit of the Lord; blue, for the Spirit of Might; and green, representing the Counsel of God. Their positive effects will be evident in our waking lives. If our spirit is submitted to God, then we will be led by the orange Spirit of Wisdom and not by the self-centered desires of our souls. The red, green, and blue light color spectrums are the three colors that are predominate in the Spirit. If we as the sons of God are led by the Spirit of God, our spirit will reflect the red, green, and blue colors of God's light.

For all who are being led by the Spirit of God, these are sons of God (Rom. 8:14).

Color is a very important concept to master in the seers realm of understanding and interpretation. Below is a color chart that will help the reader understand what the different colors that appear in their dreams or visions may represent.

It also outlines the different colors of the seven spirits of God found listed in the Bible at Isaiah 11:2 and Revelation 1:4 and 4:5.

COLORS[1]

Red: The Spirit of the Lord (see Isa. 11:2); wisdom; anointing; power; prophetic anointing; prayer; evangelist; thanksgiving; blood atonement; passion; emotion; strength; energy; fire; love; sex; excitement; enthusiasm; zeal; speed; heat; leadership; masculinity; warrior; war; sin; death; anger; rage; fighting; lust; hatred; bloodshed.

Crimson: blood atonement; forgiveness; Jesus; passion; strong emotion; washing white as snow; wine; sacrifice; death; sin.

Pink: chaste; innocence; purity; childlike; faith; feminine; female infant; lack of passion; watered down; immoral; flesh; sensual.

Amber: glory of God; purity; holiness; God is ministering; the anointing of fire (see Ezek. 1:4, 27; 8:2); idolatry.

Orange: Spirit of Wisdom (see Isa. 11:2); perseverance; powerful force; energy; balance; heat; fire; purification; persecution; enthusiasm; flamboyance; playfulness; stubbornness; strong-willed; rebellion; witchcraft; Buddhism; danger; harm; jeopardy; warning.

Gold: praise; holy; purity; God's glory; silence; divinity; tried in the fire; precious treasures; wealth; prosperity; favor; abundant blessings; heavenly gift; idolatry; defilement; licentiousness; sensuality; greed; contamination.

Yellow: Spirit of Understanding (see Isa. 11:2); soul; hope; gift of God; light; marriage; teacher; family; celebration; joy; happiness; renewed mind; optimism; idealism; wealth; summer; air; courage; welcome home; honor; sunlight; fear; coward; sissy; illness; hazards; dishonesty; avarice; intellectual pride; deceitful; timidity; weakness.

Green: Spirit of Counsel (see Isa. 11:2); growth; prosperity; wealth; health; money; provision; vigor; conscience; generosity; go; new life or beginning; tender; rest; nature; evergreen; eternal life; immortal; spring; fertility; youth; environment; aggression; inexperienced; immature; pride; envy; jealousy; flesh; carnal; mortal; misfortune.

Cyan: deals with the issues of the soul; fasting; human will; strong-willed.

Light Blue: the immature development of a person's spiritual gift; spirit of humanity; evil spirit; corruption.

Blue: Spirit of Might (see Isa. 11:2); faith; spiritual communion with God; prophet; word of God; grace; divine revelation; Heaven; spiritual; visitation; Holy Spirit; blessings; healing; good will; life; mortal; seas; skies; peace; unity; harmony; tranquility; calmness; coolness; confidence; water; ice; loyalty true blue; dependability; winter; depression; sorrow; anxiety; isolation; feeling blue; hopelessness; coldness; idealism.

Magenta: soul; emotions; love; giving; hate; fear; joy.

Plum: riches; abundance; infilling of the Holy Spirit.

Purple: authority; royalty; intercession; apostle; kingship; majestic; noble; prince; princess; queen; political power; spirituality; creativity; garments of the wealthy; ceremony; mystery; rule good or evil; arrogance; flamboyance; gaudiness; mourning; exaggeration; false authority; dishonesty; licentiousness; sensuality; Jezebel.

Indigo: Spirit of Knowledge (see Isa. 11:2); authority to heal people dealing with foundational, internal issues; heartbreak; mental disorders; stress; emotionally burned out and pain.

Violet: Spirit of the Fear of the Lord (see Isa. 11:2); increased spiritual and mental clarity; emotions.

White: love; Spirit of the Lord; holy power; purity; without mixture; light; righteousness; blameless; innocence; reverence; snow; peace; holiness of God; Christ; angels; saints;

white horse: victory; cleanliness; redeemed; simplicity; security; marriage; covenant; sterility; winter; coldness; clinical; surrender; cowardice; fearfulness; unimaginative; religious spirit; witchcraft; false righteousness; mourning for Buddhist or Hindu.

Silver: redemption; salvation; power; love; grace; mercy; life; silver cord (see Eccles. 12:6); legalism; slavery; domination; betrayal.

Gray: wisdom; age; elegance; respect; honor; reverence; stability; timelessness; great experience; maturity; wise counsel; weakness; unclear; not defined; hazy; deceived; hidden; undefined; compromise; vague; not specific; vacillation; deception; crafty; false doctrine.

Black: neutral; dusk; moved with passion; midnight hour; sophistication; formality; elegance; wealth; mystery; style; sin; grief; death; physical affliction; from the soul; enemy; famine; lack; in the dark; judgment of God; wickedness; ignorance; mourning; gloomy; evil; demonic; ominous.

Brown: compassion; pastor; humility; repentant; born again; calm; depth; natural organism; nature; richness; rust; tradition; sheep; without spirit; humanism; false compassion; self-effort; dead; tired; dried out; withered.

Brass: judgment of sin.

Bronze: forgiveness; atonement; pride; judgment.

Iron: stubborn; strength; judgment from sin.

Yellow is associated with the Spirit of Understanding, indigo represents the Spirit of Knowledge, and the violet colors represent the reverential Fear of the Lord. The three light color spectrums of yellow, indigo, and violet deal with the areas of the soul. Each person's soul is made up of the intellect, the mind, thoughts, beliefs, memories, the will, and emotions.

Isaiah 11:2 lists the seven Spirits of God, and we can find their corresponding colors demonstrated each time the beautiful circular rainbow is displayed in the heavens.

The colorful rainbow is a covenant promise that God made to mankind. The rainbow signifies God would never again destroy the world by a flood. God took the seven attributes of His spirit and assigned each one of them a specific rainbow color. When a rainbow appears in the sky it reminds us of God's covenant promise. He placed part of Himself in the colors of the rainbow. The knowledge of these different colors and what they mean help us to come into a deeper understanding of the mysteries that are concealed in God. To correctly discern the colors that coordinate with the specific color, simply overlay their colors with the verse found in Isaiah 11:2 that lists all seven spiritual attributes of God.

> *The Spirit of the Lord* [red prophetic] *shall rest upon Him, The Spirit of wisdom* [orange] *and understanding* [yellow], *the Spirit of counsel* [green] *and might* [blue], *the Spirit of knowledge* [indigo] *and of the fear of the Lord* [violet] (Isa. 11:2).

The book of Revelation also mentions the seven Spirits of God as a lampstand or menorah with seven different colored lights shining forth God's revelation (see Rev. 1:4):

> *And from the throne proceeded lightnings, thunderings, and voices. Seven lamps* [menorah] *of fire were burning before the throne, which are the seven Spirits of God* (Rev. 4:5 NKJV).

God demonstrates His glory in many different ways; through His lightning, thunder, and audible voice. His beauty is reflected in the seven lamps of fire that burn before His majestic throne. We need to embrace the fiery light of His spirit and allow the flames to burn up every sin, iniquity, and offense. Offenses come to reveal things that are hidden from God's light in our darkened hearts. God's fire will remove issues such as jealousy, hurt, grief, disappointment, and sorrow. These issues are often caused by betrayal and rejection, which, if left unresolved, lead to anger, sickness, and bitterness. There is a spiritual and physical connection between harmful negative attitudes and physical infirmity.

For every positive meaning of a color, there is also a negative meaning of that same color. Negative colors match all of our negative issues. Instead of being bright and beautiful, negative things appear dull and ugly in the realm of the Spirit. For example, jealousy is an ugly pea green color that looks and smells like gangrene. Hurt is a dark blue color that looks like bruised tissue. Grief, mourning, disappointment, and sorrow cover us in black. Betrayal is a dull or tarnished silver color. The color indigo represents our negative emotional pain related to heartbreak, mental disorders, stress, and rejection. If you have ever seen someone turn purple-red with anger, you know what that color of anger looks like in the realm of the spirit.

These attitudes and negative attributes are also associated with a terrible off-key sound and they emit a terrible odor. The combination of color, sound, and smell draws the demonic realm toward the person who is emitting them. When one demon is attracted and finds a residence, he calls for his friends and associates to take up residence, too.

COLOR AND MUSICAL HEALING

Permeating your surroundings with the correct colors, light, peace, and Classical music played in the appropriate keys can positively affect your attitude, aptitude, outlook, energy level, and the healing of your body.

The seven major organs of the body contain the seven colors of the rainbow. When the correct vitamins, colored vegetables and fruits, light therapy, or the correct sound vibrations are released, healing takes place. The Bible tells us to praise and magnify the Lord, that He inhabits the praises of His people. Praise and worship draws God into our sphere.

Jesus, who is the light of the world, spoke to sickness and disease. The sound of His anointed words and light released from His voice brought a healing presence to all who came before Him. If our eyes were opened to see into the realm of the spirit when healing took place, we could observe the different colors of the healing anointing being released. We are beings that radiate light because we come from the Father of Light in whom there is no shadow of turning.

COLOR MUSICAL KEY
RELATES TO ANATOMY

Seers are able to see and discern the ugly shrouds of color that surround harmful attitudes and spirits. They can smell their putrid odors. They hear sounds of screeching when depression, hopelessness, or despair speaks through people.

Seers who move with power in the discerning of spirits and deliverance are able to set the captives free from these negative forces. Forgiveness coupled with the blood of Jesus will release the healing anointing that moves us closer to our destiny. It is important to understand the meanings of the different colors that surround us in our waking and in our sleeping life because they communicate a message to us. The eyes of the seer discern the realms of colored light and decode their messages.

The colors that are displayed in our dreams are extremely important and are highly significant. They reflect emotional overtones and the hues of our feelings. The same color can speak both a positive and a negative message, depending on the setting and the particular symbols that are present in the dream. The Scriptures are rich with the meaning of colors. God was very specific about the colors purple, blue, and scarlet, which were to be used in the Sanctuary (Exod. 25:4-9).

Color	Key	Anatomy
Red	C	Blood, genitals, legs, muscles, bowels, lower intestines, feet problems, ovary problems, overweight, venereal diseases.
Green	F	Hearts, lower lungs, shoulders, angina, motion sickness, common cold, heart ailments, hepatitis, jaundice, liver complaints, nausea, phlebitis, thrush.
Blue	G	Throat, base of the skull, upper lungs, midriff upward, aids, fever, eczema, incontinence.
Indigo	A	Skeleton, eyes, sinuses, midriff upward, breast problems, bronchitis, back problems, diarrhea, eye problems, gland problems, hay fever, herpes complex, insomnia, menstrual pain, migraine, pain, pneumonia, quinsy (throat abscess), sinus problems, snoring, varicose veins.
Purple	B	Brain, scalp, crown of the head, midriff upward, Alzheimer's, epilepsy, womb problems
Yellow	E	Liver, gallbladder, pancreas, stomach, bowels, lower intestines, acne, anorexia, boils, bowel problems, cystitis, deafness, depression, diabetes, dyslexia, ear problems, nervous disorders, rashes, stiff neck, water retention, wisdom teeth
Orange	D	Kidneys, intestines, lower abdomen, bowels, lower intestines, asthma, bunions, catarrh, joint problems, kidney problems, knee troubles, menopause, phobias, psoriasis, sprains, warts.

By renewing our minds with the Word of God, we are able to bridge the gap between the physical, natural mind and our spirits, which respond to God. *"Let this mind (attitude) be in you which was also in Christ Jesus"* (Phil. 2:5 KJV). If we don't display Christlike attitudes we will display negative attitudes. Since our brains control everything our bodies learn, sense, know, and do, it is essential that our minds are renewed to respond by the Spirit. As David wrote:

> *Create in me a clean heart, O God, and renew a steadfast spirit within me. Do not cast me away from Your presence and do not take Your Holy Spirit from me* (Ps. 51:10-11).

Our spirits and our minds think and respond differently, but we need them both working together to walk in the Spirit. The mind is used to gather and process information and knowledge from the natural intellectual realm. Therefore, our minds have to be renewed by the Spirit of the Lord to help us process impressions we receive in the Spirit intuitively so that we have the mind of Christ. The mind of Christ allows us to move into a higher realm of understanding with a positive attitude as we strive for the high standard of perfection in Christ. Jesus is our prize.

> *I press on toward the goal for the prize of the upward call of God in Christ Jesus. Let us therefore, as many as are perfect, have this attitude; and if in anything you have a different attitude, God will reveal that also to you; however, let us keep living by that same standard to which we have attained* (Phil. 3:14-16).

God is able to adjust our attitudes as we allow Him to renew the spirit of our mind. Our spirits will sense the movement of the Holy Spirit, including any resistance, warnings (checks), or burdens in the Spirit. The more our minds are renewed by the Spirit of wisdom, the knowledge of God, and revelation, the more we will be able to move in and respond to the leading of the Holy Spirit. We are called to live according to the will of God. It is God's will that His word quickens us in the spirit to make us alive in Christ.

> *For the gospel has for this purpose been preached even to those who are dead, that though they are judged in the flesh as men, they may live in the spirit according to the will of God* (1 Pet. 4:6).

The eyes of our spiritual understanding will be enlightened to know intellectually (*gnosis*)[2] and mentally the calling God has placed on us. To acquire knowledge spiritually through revelation or a rhema word from God is (*epignosis*).[3] This type of experience or encounter brings forth light, eternal change, and spiritual fruit that remains. A new pattern of truth is established, and our minds are renewed. When the word of God is received and then applied it is able to save our souls (see James 1:21).

The *Spirit of Revelation* (*apokalupsis*) communicates a spiritual disclosure, an appearing, a coming, or an enlightening or manifestation of revelation to be revealed to our spirits.[4] *To know* (*eido*) means "to see (either literally or figuratively) to be aware of, to behold, consider, look on, perceive, see, to be sure of, to tell with a knowledge that brings understanding to the mind."[5]

> *But you did not learn Christ in this way, if indeed you have heard Him and have been taught in Him, just as truth is in Jesus, that, in reference to your former manner of life, you lay aside the old self, which is being corrupted in accordance with the lusts of deceit, and that you be renewed in the spirit of your mind, and put on the new self, which in the likeness of God has been created in righteousness and holiness of the truth* (Eph. 4:20-24).

To truly walk and see in the Spirit, every part of us must be dedicated to God. We must be totally renewed in the spirit, soul, and body or our vision will be obscured in one of these areas. We need the peace of God to sanctify us entirely.

Now may the God of peace Himself sanctify you entirely; and may your spirit and soul and body be preserved complete, without blame at the coming of our Lord Jesus Christ. Faithful is He who calls you, and He also will bring it to pass (1 Thess. 5:23-24).

The battles we experience begin in and are waged in our minds. The Bible tells us to cast down vain imaginations, temptations, negative thoughts, and everything that exalts itself against the knowledge of Christ. Human speculations and lofty imaginations cause pride which conflicts with the knowledge of God. When pride enters our heart God resists us until we repent. We must submit to God and walk in total obedience to his purposes.

We are destroying speculations and every lofty thing raised up against the knowledge of God, and we are taking every thought captive to the obedience of Christ, and we are ready to punish all disobedience, whenever your obedience is complete (2 Cor. 10:5-6).

Think of the mind as a high-powered computer with a lot of memory that can recall recorded data and respond according to the programs we have installed on the hard drive. Sometimes our environments and life experiences have programmed us to respond in error or in an inappropriate fashion. If our minds are not renewed with the Word of God and we don't install spiritual programs, our minds will reject the spiritual truths God sends us. They simply will not compute to the natural mind.

But a natural man does not accept the things of the Spirit of God, for they are foolishness to him; and he cannot understand them, because they are spiritually appraised. But he who is spiritual appraises all things, yet he himself is appraised by no one. For who has known the mind of the Lord, that he will instruct Him? But we have the mind of Christ (1 Cor. 2:14-16).

Because the mind set on the flesh is hostile toward God; for it does not subject itself to the law of God, for it is not even able to do so (Rom. 8:7).

Our natural or carnal mind does not agree with God, but it is at enmity with Him. The natural self says one thing and the spirit says another, causing us to be confused or be double-minded. The spiritual training we receive through the Word will enable us to make the right decisions when situations present themselves. *"Train up a child in the way he should go, even when he is old he will not depart from it"* (Prov. 22:6).

When we are able to align our spirits with our spiritually-renewed minds, a supernatural transformation takes place in God's kingdom of light. When God's light shines, our hearts will be illumined to make the correct choices as He guides us upon the right path. We will shine in the darkness bringing God's eternal light to bear.

The eye is the lamp of the body; so then if your eye is clear, your whole body will be full of light. But if your eye is bad, your whole body will be full of darkness. If then the light that is in you is darkness, how great is the darkness (Matt. 6:22-23).

When our spiritual eye is clearly focused on God it shines like a lamp. Spiritual harmony, transfiguration, and transformation take place, releasing great light. The light of God's presence and power increases in our lives when we move from the good, to the acceptable, and finally manifest the perfect will of God. Jesus' face and clothes shone with the glory of God's light.

And He was transfigured [metamorphoo: "to transform, change, transfigure or transform]⁶ before them; and His face shone like the sun, and His garments became as white as light. And behold, Moses and Elijah appeared to them, talking with Him (Matt. 17:2-3).

And do not be conformed to this world, but be transformed [metamorphoo] by the renewing of your mind, that you may prove what is that good and acceptable and perfect will of God (Rom. 12:2 NKJV).

If our eyes are focused on the rhema Word of God's kingdom, which brings light, we won't be distracted by the natural ways of the world, but we will be full of God's light. When our minds and spirits are united, we are able to receive and release the blessings of Heaven. If we walk in the light as He is in the light we will have true fellowship with God. He will cause all of our enemies to be at peace with us. They may attack us on one way but God will defeat and scatter them in seven different directions.

The Lord shall cause your enemies who rise up against you to be defeated before you; they will come out against you one way and will flee before you seven ways. The Lord will command the blessing upon you in your barns and in all that you put your hand to, and He will bless you in the land which the Lord your God gives you. The Lord will establish you as a holy people to Himself, as He swore to you, if you keep the commandments of the Lord your God and walk in His ways (Deut. 28:7-9).

When we follow after God He will establish and command His blessings on us.

ENLIGHTENED UNDERSTANDING

God's light shines in the soul in accordance with our level of spiritual understanding, consciousness, or the awareness that God is with us wherever and in whatever state of being we may be at that time. We will always gain more of His light if we are faithful with the little God has given us.

Seers are shown premonitions of future events. Righteous people are given advance notice of the future through dreams and visions. This insures that they have plenty of time to prepare and align themselves for success and advancement. Therefore, it seems that the dreams of the righteous are delayed, but the dreams of the wicked happen quickly. They are not allotted time to change because their hearts are rebellious and hard. We are not to despise the small beginnings (see Zech. 4:10). If we despise our small beginnings, we will never get to the abundance and overflow. God is continuously creating us anew; His divine providence is always looking after us. We grow in understanding from glory to a higher level of glory and understanding. Seers who pursue greater spiritual perfection will receive knowledge of great importance.

Seers have the ability to see divine intervention at all times if people are truly living in the measurement of God's righteousness. People of merit are able to ascend above and see the things God wants them to see. If people are not virtuous or pure, they can be seized or pulled aside into a false dark realm. God says, *"I am the light of the world"* (John 8:12). He has called each one of us to be that light. You are the light of the world.

Light symbolizes the earthly service of the *tzadik*, or righteous individual, who is described as God's chariot or messenger in this world. The prophet Elijah was nothing more than a revelatory vessel that God used to communicate His heart and plans to people. Elijah was not of greater value than Nehemiah, who stood in the presence of King Artaxerxes as a cupbearer and then restored the wall of Jerusalem. Each of us is important because we have an individual calling that no one else can fulfill. We are righteous because of the blood of Jesus Christ that covers us.

In God's wisdom, He gradually reveals the unknown, hidden mysteries as we are prepared to seek His heart and mature in our understanding. Everything that has been said behind closed doors will one day be revealed in God's light.

> *But there is nothing covered up that will not be revealed, and hidden that will not be known. Accordingly, whatever you have said in the dark will be heard in the light, and what you have whispered in the inner rooms will be proclaimed upon the housetops* (Luke 12:2-3).

God creates a strong foundation of unified faith within us. Faith draws the knowledge of Jesus to us. Faith enables us to obtain an increased measure of spiritual maturity within our hearts. The knowledge of the secrets of the kingdom of Heaven is given to believers in abundance. Earthly circumstances cannot limit eternal spiritual beings that are controlled by faith. People do not live on bread alone, but by the creative, proceeding word from the mouth of God. When we pray, God hears us. When we decree, God establishes it for us so His light continually shines on our path.

> *You will pray to Him, and He will hear you; and you will pay your vows. You will also decree a thing, and it will be established for you; and light will shine on your ways. When you are cast down, you will speak with confidence, and the humble person He will save. He will deliver one who is not innocent, and he will be delivered through the cleanness of your hands* (Job 22:27-30).

In time and space, there are dimensions of the past that try to imprison and define us. The present dimensions try to limit and contain us, while the future calls us to operate in eternity where there are no limits prohibiting us from becoming who we are destined to be in Christ. As eternal beings, we will continue to evolve throughout the eons of time into the expanses of eternity transforming into His image from glory to glory.

ENDNOTES

1. Barbie L. Breathitt, *Dream Encounter Symbol Book,* Volume I, (Self-published, 2008).

2. Strong, *Strong's Exhaustive Concordance*, Greek #1108.

3. Ibid., Greek #1922.

4. Ibid., Greek #602.

5. Ibid., Greek #1492.

6. Ibid., Greek #3339.

Chapter 3

VISUAL CONTACT WITH LIGHT

Seers are a point of visual contact to the concealed power of God's presence. Seers are people who serve as doors to the infinite light of God in order to allow the created reality of the Spirit to come into existence in the natural. It is difficult to envision or imagine a spiritual God from a fleshly or natural perspective.

When people, who are created in the image of God, contemplate their own existence or their souls, they are trying to comprehend God, the Creator of flesh. God created people in His image from the "dust" of the earth. It is hard for us to comprehend a Creator who is infinite when we are finite.

The dust we are created from has the ability to record information and sound. Each of us is a testimony that carries a recording of the Father in our DNA—we are living data. At the end of our lives, that data is retrieved because God needs that piece of the puzzle. We are called to Heaven to give testimony of our lives and who God is.

When God created humanity, He created us out of dust. The dust we are formed from has the ability to record and remember the mighty acts of God. The Bible tells us that if we don't praise God, the very rocks will cry out, giving testimony of His wonderful greatness (see Luke 19:40). Rocks have ability to record and reflect what God is doing. All of creation testifies of God's existence. That is why people are without excuse. No one can deny God's existence. The dust that forms our body records everything we hear, see, say, and do. Even the sand is used for memory chips.

That is why the Bible tells us not to place anything unholy before our eyes; our bodies record the images we see and the words we hear. God has placed an image center within us. God projects images of Himself, His Word, the anointing, angels, and dreams and visions that contain His plans into our spirits, and we record them. This is how we are able to recall spiritual things when they are needed.

The images God sends us are scripted on our hearts. Our souls are scripted by God so that we can become like the images God places within us. We record everything we see. When we stand in Heaven, the Bible tells us:

> ...*We will all stand before the judgment seat of God. For it is written, "As I live, says the Lord, every knee shall bow to me, and every tongue shall give praise to God." So then each one of us will give an account of himself to God* (Rom. 14:10-12).

Our own tongues will be there to testify against us. The words we have spoken will either justify us or condemn us. We will give an account for every word we have spoken. Every word that is released from our mouths goes into eternity and is recorded by the earth. Science can now go back in time and retrieve historical speeches that were given when there were no recording devices present (Matt. 12:36, Rom. 14:12, Heb. 13:17, and 1 Pet. 3:15).

Every word we have ever spoken remains in the airways. The whole earth is recording our words and actions because it is composed of a large magnet, rock, and dust. It is necessary to place a guard upon the words of our mouths. We should be people of few words because we will give an account for our words. The words that we speak should be the written Word of God that becomes the living Word, the creative Spirit of God.

We create the world that we exist in. We create our own lives. If we are not prospering, it is because of the words we have released that have shut doors, released curses, and brought in spirits of darkness rather than the angelic realm. It is the Holy Spirit who wills to open doors before us. Our words create. Within our words are the power of death and life (see Deut. 30:15-20, Deut. 31:1).

When Jesus created the earth, He spoke a word that released light. The light and power of His words caused things to come into being. His words separated darkness from light. Jesus created the worlds just by speaking a word (see Gen. 1:1-31). If God could speak the universe into existence, we have the ability to frame our own individual lives and world (see Heb. 11:3). Seers look through the spiritual windows to gain revelation from other dimensions.

Seers are windows into the dimension of eternity and time. Time carries the aspect of history (His Story)—time past, time present, and time future. The beautiful thing about the vision or dream realm is that God can pull us out of whatever time we are in and insert us back into the past or into the future. People often dream about a house they lived in as a child or visiting their grandmother's home, or they dream they are back at an apartment where they lived during their college days. When this happens, God is pulling us out of our present and taking us back to a previous time to reveal something we need to know to bring healing or restoration to our present time.

God continually reveals another measure and dimension of Himself to us as we come into an understanding of who He is.

Everyone is at a different level of spiritual development, hearing, and seeing, but no matter where we are, there is always room for increase, always need to climb to the next rung of the ladder or dimension of revelation. When everything seems to be gone or dried up, it is time to relocate, dig a new well or transition into the next level of anointing.

The New Testament shares an example of the audible voice of God speaking from Heaven when Jesus foretold of His death (see John 12:27-30). Some who stood by didn't hear anything. Others who were present in the crowd heard God's voice manifested in thunder, while still others thought an angel had spoken.

> *"Father, glorify Your name." Then a voice came out of heaven: "I have both glorified it, and will glorify it again." So the crowd of people who stood by and heard it were saying that it had thundered; others were saying, "An angel has spoken to Him." Jesus answered and said, "This voice has not come for My sake, but for your sakes"* (John 12:28-30).

Jesus moves as one with His Father. He is intimately acquainted with His heavenly Father in every aspect, dimension, and possible manifestation. The Father always shares His secrets and mysteries with Jesus. Jesus shares them with the Holy Spirit and now the Holy Spirit reveals them to us. We are called to daily walk with God so we can be transformed into His image.

The Bible tells us that Enoch walked with God and then was not because God took him (see Gen. 5:24). God took and transformed Enoch into His image and likeness so that no one could find him. Enoch was gone, totally consumed by God. Earlier in his life, Enoch was transported into the heavenly realms on many occasions. God would return Enoch to earth and plug him back into time, and Enoch would teach people what dwelt in the future because he had seen it in the heavenly realms.

Enoch was able to impart futuristic revelation knowledge to the people of his time. This is also happening in our time. There is an acceleration of the anointing that is being released in revelation knowledge. God is catching people up out of the now to move them into the heavenly realms of the future to reveal things to the Church. Secrets and mysteries that have been concealed in God's Word since the beginning are now being revealed.

Chapter 4

SEERS ARE SHEPHERDS OF GOD'S GLORY

Seers are shepherds or stewards of God's glory. Therefore, seers are windows into a dimension of eternity in time. Time is linear. Time carries the aspects of history—time past, present, and future. But concerning the things of God, there is only what is *always*. The eternal nature of God transcends time barriers.

Although revelation knowledge has always been and always will be in God, it is the invisible realm of light that appears as nothing in the natural realms of time. God moves us into the supernatural realm outside of time. When we step into eternity, we are able to look past the natural realm and see into the invisible realm of the spirit. God trains us to do this in our sleep. During sleep, we are not conscious, but the subconscious is connecting with God's Spirit. God opens our eyes to see as we sleep. We gaze past the natural spectrums of color to see the different colors of the spirit. In the realms of the spirit, revelation is vibrant, colorful, and resounding with the fullness of life. Ecclesiastes 1:9 tells us that there is nothing new under the sun; what is has always been in God. We recognize angels and discern things in the realm of the spirit.

However, not every encounter we have in the spirit is of God and the kingdom of light. Sometimes demonic forces come, and we are battling or warring in the spirit in the night. Our spirits have to be trained to discern between the holy and the profane, the true and the false, the good and the evil. God trains us in our sleep. He speaks to us spirit to spirit so that our minds and carnal reasoning are not engaged. We can't argue with God or tell Him all the reasons why we are not qualified when we are asleep. God bypasses our minds and speaks to our spirits. Usually, spiritual encounters don't come when we are wide awake. God comes to have face-to-face encounters with us while we are asleep.

I used to be jealous of Moses because God spoke to him face to face. I asked God to visit and speak to me that way, too. To my surprise, God told me, "I do. Every night I come to hold you in a loving embrace. I visit you face to face in your dreams." The Song of Solomon speaks of the banner of love being placed over the bride in the way the lover comes to hold his bride. He places his left hand behind her head and lovingly embraces her lower back with his right. For women this position brings emotional healing and security. *"Let his left hand be under my head and his right hand embrace me"* (Song of Sol. 2:6). Everything that God does in the Scripture is a picture of how much He loves His bride, the Church. He is coming to visit and hold us in an intimate embrace of love.

God exists outside of time because He is eternal. Therefore, time cannot perceive or reveal what God has yet concealed. Understanding and revelation require the seven spirits of God to move our spirits into eternity or the fullness of God. God alone knows the fullness of time when mysteries are to be revealed. Seers must step out of real time and enter into the eternal realm of the Spirit, where time does not exist, in order to receive understanding of revelation knowledge from God.

God speaks to us by the spirit and not through our carnal reasoning. We then become windows, gateways, or bridges that allow God to come out of the invisible and be able to manifest. If our eyes were opened to see into the realm of the spirit, we would see the different rainbow colors that represent the different realms of anointings and their manifestations of power. As we speak, pray, sing, and worship, our words form colors and the cloud of glory manifests God's presence. When the presence of God comes in a tangible form, we can each receive our specific needs.

Every one of us has different DNA that produces its own individual sound and releases its own light. If you were to take your DNA strands and plug them into a musical instrument, your life would play a unique song to the Lord. When God takes each one of our life songs and places them together in harmony, they begin to release the new sound. When that sound comes into unity, it releases one voice that brings forth the clarion call of God. The gates of hell cannot stand against the voice of God speaking through His Church.

The process of life begins with conception. When the sperm penetrates the egg, light is released. Then the person continues shining throughout life with the process of growth—infant, toddler, child, teenager, and finally adult—unless the process is cut short by death. Millions of our cells are dying and being born everyday. In a year's time, you will be a whole new person. God is transforming you. You are a different person now than who you were ten years ago. Your belief structures have changed. God has radically changed, remolded, and increased you so that you are not the same person. You don't even have the same realm of influence or the same friends any more. That which you used to partake of in the past has nothing to do with you now. You are a new creation.

This same process is mirrored in the realm of the spirit to bring us to spiritual maturity. The closer we get to God, the more we are broken, the pruning comes, and the more the fire is turned up. The more of God's light we release, the more of His image we reflect. God can trust us with His secrets when we walk in His ways; no longer bondservants, we become the friends of God.

Passion for God releases a hunger to know Him in dimensions and ways we have never known Him before. God expands that which is within us so that we can mirror Him as an ambassador. We are called to bring His light before kings in order to impact and change the world.

Holiness is required to access spiritual realms of truth. Those with clean hands and pure hearts will see God! Sin blocks our ability to enter into God's presence, but His blood and Word wash us white as snow. When the living Word and the blood of Jesus are applied to our lives, we are cleansed. This process makes us pure vessels of honor that are fit for the Master's use.

THE WORLD OF THE SEER

The seer's world is much like that of C.S. Lewis' fanciful Narnia, where the unusual creatures speak, sharing their hidden wisdom and secrets. They walk on their hind legs, wield swords, and exist in a world all their own. These beings of darkness and light clash as two opposing kingdoms collide, battling for control. The realms of darkness contain the incantations of witchcraft, spells, curses, sorcery, black and white magic, and fiery darts of the wicked one. They use sickness, disease, jealousy, control, rebellion, hatred, murder, lies, demons, principalities, and powers to rule in wickedness. They spin a web of treachery, trickery, and deception.

Seers are able to observe their darkness, hear their vile words, and feel the pressure of their grasping claws. A seer smells the stench of the demonic. They can even taste their diabolic schemes. They have trained their bodies to read the pressures, invisible signs, and signals like blind people are able to read Braille.

God's seers are His special agents sent to tear down and destroy the works of darkness with the glory realms of heaven. Seers remove evil and replace it with the goodness of God. They break curses by releasing blessings that cause increase and multiplication. The training of a seer is aggressive and extensive.

FLEDGLING SEERS

Many fledgling seers shut their seeing gifts down in their infancy, before they have time to develop their ability to see the beauty of God's Spirit realm. They could not bear to view the gruesome images of devilish wreckage. Their nights were full of torment and terror. The demons of fear and nightmare would dance in and out of their rooms. This left them with the feelings of dread and despair. Horror hung around their necks like a dead man's noose. They begged to have their eyes blinded to the dark creatures of the night. They didn't want to see this horrible realm. They shut down their gift before they learned to battle these menacing enemies with their spiritual weapons. Once they are trained to operate their spiritual God-given gifts in authority and power, no weapon formed against them will prosper (see Isa. 54:17).

BARBIE'S STORY

As a young girl, I was terribly afraid of the dark. There were four of us children growing up together, so two of us shared a room with each other for many years. That brought some level of comfort, knowing there was another person in my room at night, but it didn't alleviate the dread I felt when scary visitors appeared in the night.

Everyone remembers the notorious "Boogie man" who lived under the bed or the Frankenstein monster who occupied the closet. I can still remember seeing thousands of roaches and snakes crawling over my clean white sheets at night. And they said, "Don't let the bedbugs bite!"

When I was growing, up the scariest movies or television shows were *The Edge of Night, The Dark Shadow* (the Shadow knows what lurks and goes bump in the night), *The Blob, The Swamp Monster in the Black Lagoon,* any vampire and werewolf movies, *The Headless Horseman,* and *Godzilla.* These movies would be considered mild or even comical compared to horror movies in our present day.

When I would watch any type of horror movie, my spirit would record the monstrous images and fear would well up in my heart. My parents forbade us from watching things with witches, magic, or horror but I did it anyway. When I was being trained as a seer, my negative exposure to the magical or mystical realm consisted of the hilarious comedies *I Dream of Jeannie,* with Barbara Eden, and *Bewitched,* with Elizabeth Montgomery. Evil, witchcraft, and horror movies have continued to grow in their explicit content which releases fear.

We were shocked when *The Exorcist* came out, with her spinning head and projectile pea-green soup-like vomit. After all, "demons didn't live in America"; I'd been told they were only in the bush country of Africa. But look at where we were then and where we are now! We have come a long way in these few short years. There is no comparison of the past where we laughed about evil, to the present where witchcraft is practiced on television. The horror flicks of my day are like comedy relief compared to the sorcery and demonic expressions on the big screen today.

Today's children (and adults) are being trained to become witches by studying Harry Potter and Vampire Diaries. They can check out or buy books on witchcraft, incantations, and curses at their school book fairs or publicly funded neighborhood libraries. The Internet also offers a large variety of occult-training Websites. Children are cutting their spiritual teeth on the black arts and routinely entertain demonic spirit guides as their invisible friends.

VAMPIRE VAPORS

I still remember the sheer terror I felt when I was a pre-teen when a demonic presence entered my room. People call demons many things—spirits, the Boogieman, monsters, ghosts, or simply your imagination. Demons have always struck terror in the hearts of people. But once we learn how to conquer and defeat them with the power of God and the name and blood of Jesus, we do not need to fear them any more.

I was one of four children raised in a conservative Christian home. Dad was a lawyer and an elder in the Presbyterian Church where we faithfully attended every Sunday. Mother was a devoted wife and a stay-at-home mom, church volunteer, P.T.A. president, and Aglow president. We all led active lives. We were not allowed to watch horror movies in my home, but like most children, I would occasionally sneak a peek. When Mom would leave the house for any predictable length of time, I'd turn on the forbidden television show and feast my eyes on horror.

The problem with being a seer is that you are already hypersensitive in the visual realm. You are able to imprint and vividly remember every dreadful monster and often the venomous words they speak. God has given us an imagination and a memory that is able to record the great works and wonders of our Creator. But our image center will also record the horrors of the darkness. This is why it is so important to guard the eye gate to your soul and only allow pure, precious things to enter. Watching violence, horror, and evil will dull your spiritual eyes so they become blind and non-receptive. We can train our natural and spiritual senses to see good or evil.

Once, while watching a horror movie, I discovered that vampires could vaporize, that they could float unsuspected in a watery mist, and then materialize to attack their victims. This new knowledge made me afraid to take hot steamy showers. If during my shower, I momentarily forgot my fear, I could close my eyes to rinse the shampoo from my hair. But if I remembered that vampires could vaporize, I knew when I opened my eyes he'd be there, poised with his awful fangs, ready to stab my juggler vein and suck the life out of me.

I didn't feel safe until the condensation evaporated from the mirror and the cloud of mist left the bathroom. One good thing about my particular flavor of fear was that I wasn't one for long showers. I was in and out of the bathroom as quickly as possible. This made it more convenient for the other five family members who shared one small bathroom. That's a family of six and maybe one or two vampires sharing one bathroom.

Not only was I afraid of vampires but I also feared things that would appear in the dark. I would not go outside alone at night. Sometimes when fear gripped me I would imagine a monster was after me. I would become terrorized and run to the safety of my home. Fear would come at night and during the day.

BLOOD RED EYES

I was raised in a three bedroom, one bathroom Spanish stucco home where my father had been born in Lakeland, Florida. Early one morning, before the sun was up, my family was congregating in and near the bathroom waiting their turn to use the facilities. Dad liked to read the paper on the porcelain throne, so Mom asked me if I would go out to the front yard to retrieve dad's newspaper. I was ten years old but I still didn't like the dark. And I especially didn't like to be left alone in the dark. I knew all about vampires, because I was dreadfully afraid of them. I knew from watching horror movies that vampires had to be back in their coffins before the sun rose. So I thought I could brave the darkness of dawn, just this once and get Dad's paper for him.

I had been chosen and given the honor of retrieving Dad's paper. So in obedience to Mom's request, I headed toward the front door. I cautiously peeked out through the curtain that draped the door. The coast looked clear, no vampires! I slowly opened the deadbolt so it didn't make a sound and stepped out on the tile porch. I saw my goal. The newspaper was across the porch, down the steps, seemingly miles away, resting on the curb at the end of the sidewalk.

I took a deep breath to steady myself. But before I could take another step on that cold floor, I saw a large pair of blood-red eyeballs appear. They were intently peering at me from the top of the hedge. The two oversized eyes just glared at me. I was seeing evil in the realm of the spirit. For an agonizing moment, terror paralyzed me. I couldn't even scream. I completely lost my voice. My pulse shot up and my heart began to pound as if it was going to explode out of my chest. I was frozen, focusing on the devilish eyes for what seemed like an eternity. When I was finally able to break my gaze, I turned toward the door to make my escape.

I flung the screen door open so wide it almost came off the hinges. Crashing through the heavy front door, I fled from the blood-red eyeballs. I ran through the living room to the supposed safety of the bathroom, where I finally rediscovered my vocal cords. Dancing in hysteria, I let out a bloodcurdling scream. I screamed so loud the sound waves almost knocked mom's bobby pins out of her hair. I was traumatized! And now, so was everyone else in the house.

Mom demanded, "What is wrong with you?" "Get a hold of yourself!" "Where is your Father's newspaper?"

I responded, "It's still outside!" "I'm not going out there again! There's a pair of big glowing red eyes looking at me over the parapet."

All mother would say is, "Young lady, get control of yourself! You are going to scare the children!" *What did she think I was?* "Now, march yourself right back out there! You will get that paper for your father. Stop all your shenanigans, or I will get my belt and give you something to be afraid of!"

I thought, "*Who cares about a beating with a belt?*" I was more afraid of the blood-sucking eyeballs that wanted to glare me to death.

Looking back, I find it interesting that as a child I saw a pair of intimidating blood-red eyes peering at me. Their purpose was to strike so much fear into my heart that I would shut down my seer gift. But, God protected me and has allowed me to write a book to help train the next generation of seers.

I also remember that the first beautiful vision I saw, as a child, was of Jesus. His face was handsome, tan, gentle, and warmly inviting. I wanted to run into Him. He was covered in a spirit of peace and love. His loving arms were opened wide, inviting me to rest in His embrace. But the thing I remembered the most was His beautiful, crystal clear blue eyes that radiated His eternal compassion. His transparent eyes were so kind and accepting. He looked deep into me. He knew me totally, yet loved me completely. I thought, "*How can Jesus' eyes be blue when He is Jewish?*" I was expecting them to be brown. Yet Revelation 19:12, tells us that, His eyes are a flame of fire and the hottest fire is blue. If we are able to see the hideous dark realm of the spirit we can also see the beautiful realms of glory.

Seers can see the supernatural, invisible realm of the spirit with their natural and spiritual eyes. The enemy wanted to close me off from seeing. But his plans failed and his weapons didn't work. His plans to stop me only made me stronger and more determined to see God. Most young seers make the mistake of turning off their seeing gift by shutting down their spiritual eyes before they learn to use their spiritual weapons to overcome the elements of darkness.

For seers, learning to understand the realms of angels and becoming experts in spiritual warfare is essential for their survival. We are destroyed for a lack of spiritual knowledge. The enemy's commission is to kill, steal, and destroy everything that is precious in life (see John 10:10). Our commission, as believers, is to destroy the works of evil and establish the kingdom of God (see 1 John 3:8). The Bible tells us that no weapon formed against us will prosper if our life is submitted to God. But it also tells us that we are destroyed for a lack of knowledge when we don't seek to know God. Death is the enemy of life. Jesus came to give us salvation and eternal life through His life, death, and resurrection from the dead.

OVERCOMING THE SPIRIT OF DEATH

I have met death and won by the grace of God. Grace can be defined as the aggressive mercy of God. I was living in Franklin, Georgia, in 1982. Having just graduated from the University of Georgia, as a veterinary technician, I was employed by my then fiancé's animal clinic. I was attending his Methodist church, where most of the pastor's sermons came from articles that had been published in the Reader's Digest. Needless to say, there was a spiritual vacuum in that small town. Many people were depressed, some to the point of suicide.

One of the local contractors, who attended our church, was found sitting under a tree with a bullet in his head. Life had become more than he could bear with the little spiritual food he was given. When that happened, I began to cry out to God in prayer for revival, and God heard my prayers. He began to release more angels into the airwaves over Franklin. The light in that little community began to increase as God's presence pierced the darkness. The kingdoms of darkness and light began to clash.

One night, as I was drifting off to sleep, the spirit of death invaded my house. I felt its eerie presence when it entered the back of my old country home. The enemy always tries to sneak in the back door. He knows his presence is not welcome. Although I was in the front bedroom, I felt a cold, lingering presence sweep over my body. My spirit was awakened to the impending life and death battle that approached.

The spirit of fear rushed into my room. Fear was so strong that my body was paralyzed. I lay there motionless, unable to move. My mind battled a spirit of confusion that came to torment me. A lying spirit began to chant its hideous lies at the top of his voice. Condemnation, doubt, and unbelief were the next to manifest. They all led the way for death to come in and to try to steal my life prematurely.

Spirits of darkness began to fill my room. They swirled around like a black hazy fog rolling in to smother any hope of survival. My heart was pounding so loudly that I could feel each beat in my throat. I struggled to gain a voice to protest this demonic intrusion when an ape-like creature wrapped his hairy arm around my throat in a death-like grip. No words were able to escape my mouth.

Then a lying spirit leaned in so close I could feel its cold, icy lips as he whispered in my ear, "You can't do anything about this. You are going to die. You can't stop us because you can't speak. You are our helpless victim." He jeered, "Where is your God when you need Him? He can't help you. He can't hear you. God has forsaken you." It seemed like all the imps of hell had crowded into my bedroom to take my life. This same army of murderers, liars, and thieves reported that they had taken my friend's life through the spirit of suicide a week prior. And now they were in my bedroom, poised to extinguish my life.

After the stage was set, the spirit of death made his grand entrance. Death manifested by walking through the wall in the corner of my bedroom. He stood about eight to ten feet tall. His broad, solid shoulders looked like he was wearing football shoulder pads. He wore a thick, long black cloak that hung to the floor. He was shrouded in pitch black darkness. His facial features were obscured by the total depths of evil shadows.

He approached my bed to carry out his diabolical, murderous scheme. My heart pounded, and my mind raced. Death had come to destroy me. What could I do? *I don't want to die! I am too young to die! I have my whole life to live. What will people think?* Suddenly, I could see the newspaper headline that read, "Young Woman Mysteriously Dies in Sleep." My heart began crying out to God. Please protect and defend me. *What are the weapons I use in this situation? How do I defeat death? Is it my time to die?*

In my desperation, I asked for the biggest, strongest angel in the Bible. You know the angel in Revelation that comes down from Heaven clothed with a cloud. The angel I called for was so big he wore a rainbow on his head. He is described in Scripture as having a face as bright as the sun, and his feet are like pillars of fire. He is so enormous that he is able to place one foot on the sea and the other on the land. When he cries out, his voice is like that of a lion that releases a sound like thunder (see Rev. 10:1-4).

I didn't want to mess around with little, naked flying baby angels. No! Not when I was wrestling with Death. I wanted the biggest, baddest angel I could think of. I knew something had to happen quickly. Death would just backhand little angels around like gnats or bounce them off the walls of my bedroom with his steely sickle.

Suddenly, I heard the whisper of the Holy Spirit's voice. He spoke to my fearful heart. I was looking for comfort, keys, and weapons to combat the spirit of death. The Holy Spirit spoke these words to me, "Barbie, if death touches you, you will die!" That was not what I wanted to hear. How was I going to stop a monstrous spirit of death from touching me when he was only feet away? Death was radiating spirits of hatred and murder toward me. How could I stop death from touching me?

Suddenly into my spirit the answer came. "Use the powerful name of Jesus and My blood!" I mustered all my strength and simply thought, *Jesus!* Just the thought of Jesus caused the ape-like creature to loosen his death grip on my throat. When my thoughts turned to Jesus, the angels were released to rebuke the demon who had me bound. Then I barely whispered, "In the name and by the blood of Jesus, I bind you and command you to go!"

As soon as I spoke those words, it was as if the spirit of death hit an invisible wall. His forward progress was stopped cold. All he could do was release a spirit of fury and rage. He projected his cold, murderous hatred toward me. Death was bound, frozen in space and time. But I could still see him. A few seconds later, the darkness of death disappeared from sight with the legion of evil following behind him.

I wish I could say that I bravely sprang from the bed and rebuked the demons for coming. But I cannot. I lay there terrorized and exhausted. My body still felt paralyzed. It took me a long time to navigate the thick fear that hung in my room. I pondered that dreadful experience for many weeks. I sought God for answers to the myriad of questions I continued to ask. I rehearsed this event over and over in my mind. I never wanted to encounter that level of darkness again.

The Holy Spirit gave me understanding and several strategic kingdom keys.

The Comforter reminded me of the passage that says, *"My people are destroyed for a lack of knowledge"* (Hos. 4:6; see also Isa. 5:13). In my ignorance, I had prayed for the wrong angel. But because I often prayed for God's mercy and grace, He dispatched the correct angels. He explained, "Barbie, when dealing with the spirit of death, one requires the opposite spirit, which is Resurrection Life! Therefore, the correct angels for that particular assignment would have been the Resurrection angels. Yes! I sent the very same Resurrection angels who served Jesus at His tomb. They participated in His resurrection from the dead." Holy Spirit said, "Heaven sent the Resurrection angels to stand between you and death."

I finally understood what had happened on that dark, dreadful night. I realized death had disappeared in a moment, as if he had been swallowed up. Although I didn't see the Resurrection angels step in front of death to protect me, I knew it was a reality, and it was a lesson well learned. The Resurrection angels had become a wall to protect me from the sting of death.

> *So when this corruptible has put on incorruption, and this mortal has put on immortality, then shall be brought to pass the saying that is written: "Death is swallowed up in victory." "O Death, where is your sting? O Hades, where is your victory?" The sting of death is sin, and the strength of sin is the law. But thanks be to God, who gives us the victory through our Lord Jesus Christ. Therefore, my beloved brethren, be steadfast, immovable, always abounding in the work of the Lord, knowing that your labor is not in vain in the Lord* (1 Cor. 15:54-58 NKJV).

If seers have to endure visions of death, darkness, and corruption, they are also graced with seeing the beautiful, rapturous realms of God's light and glory.

SEERS UNIFY GOD AND MAN

Seers are God's system of unification. Seers are used like connectors or conduits to plug people into God. They can be used as bridges, gateways, doors, or windows between God and humanity's ability to understand revealed mysteries. Salvation is God's system of reconciliation; therefore, it has a contingency, an unforeseen event or eventuality of fulfillment. We are saved when we accept Jesus Christ as our Savior yet we are still being saved daily—as opposed to, what is, will always be, regardless of whether understanding takes place or not. What we used to do and be; the person who we were becomes something completely new and different. Our ways of handling problems and looking at others changes for the better. Now every situation in our life miraculously works out for our benefit. Everything that our hands touch prospers. We become a new creation, a new person that is carefully fashioned upon the Master Potter's wheel.

When the Lord gives a vision, He is bringing unity to Himself through the vessel He uses. We see the blueprint of the goal or high calling God is placing on our lives. God is expanding what has always been and mirroring it in that person. Magnification has to do with vision. Amplification has to do with hearing. Hearing the Word of God releases faith. In this sense, amplification is not the process of making something louder; it is the process whereby God reveals Himself through the lives of individuals who have an understanding of His Word.

When we hear the still small voice of God, we are to shout it from the roof tops so that it multiplies in the lives of those who hear the voice of God. With every revelation, the breath of His Spirit is uttering His love, His secrets, and His mysteries to the hearts of people. When we seek Him with all of our hearts, we will find Him (see Jer. 29:12-14).

The angels bring understanding and skill to us through the gateway of our hearts. As we sleep, God releases angelic messengers to come into our dream lives to reveal the meaning of mysteries so we can decipher what God is speaking to us through symbolic language. Our carnal reasoning cannot understand or figure God out. To come into spiritual understanding, we must enter into the rest of the Holy Spirit's embrace and engage with the angelic ministers of fire that come to give us revelation knowledge in the spirit.

Chapter 5

THE PARABOLIC LIFE OF A SEER

The seer is right brain dominant, seeing things in abstract, symbolic forms. Seers are very parabolic, speaking in metaphors and analogies and seeing in cartoon forms. This makes the seer an expert dream interpreter. As the dream is being told, the seer is able to enter into the dream and watch the scenes unfold.

Seers tend to live out the visions they see in their own lives. Because they see in the realms of the Spirit, it is often difficult to communicate what they are seeing accurately through spoken language so they tend to talk in riddles or fragments. Similarly, Paul found it difficult to express the visions he beheld and the words he heard while in the heavenly realms of Paradise (see 1 Cor. 12:4). It is difficult to master a heavenly inspired language when one dwells on earth. That is the beauty of dreams they help us bring the communications of heaven to earth.

DREAMS AND VISIONS

God speaks to both prophets and seers through dreams and visions. Dreams rain heavenly wisdom down upon our open hearts so we can receive God's saving knowledge. In this way, dreams help to ensure our right standing and continued spiritual growth. God sends us dreams from Heaven that speaks the truth to us in love so we can grow up into Him.

Prophets and seers have practiced developing their skills in understanding a spiritual language, as well as dreams and visions. They maintain a relationship in the presence of God to discover all they need to know about life. A good dream interpreter will be able to give insight with understanding to help illuminate God's faith message for difficult circumstances. A series of dreams may also reveal the dreamer's strengths, weaknesses, and spiritual gifts as the group of dreams is dissected.

Dreams are God's night parables that direct our paths and speak to our daily needs in life. These dream events and awesome promises come while we are sleeping. To understand the dreams of the night we need to develop our mind's eye or imagination.

The Bible indicates that revelation knowledge, dreams, information, and communication come from different sources.

Dreams can come because of busyness and too much activity. Ecclesiastes 5:3 says, *"For the dream comes through much effort and the voice of a fool through many words."* Also, Ecclesiastes 5:7 says, *"For in the multitude of dreams and many words there is also vanity. But fear God"* (NKJV).

Dreams that are not of God are usually fragmented or incomplete. It is very difficult to remember the dream sequence. They will quickly evaporate and be completely forgotten. Test the dream, vision, or revelation. Do we see the whole picture or just a portion? Are we able to recall the details and gain understanding? If God is truly speaking, He will repeat the dream or speak in another way so we will finally perceive His message. God will also give the same dream to a family member, husband, wife, or close friend so we know He is speaking to us. Sometimes God will also use someone to warn us of a certain action. If we continue on that path, we will suffer the repercussions.

While he was sitting on the judgment seat, his wife sent him a message, saying, "Have nothing to do with that righteous Man; for last night I suffered greatly in a dream because of Him" (Matt. 27:19).

God will guide us to make the proper decisions through dreams.

And Joseph her husband, being a righteous man and not wanting to disgrace her, planned to send her away secretly. But when he had considered this, behold, an angel of the Lord appeared to him in a dream, saying, "Joseph, son of David, do not be afraid to take Mary as your wife; for the Child who has been conceived in her is of the Holy Spirit" (Matt. 1:19-20).

Some dreams come because of our own souls' desires or longings.

It shall even be as when a hungry man dreams, And look—he eats; but he awakes, and his soul is still empty; or as when a thirsty man dreams, and look—he drinks; but he awakes, and indeed he is faint, and his soul still craves: so the multitude of all the nations shall be, who fight against Mount Zion (Isa. 29:8 NKJV).

Some sexual dreams defile the flesh. They come from a demonic spirit of lust, fantasy, perversion, or carnal desires. *"Likewise also these dreamers defile the flesh, reject authority, and speak evil of dignitaries"* (Jude 8 NKJV).

Dreams and revelation must be judged. Deuteronomy 13:1-5 explains it this way,

If there arises among you a prophet or a dreamer of dreams, and he gives you a sign or a wonder, and the sign or the wonder comes to pass, of which he spoke to you, saying, "Let us go after other gods"—which you have not known—"and let us serve them," you shall not listen to the words of that prophet or that dreamer of dreams, for the Lord your God is testing you to know whether you love the Lord your God with all your heart and with all your soul. You shall walk after the Lord your God and fear Him, and keep His commandments and obey His voice; you shall serve Him and hold fast to Him. But that prophet or that dreamer of dreams shall be put to death, because he has spoken in order to turn you away from the Lord your God, who brought you out of the land of Egypt and redeemed you from the house of bondage, to entice you from the way in which the Lord your God commanded you to walk. So you shall put away the evil from your midst (NKJV).

THE MIND'S EYE

The imagination is a power tool that can be used to create wealth, invent and understand the images God projects to our soul. Some call the imagination the mind's eye. The *mind's eye* can be defined as: "the human ability for visual perception, imagination, visualization, and memory. In other words, the mind's eye is one's ability to see things with the mind." Because many dreams are symbolic mysteries, God's guidance is necessary to uncover their hidden meanings. God intended that we get to know Him better through this process of discovering the meaning of our dreams. Our image center is a vehicle that the Holy Spirit can access if we are open to him. The Holy Spirit will give us dreams in the night or streams of thought during the day to bring revelation and direction to our lives. The more we develop our image center the more God can speak to us through thoughts, impressions and pictures.

PICTURES AND IMPRESSIONS

God speaks to us through a personal picture language that is full of symbols. God begins to show us things we would not naturally know during the course of our everyday lives. He often shows us pictures and impressions that pass across the mind's eye. By communicating in this way, God works to strengthen His relationship with us. He takes us on a journey of supernatural guidance through the Holy Spirit and teaches us to discern between good and evil influences.

Whether specific dreams are to reveal hidden issues, to inspire us to greatness, to keep us out of harm's way, or to provide insight into the world around us, God leads us through a revelatory cycle of dreaming to build a transitional bridge. This connection is where our dreams become the link between His infinite wisdom and our finite thinking. It is God's desire to draw us by the Holy Spirit to a place of acknowledgement that this bridge is a point of crossing from the limited realm of our plans to His limitless realm.

GOD COMMUNICATES THROUGH DREAMS

Dreams are one way that God chooses to communicate what He sees in us. A dream is a picture language. Because pictures are easily imprinted on our spirits and minds, we can recall the images back to remembrance. God speaks in a language of signs, symbols, puns, riddles, and mysteries through dreams. God also speaks to the positives of what we are and what we can become, rather than emphasizing the negatives.

The Bible, however, reveals to us that dreams are one of the ways that God speaks to us (see Job 33:15; Num. 12:6). The key to understanding God's dream language is using a biblical basis to interpret the symbolism. We must rely on the Holy Spirit as our source of revelation, understanding, wisdom, and proper application. Dreams are one of the vehicles that God has chosen to show and tell us who we are called to be in Christ. His desire is for us to reach our full potential and to be successful. Not all dreams are inspired by God. But we can still benefit from the script they reveal if we learn how to decode their hidden messages by recording our dreams with an open mind, honesty, thankfulness, and objectivity.

SEERS NOTED IN SCRIPTURE

Nine Old Testament Seers

- Samuel was a Priest and governmental advisor (see 1 Chron. 29:29; 1 Sam. 9:11-14).

- Hanani was the grandson of Samuel (see 2 Chron. 16:7).

- Iddo was a Priest (see 2 Chron. 9:29).

- Gad was a governmental advisor (see 1 Chron. 29:29).

- Amos was a shepherd-prophet, a herdsman who was a tender of sycamore fruit (see Amos 7:12).

- Asaph was a worship leader; he wrote Psalms 50 and 73 through 83 (see 2 Chron. 29:30).

- Jeduthun was a worship leader and the king's seer (see 2 Chron. 35:15).

- Heman was a worship leader; he wrote Psalm 88 (see 1 Chron. 25:5).

- Zadok was the Chief Priest (see 2 Sam. 15:27).

- Balaam, Daniel, Elisha, Ezekiel, and Zechariah all operated as seers through dreams and visions, but were not given the title seer.

Prophets and seers are both equally valid and needed ministries, although they receive their revelation in different manners. In the past people sought both the prophet and the seer for revelation knowledge.

Formerly in Israel, when a man went to inquire of God, he spoke thus: "Come, let us go to the seer" [ra'ah]; for he

who is now called a prophet [nabiy'] was formerly called
a seer [ra'ah] (1 Sam. 9:9 NKJV).

Gad was a governmental advisor, and Asaph was a worship leader. Both of these men were seers in David's court,
while Nathan was considered a prophet. Samuel the seer was
both a priest and a governmental advisor, while Iddo the
priest was only a seer. Seers and the way they functioned and
the office they held were as diverse as people are today.

> *Now the acts of King David, first and last, indeed they are*
> *written in the book of Samuel the seer [ra'ah], in the book*
> *of Nathan the prophet [nabiy'], and in the book of Gad*
> *the seer [chozeh]* (1 Chron. 29:29 NKJV).

> *And he stationed the Levites in the house of the Lord*
> *with cymbals, with stringed instruments, and with harps,*
> *according to the commandment of David, of Gad the*
> *king's seer [chozeh], and of Nathan the prophet [nabiy'];*
> *for thus was the commandment of the Lord by his prophets*
> (2 Chron. 29:25 NKJV).

The seer, generally termed *chozeh* or *hozeh*,[1] was one who
saw into the spirit realm and spoke what was seen. *Chozeh*
refers to a separate function that is different from *nabiy*,[2]
which was a standard term for a prophet and was also used
as the word for *vision*.

We can learn a lot from the Hebrew spelling of a word. For
example, the meaning of the word *chozeh* is as follows. *Chet*
means "man's ability to transcend limits of physical existence,
divine grace that enables one to abound in God's strength,
and a new beginning or birth into resurrection life."[3] Being
the eighth letter in the Hebrew alphabet, *Chet* eludes to
humanity's ability to go beyond or transcend the limitations
of the physical world. It speaks of resurrection power, new
birth, or a new beginning—to swell with revelation so one
can abound in spiritual strength. For us to apprehend this

free gift of God, grace is necessary. Grace refers to the divine attribute of the Gracious One, who favors people with His kindness. God gives us eternal life, the virtue of the spiritual heritage, which allows our spirits to prosper. The power of sin is broken; it no longer has a hold on us, but only has the potential to limit us if we surrender to it. We need to develop our ability to look beyond and see the Beautiful One, full of grace and mercy.

The Hebrew word *Ayin* means "the awakening eye, a wellspring, the seer who perceives the declarations of God with understanding."[4] *Ayin,* or the number seventy, represents perfect spiritual order being carried out with significant spiritual power throughout the nations and peoples of the world through God's judgment. In God, judgment does not carry a negative connotation of destruction, but it weighs and measures things on His perfect scales of justice. God's judgment brings balanced order and justice. God's judgment brings a time of supernatural alignment and establishes strategies that bring prosperity. Everything that can be shaken will be shaken so the unshakable kingdom of God can be established with us.

Ayin represents God's administration of the world through His eye or visionary insights. Moses appointed seventy elders to help him administrate, judge, or oversee Israel. Seventy is the number of multitude prior to increase and it relates to the Lord's disciples. We are the disciples of God. *Ayin* has to do with the eye and its relationship with light bringing revelation. We don't see light. Light doesn't enable us to see, but it makes that which was unseen possible to see. When God enlightens the eyes of our understanding, we know the hope of His calling. Enlightenment allows us to see the riches, wealth, and creativity of His glory. God's light enables us to see past the veil into the unseen to bring forth revelation that has never been seen before.

Zayin, the Hebrew number seven, means "Spirit, sustenance, and struggle."[5] People struggle to grow and understand their purpose through life. People strive for their completeness, wholeness, fullness, spiritual perfection, balance, and alignment with God. God gives us a vision of who we really are in the realm of the spirit that shows us what we are called to accomplish in this life. Throughout life, people are going to try to dictate what we can do. They will try to define who we are or who we are called to become; if we allow them, they will steal our destiny. If we stumble or fall, God doesn't criticize us. He picks us up, dusts us off, and lovingly sets us on the path again. God is an encourager who empowers us to accomplish great things.

Life is a spiritual journey of development, purification, and consecration. *Zayin* being the seventh letter in the Hebrew alphabet denotes the spiritual values that were the purpose of creation. God created the world in six days and rested on the seventh day. We enter into possessing the promises of God by resting in them. God created a perfect image of who we are from before the beginning of time. All of our days are numbered and ordered. Our dreams reveal the blueprints God has planned for us. When we enter into rest, the Spirit of the Lord comes to visit us with dreams and visions. He imparts gifts, callings, and anointings that will transform and empower us to change. We are created in His image. We grow into His likeness through seeing Him and becoming like Him.

The number seven represents God's own essence and centrality. Seven denotes all directions: east, west, north, south, up, and down, as well as the center of everything, where Jesus the holy one represents what we should focus upon. Every direction surrounds a person wherever they are; the seventh position, Jesus, is the center of it all. Jesus should be at the center of each of our lives. The whole universe revolves around Jesus and the seven spirits that are represented in the Holy Spirit as One God (see Isa. 11:2).

We have an ability to know Him in every dimension of life; no matter where we look, we can see His hand of protection and provision watching over us. The Holy Spirit brings us into the centrality of knowing God in ways we have never known Him before. God is always revealing Himself to us in a new dimension, but we will never know God completely. We are eternal beings in a process of discovering Christ. The angels in Heaven continually announce "Holy!" every time God reveals another aspect or facet of Himself. God surrounds us with His presence.

The creatures within the wheel within a wheel moved in a straight line following the leading of the Spirit (see Ezek. 1:15-18). There is a plumb line that is dropped from Heaven. It is like a ladder that allows an eternal ebb and flow of His presence. Our subconscious aligns the conscious, enabling it to follow the Holy Spirit, not the soul, which allows destiny to be accomplished. When the two ends of a straight line come together in a loop to meet, it forms a perfect circle. Circles represent eternity and God's covenant. The *Zayin* part of being a seer is the struggle of becoming who God has called us to be in the fullness of it, by removing the limitations.

If we put all three letters together for *chozeh*, the Hebrew word for "seer," Chet, Ayin, and Zayin we have a picture of a threefold cord, which is not easily broken. This cord symbolizes a vehicle that helps people, in the midst of their struggles, to go beyond physical limitation and unite to the breath or spirit of God. A proper understanding of the Hebrew words will give us a greater understanding of how the seer and developing our own ability to see beyond the natural will help us to transcend limitations and reconnect with God. In this way, we know God in Spirit and in truth so that His Spirit may flow to, in, and through us.

Our subconscious is where God deals with us in dreams and visions. It is our subconscious that begins to align with God so we can be conscious of knowing Him. We have to know Him more than just through head knowledge. True knowledge of God has to be transferred into our innermost being, where the spirit resides. God communicates to us through the Holy Spirit who resides within us. The Spirit leads us into the deep things of God. God speaks through spirit-to-spirit communication, revealing truth that brings forth eternal change in us. Without spiritual communication, we will always be striving to make changes in our lives, but we will never accomplish our goal.

We operate out of the soul realm which is the mind, will, and emotions. If we approach things in life through our souls, we will continue to go around the mountain and around the mountain of wilderness wanderings. Once we exit the wilderness, with our head resting on our Beloved, we will hear His still small voice and know Him in truth. For the most part, we only know God in a form. God leads us through the Holy Spirit so we can know Him Spirit to spirit, which brings the transformation we desire. Our spiritual transformation allows the image of Christ to manifest in this earthly realm. Transformation allows the kingdom of God within us to be established.

God extends a plumb line from Heaven. We must not measure or compare ourselves by each other, but by Jesus the heavenly plumb line or standard. When we look at Jesus, God's plumb line, we will strive to line up to His standard of excellence. Think about eternity as a straight line. If we join the two ends of that straight line, it forms a circle or a wheel. If we join two lines in a circle, they form a wheel within a wheel. In Ezekiel, the creatures in the wheel move with God; wherever the anointing goes, it follows in a straight line. A timeline is linear. If we connect the ends of a line into a circle, we now have a representation of eternity. If we drop a plumb line down the center of the circle, we can measure ourselves according to God's standard and begin to line up with His perfect plans and purposes for our lives.

If we open the line of the circle up again, we have two lines that intersect, making the cross of Jesus, which must be the center focus of our lives. We must take up our cross daily and follow Him into eternity. If we keep our eyes focused or centered on what Jesus did for us through His death on the cross, then everything in our lives will revolve around Him. Eternity is all about the cross and us being transformed into His image because of the blood Jesus shed for us. Jesus died on the cross to restore us back to God; yet sometimes it is still difficult to communicate to a God who is spirit.

There are times in life when we think God is not hearing our prayers. It seems our prayers are bouncing off the ceiling and God has stepped away from us. In reality, God has moved deeper into the realm of the Spirit to draw us out of the soul realm so we can be closer to Him in spirit and in truth. We discover a better way to connect with God's wisdom. As we commune with God, our consciousness begins to know Him because He touches us in our subconscious. This process enables us to understand God in a deeper way.

The inner self will accept or reject these positions and will identify with success or failure to their purposes according to the measure that Christ is central in our lives. *Zayin* represents the spirit of this struggle: "Is it real or not?" Life is the struggle for us to discern what is real and what is not real. We understand that the realm of the Spirit is the most real realm. It is eternal and tangible. That is why God has called us to know Him in and by the Spirit.

Hei means "divinity, discretion, refinement, and specificity."[6] *Hei* is represented by the number five; it also speaks of God's grace, gentleness, and favor. Without God's great grace, none of us can make it. Jesus suffered five major wounds on the cross. Jesus' act of love bought our redemption, and His saving grace leads to our freedom through the atonement. *Hei* is the exhalation of breath. (Try it. Place your hand over your mouth and say, *"Hei,"* pronounced "hay".) Little effort is made; yet it carries great significance. *Hei* speaks of the exhalation of breath. The Holy Spirit is breath. Angels are made up of light, fire, wind, and the breath of God. The spirit realm is full of all of those different dimensions. Breath comes forth with very little effort. It means that we don't have to do a lot—but just breathe. God finds pleasure in knowing us as His children, not in what we do or don't do.

Hei is part of Adonai's name; the structure of His fiery substance is air, wind, or breath; that which expands continually. *Hei* symbolizes God's readiness to reach out, to extend grace, to forgive, and to receive a repentant person into His loving embrace. Breath is the only thing in existence that carries the boundary of God. If we have breath, we have life. If we lose our breath, we die. Breath is a boundary determined by the one who created or released Himself into us through the breath of life. God is Spirit. The goodness of God's grace and favor allow us to repent. *Hei* represents repentance—a returning to God. God gives and He takes away; blessed be His name.

When God created Adam, He breathed into him the breath of life, and Adam became a living being. The more of the breath of God or the breath of the Spirit we have in us, the more alive we become. The more of the anointing we carry, the more we are transfigured and transformed into His image. The breath of God's spirit empowers us to do the great things God has called us to. It's as simple as surrendering to His presence and breathing Him in. When we are stressed, fearful, or anxious, what do people say? "Relax, just take a deep breath, and breathe it all out." Breathe out the bad and breathe in the good. We breathe in of His Spirit, and we exhale stressful things of darkness, sickness, limitations, or depression. Those negative things are nothing but a spirit or a breath that can be breathed out.

ENDNOTES

1. Strong, *Strong's Exhaustive Concordance,* Hebrew #2374.

2. Ibid., Hebrew #5030.

3. Breathitt, *Dream Encounter Symbol Book,* Volume I.

4. Breathitt, *When Will My Dreams Come True?*

5. Ibid.

6. Ibid.

Chapter 6

THE POWERFUL WEAPON OF PRAYER

Prayer is a powerful weapon when it is fueled by God's loving grace. The Word of God is a mighty sword. If we will trust the Lord, He will fight our battles for us. As He did for Elisha, God can both blind our enemies and reopen their eyes at the right time (see 2 Kings 6). God's anointed word will not return void. He promises that His Word will accomplish what it is sent to do (see Isa. 55:10-11). The angels respond when they hear the Word of God spoken with a heart of love.

> *Bless the Lord, you His angels, mighty in strength, who perform His word, obeying the voice of His word! Bless the Lord, all you His hosts, You who serve Him, doing His will* (Ps. 103:20-21).

The Lord will reward and prosper us as we bless and take care of our enemies, return good for their evil, and return love for their hatred.

> *If your enemy is hungry, give him food to eat; and if he is thirsty, give him water to drink; for you will heap burning coals on his head, and the Lord will reward you* (Prov. 25:21-22).

The coals of fire are there to burn up, destroy, and remove the negative spiritual influences over our enemies' minds.

Our kindness will demonstrate God's love in action. Their harmful responses will eventually change if we continue to act in love. We must persevere in doing good; we must seek His glory and continually honor God, who gives eternal life. As David wrote, *"You prepare a table before me in the presence of my enemies; You have anointed my head with oil; my cup overflows"* (Ps. 23:5).

God is able to abundantly bless us when we are obedient to His Word. We must view others with God's eyes of love. Seeing as God sees empowers us to act like God acts. God anointed Jesus with the Holy Spirit and power (see Acts 10:38), and God's presence with Jesus empowered Him to do good and to heal all who were oppressed by the devil (see Acts 10:38). Never lose heart; doing good must become a lifestyle. Use every opportunity that comes your way to be kind to others. If we don't become weary in doing good, in time we will reap the full benefits of God's blessings (see Gal. 6:9, 2 Thess. 3:13).

When we respond in love, God will open our spiritual eyes to see as He sees. Jesus was and is the greatest seer who ever lived. When Jesus turned His heart of love towards His heavenly Father in prayer, the realm of vision opened. Holy Spirit connected Jesus to heaven. Holy Spirit opened Jesus' ears to hear and His eyes to see. The Holy Spirit is also our lifeline to heaven.

THE POWER OF LOVE

Love is the greatest power in the universe because it unlocks true, clear vision. We need to see everything and everybody through the eyes of love. Because Jesus loved His Father, He was able to observe what His Father was doing. Love is personified in Jesus; He is the gateway to the mystical realm. The Son of God watched His Father, and then He followed His Father's actions in like manner. The more we love, the wider and clearer the scope of our vision becomes. God shares His secrets with His trusted, intimate friends.

For example, the Bible tells us that Jesus did whatever He saw His Father doing in Heaven (see John 5:19). Jesus was a man who prayed. While in prayer, He saw His Father healing the paralyzed man at the Pool of Bethseda (see John 5:1-9). This particular man had suffered for thirty-eight years. God's merciful favor selected this one man above all the others who were present.

Jesus was in Jerusalem to celebrate the Jewish festivals. He passed by the five covered porches at the Sheep Gate. This is where the outcast, infirmed, deformed, crippled, and paralyzed gathered to rest beside the healing pool. God highlighted a crippled man to Jesus in a vision so He would recognize him in the crowd. Jesus knew the extent and duration of the man's sickness. God also gave Jesus the key to unlock his crippling prison. The Word says that when Jesus saw the crippled man, He asked, *"Do you wish to get well?"* (John 5:6). The paralyzed man answered like most, responding with hopelessness and an excuse, not with faith. *"Sir, I have no man to put me into the pool when the water is stirred up, but while I am coming, another steps down before me"* (John 5:7).

This man did not display faith or any type of belief in Jesus' power to heal. Yet Jesus' compassion drew the man so that He could deliver the man from his desperate state. Jesus' compassion healed the man in his darkest hour of despair. Jesus lovingly gazed upon the man and commanded, *"Get up! Pick up your pallet and walk"* (John 5:8). Immediately the man was well! He picked up his mat and started walking. What a powerful miracle!

The love of God was manifested through Jesus, who always personified love. Love is the power that opens spiritual gateways for vision, provision, and power. Love is the spiritual force that empowers us to see into the realms of the Spirit and empowers us to operate in the spiritual gifts.

The more we love, the more we are able to behold, hear, and see. First Corinthians 14:1 tells us to pursue love and then to desire spiritual gifts. Without love being established first as a strong foundation in our lives, the gifts, although they are from God, will only make noise. In other words, we will say, "Be healed," but nothing will happen. We will prophecy, but it won't come to pass if it is not riding on the foundation of love. We may be greatly gifted, but if we are not full of love, we are a gifted nothing, and nothing of eternal importance will take place in our lives. Everything that is accomplished in the kingdom of God is accomplished by His Spirit of love.

The first commandment with a promise is: *"Honor your father and mother, that your days may be prolonged..."* (Exod. 20:12; see Eph. 6:1-3). Likewise, we are called to love God with all of our hearts, minds, bodies, and spirits (see Deut. 6:5). Then we are commanded to love humankind, even our enemies, as ourselves (see Matt. 5:44). It is the perfect love of God that casts out fear and brings clarity with laser-like precision to the gifts of God (see 1 John 4:18).

Jesus delighted in hearing His Father's knowledge, wisdom, and counsel. Jesus sensed His Father's presence and felt His loving touch. The Father's strong arms strengthened Jesus in the spirit of might. A glance of the Father's eyes would direct His path. As it says in Psalm 32:8, *"I will instruct you and teach you in the way you should go; I will guide you with My eye"* (NKJV). The Scriptures tell us that Jesus didn't do anything on His own. He only acted when He saw His Father moving.

> *Therefore Jesus answered and was saying to them, "Truly, truly, I say to you, the Son can do nothing of Himself, unless it is something He sees the Father doing; for whatever the Father does, these things the Son also does in like manner"* (John 5:19).

Seeing past the surface or superficial involves all the senses. When we totally surrender to God's presence and leading, we are able to experience God and receive His guidance. Blind people must see by feeling things with the touch of their hands. Their fingertips begin to draw a visual picture for their blind eyes. Until our spiritual eyes are opened, we are like blind people trying to feel our way through life in darkness.

Faith enlightens our heart to see what God sees and, in obedience, to do what God does. Faith is not blind; it has perfect sight and spiritual clarity. If we take away faith, we remove true vision. Abraham saw what God was doing and became the Father of Faith (see Acts 7:1-8, Rom. 4:16-17). Jesus said in John 8:56, *"Your father Abraham rejoiced to see My day, and he saw it and was glad."* God saw all that He had made, and behold, it was very good!

If we are not seeing God clearly, if we ask, God will teach us how to love Him more. Learning of His love will open new avenues of expression to us. Love will open our eyes to see as God sees, to hear what God says, and to do as God does. God is love. The more love we possess, the more godly we will become.

OUR TRUE STATE

Once we recognize our true state of being wretched, miserable, and spiritually poor, blind, and naked, our new day of seeing truth and walking in abundance will begin. But if we continue to say, *"I am rich, and have become wealthy, and have need of nothing,"* we will remain naked, covered in shame, blind, and undisciplined. This is what Jesus said to people who thought like this:

> *Because you say, "I am rich, and have become wealthy, and have need of nothing," and you do not know that you are wretched and miserable and poor and blind and naked, I advise you to buy from Me gold refined by fire so that you may become rich, and white garments so that you*

may clothe yourself, and that the shame of your nakedness will not be revealed; and eye salve to anoint your eyes so that you may see. Those whom I love, I reprove and discipline; therefore be zealous and repent (Rev. 3:17-19).

The love of the Lord brings forth fruitfulness in our lives. His reproving fire is a necessary discipline that comes into our repentant lives. Our spiritual eyes will not be opened to see truth unless we allow God's fire to purify our heart. The fire of God comes to fashion us into pure golden vessels of honor. Only after God's fire has purged the dross from our life can we contain His glory. Only then can His image be seen in us and His power flow through us. When His image is formed in us, people will be drawn to us because we will contain His light, love, and wisdom. When the fire of God has cleansed us, our eyes will see people the way God sees them. God sees people for who they are, who He created them to become, not for who they are currently. God's fire will transform us into ministers of fire.

THE REFINING FIRE

An Old Testament example of men being turned into ministers of fire is found in Daniel 3:14-28. Shadrach, Meshach, and Abednego provoked the wrath of King Nebuchadnezzar because they didn't respect his gods and they refused to worship the gold statue that he had erected. The king offered them a second chance to escape a sure death if they would bow their knees and worship the statue. Here is what they said:

Shadrach, Meshach, and Abednego answered the king, "Nebuchadnezzar, we don't need to explain these things to you. If you throw us into the hot furnace, the God we serve can save us. And if he wants to, he can save us from your power. But even if God does not save us, we want you to know, king, that we refuse to serve your gods. We will not worship the gold idol you have set up" (Dan. 3:16-18 ERV)

Nebuchadnezzar's face turned purple with rage, and he ordered the furnace fired up seven times hotter than usual. Strongmen tied Shadrach, Meshach, and Abednego's hands and feet, and they threw them fully dressed into the roaring furnace. The flames from the furnace killed the strongmen who bound Shadrach, Meshach, and Abednego. But the same flames that destroyed those who sought to bind and destroy the men of God, also set the men of God free.

It is the same for us today. When the fiery trials come to test and try us, the flames of persecution will only burn away the wrong thought patterns, the things and individuals that hinder or bind us to the natural realms of existence. We will see the wrong our enemies are doing against us consumed by a God who is able to turn their evil to our benefit and good. God offers His protection to those who love and serve Him. The fire of God will burn up their wrong ways of thinking and set the captives free to move into God's presence, true liberty, and freedom. They will no longer be slaves to the evil impulses and spirits that drive them. Their eyes will be opened to see and know the truth.

When King Nebuchadnezzar drew near and gazed into the fire, God opened his eyes to see. He was surprised to see Jesus walking in the fire with Shadrach, Meshach, and Abednego. Alarmed and confused, the king jumped up and said, *"Was it not three men we cast bound into the midst of the fire?"* (Dan. 3:24). When his advisers agreed, the king said, *"Look again! I see four men loosed and walking about in the midst of the fire without harm, and the appearance of the fourth is like a son of the gods"* (Dan. 3:25). Then Nebuchadnezzar went to the door of the raging furnace and called, *"...Come out, you servants of the Most High God, and come here"* (Dan. 3:26).

As with Shadrach, Meshach, and Abednego, the fiery preparation that God allows us to walk through will not harm us, but will cause Jesus' image to be imprinted upon us. The world will no longer hear or see us, but the Christ in us will come forth shining.

After their deliverance from the fire, many important government leaders and king's counselors gathered around Shadrach, Meshach, and Abednego to examine and question them. They discovered that the fire hadn't so much as touched the three men—not a hair was singed, not a scorch mark was on their clothes, not even the smell of fire clung to them! Only the ropes that had tried to bind, hinder, and limit them were removed. World leaders will be drawn to gain supernatural counsel and wisdom from those who successfully walk through the fire with God.

Nebuchadnezzar declared,

> *Blessed be the God of Shadrach, Meshach and Abednego, who has sent His angel and delivered His servants who put their trust in Him, violating the king's command, and yielded up their bodies so as not to serve or worship any god except their own God. Therefore I make a decree that any people, nation or tongue that speaks anything offensive against the God of Shadrach, Meshach and Abednego shall be torn limb from limb and their houses reduced to a rubbish heap, inasmuch as there is no other god who is able to deliver in this way* (Dan. 3:28-29).

These three men demonstrated great faith, conviction, and courage. They saw God deliver them from an impossible situation. They walked and talked with the fourth man in the fire. Jesus still walks with us in the fiery furnaces of life to comfort and give us wisdom in our times of testing and fiery trial.

The three Hebrew slaves possessed the same mindset Jesus possessed when *"...He humbled Himself and became obedient to death—even the death of the cross"* (Phil. 2:8 NKJV). God's desire is for us to utterly abandon ourselves to His will, even when it looks like circumstances are hopeless or out of control. God is always in control. We must choose to trust in His purposes and sovereignty. God will never disappoint us. Instead, God often delivers us by walking with us or carrying us through the troubles until we are strong enough to walk out of them.

These three men of godly character had the same resolve as Job when he said, *"Though He (God) slay me, yet will I trust Him..."* (Job 13:15 NKJV). When we willingly relinquish our life and live for Jesus and for the benefit of others, we gain eternal life. When we invite the Holy Spirit into the depths of our being He begins to create a beautiful wholesome spirit within us. Without a pure heart no one will see God. When our heart pants after Jesus, like a deer pants for water, we become His intimate friend instead of a bondservant. God shares His secrets with friends like Shadrach, Meshach, Abednego, and Job. The Bible is full of examples of individuals who developed a cherished personal relationship with God.

GOD WAS PROUD OF JOB

Job is one of the best examples of a man who loved God with his whole being. He learned to hear God's voice and sense His presence through many diverse ways. Before Job had a personal encounter with God, he knew God in an imperfect way. Job only knew God through the rumors and stories he had heard about God. But after Job had a firsthand visitation, he experienced God. Job had a face-to-face introduction not just a dream. Job saw God with his own eyes. Job repented because he was ashamed of his limited knowledge of God. He retracted everything he had ever said about God. Job changed his heart and life.

GATEWAY *to the* SEER REALM

God bragged on Job to Satan because Job was God's friend. He had great character and integrity. Job was a man of his word, an honest, God-fearing man who was passionately devoted to God. He respected God and refused to do evil. Job was the most influential man in the East! Job had three daughters and seven sons. He owned vast herds of livestock, had many servants, and was the richest man in the East. Job always sought the Lord to forgive his children's sins.

When the Lord met with His angels, Satan the Accuser was there with them. The Lord inquired of Satan, *"Where have you come from?"* (Job 1:7 NIV).

Satan replied, *"From roaming through the earth and going back and forth in it"* (Job 1:7 NIV).

Then the Lord said to Satan, *"Have you considered my servant Job? There is no one on earth like him; he is blameless and upright, a man who fears God and shuns evil"* (Job 1:8 NIV).

Satan snarled,

> *Does Job fear God for nothing? ...Have you not put a hedge around him and his household and everything he has? You have blessed the work of his hands, so that his flocks and herds are spread throughout the land. But stretch out your hand and strike everything he has, and he will surely curse you to your face* (Job 1:9-11 NIV).

The Lord replied, *"Very well, then, everything he has is in your hands, but on the man himself do not lay a finger"* (Job 1:12 NIV). God removed the fiery hedge of angelic protection from around Job so that Satan could bring loss, destruction, and death. God allowed Satan to touch Job's flesh with boils and great pain. He touched Job's soul with grief and sorrow. Job lost it all.

Sometimes, in order to see beyond the surface into the deep things of God, we need to battle through life experiences. Battles reveal the condition of our hearts. Too often we see losses as a hardship because we don't look beyond the obvious into the hidden truths God is trying to reveal. Dreams have an ability to take the dreamer into the realms beyond where God's creative words become spirit and truth. When we speak God's words of life into an atmosphere, that atmosphere changes and God's kingdom comes. The atmosphere of the kingdom of God brings forth revelation, power, light, anointing and spiritual insight. It is for us, the believer, to know the kingdom truths that are hidden in Scripture; and often they come to light as Holy Spirit reveals them in the dreams of the night.

> *In a dream, a vision of the night, when sound sleep falls on men, while they slumber in their beds, then He opens the ears of men, and seals their instruction, that He may turn man aside from his conduct, and keep man from pride; He keeps back his soul from the pit, and his life from passing over into Sheol* (Job 33:15-18).

The word *dream* in Hebrew is *chalom*, spelled: *Chet, Lamed, Final Mem*.[1] The word itself can be a symbolic representation of "the yolk of an egg where new life is formed" or "revelation that comes to restore one back to health."[2] This Hebrew word tells us that we can find answers to life's questions in our dreams. Dreams can restore us to health through intimacy with God. The esoteric meaning of the word *dream* is seen in the spelling. Hebrew alphabet is a symbolic picture language. The *Chet* shows a bonding to or a binding with God. The Chet represents a new metaphysical beginning that is connected to the supernatural. The higher divine influence of heaven comes into the natural realm and physically touches earth. The letter is symbolized by a fence that is divided to reveal a mystical protection.

The *Lamed* shows us instruction from Heaven. It is the tallest letter of the Hebrew alphabet. The Lamed is shaped like a shepherd's staff so it speaks to taking control of a negative situation to bring deliverance by speaking God's word with authority. God's throne of glory brings forth His teaching, discipline, chastening, and purpose here on earth so the quality of man's highest endowment may be realized. It also represents Christ the Eternal Shepherd's ascension back into heaven.

The *Final Mem* represents two forms, the hidden, concealed and the revealed mysteries of God. It symbolizes both Moses and Messiah; chaos, trial, and testing through the forty years in the wilderness. Mem is symbolized by water, the mighty flowing of the Holy Spirit and the blood of Jesus that flows to cleanse and heal us from all sickness and disease. It is in our dreams that we bind ourselves to God as He reveals His hidden mysteries to us.

By looking at the various translations of these verses in Job 33, we can get a broader understanding. Many Hebrew scholars and academics throughout the generations past and present have agreed that sealed instructions form a covert bond to the dreamer. This indicates that we receive personal messages about our future that are hidden or concealed in the dreams.

God opens the eyes of our heart to gain an intimate spiritual understanding of the dream. God will open our ears to hear and our eyes to see the plans He has for our future. God-given dreams can be more than prophetic (foretelling the future); they can be a disciplined way of searching out what has been hidden in a dream. We will discover the language of dreams is the way in which God reveals His intimate secrets to us. If we do not diligently seek God to understand the meaning of the dream, He seals the dream's instruction so we cannot benefit from the revelation it holds for our future.

During sleep, God can become very intimate with us. During sleep our souls do not slumber, but they actively search the spirit realm for the revelations of God. Our spirits are not influenced or restricted by the limitations of the physical body while we are asleep. In the dreams of the night, we are able to see ourselves as God sees us in the past, present, and future.

SEALED DREAMS

Sealed dreams are not remembered because God seals them in our subconscious until the preparation process is complete in us. Then the seal is broken. Upon hearing, seeing, and walking through a situation in life, our past dream is recalled and remembered. This is what some call a *déjà vu* (or "already seen") experience. Years ago, the dreamer dreamed the experience, interacting with the characters of the dream. It was sealed and forgotten. In the fullness of time, when the dreamer is walking into the situation in real time, the near memory is triggered and the dreamer recalls the previous dream events. The dreamer then follows the script that was written in the past dream. This invokes the feeling of *I've been here or done this before.*

Job 33 gives us some great insights into the various ways that God communicates with us. God speaks to people in many different ways, yet if we have hardened our hearts, if we are not careful to listen or have not attuned our spirits to understand His ways, we will not prosper. One of Job's friends, Elihu, said to him:

> Look, in this you are not righteous. I will answer you, for
> God is greater than man. Why do you contend with Him?
> For He does not give an accounting of any of His words
> (Job 33:12-13 NKJV).

First and foremost, God speaks through His written Word. God speaks once or twice through our state of affairs. God speaks through the circumstances and situations that surround our lives. God speaks through friends, family members, employees, music, books, movies, newspapers, radio, television, and billboards—just to mention a few. If we ignore God's promptings or we don't perceive what He is saying, God will speak to us through dreams or visions of the night to get His message through to us. The quality and clarity of the dreams depend on our spiritual level. Dreams are a shadow of prophecy.

Elihu continued, *"For God does speak—now one way, now another—though man may not perceive it"* (Job 33:14 NIV). Sometimes the only time God can speak to us is while we are asleep. One of the best and easiest times to receive the understanding of a dream is during the twilight time of sleep. Twilight is the time right before falling asleep or waking from sleep. It is easier to remember and receive the interpretation of a dream during this time. Interpretations often follow the life circumstances of the dreamer. They will also follow the specific positive or negative words the interpreter chooses to use in the interpretation because dreams follow the words of the mouth.Our words carry the power of life or death, good or evil, prosperity or poverty. Choose your words wisely. Much wisdom is needed for dream interpretation.

While we sleep, our subconscious spirits are actively searching, but our minds are not at full capacity. God will speak when we are in a deep sleep. He may take us past several layers of our subconscious so that we are not able to argue with Him. In this state, we focus and concentrate on the brilliant, colorful, lucid dreams God gives. God's ways are higher than our ways. So God speaks in one way and then another to turn us from our plans and hurtful deeds. He conceals pride from us to keep us from death at the hands of the enemy.

Now let's look at the passage in Job 33 more carefully. It starts by highlighting three types of dreams. First it says, *"In a dream, a vision of the night..."* (Job 33:15). This refers to prophetic dreams in which every detail is significant because it comes with angelic presence, like Jacob experienced (see Gen. 28:12). In these visions of the night, God clearly opens the morally-wise person's understanding to gain spiritual knowledge. Next it says, *"...when deep sleep falls upon men..."* (Job 33:15). This refers to the ordinary hidden or difficult-to-understand dreams that everyone experiences. Third, it says, *"...while slumbering on their beds..."* (Job 33:15). This can refer to a self-induced dream state. These are the three types of dreams. This is their purpose:

> *Then He opens the ears of men, and seals their instruction. In order to turn man from his deed, and conceal pride from man, He keeps back his soul from the Pit, and his life from perishing by the sword* (Job 33:16-18 NKJV).

If we continually ignore God's voice or rebelliously refuse His instruction, sickness will chasten us on a bed of affliction. When we are rendered helpless or confined to bed, we have plenty of time to reflect on life, to listen to and consider God's ways.

> *Man is also chastened with pain on his bed, and with strong pain in many of his bones, so that his life abhors bread, and his soul succulent food. His flesh wastes away from sight and his bones stick out which once were not seen. Yes, his soul draws near the Pit and his life to the executioners* (Job 33:19-22 NKJV).

When we become sick, if we humbly inquire, God will show us what has caused the sickness. He will send a messenger, a dream-interpreter or one who understands the ways of God. The Bible tells us that interpreters of dreams are rare; they are one in a thousand (see Job 33:23). If the afflicted person listens to the interpretation of the dream and repents, the messenger will pray to deliver the person from the disease. The one who is skilled at hearing God's voice and who understands His ways will possess the power to heal. God is gracious and merciful. He doesn't want anyone to perish, especially from sickness. God is a healer.

If there is a messenger for him, a mediator, one among a thousand, to show man His uprightness, then He is gracious to him, and says, "Deliver him from going down to the Pit; I have found a ransom"; His flesh shall be young like a child's, He shall return to the days of his youth. He shall pray to God, and He will delight in him, He shall see His face with joy, for He restores to man His righteousness. Then he looks at men and says, "I have sinned, and perverted what was right, and it did not profit me." He will redeem his soul from going down to the Pit, and his life shall see the light. Behold, God works all these things, twice, in fact, three times with a man, to bring back his soul from the Pit, that he may be enlightened with the light of life (Job 33:23-30 NKJV).

In Job 33:14, we see several different levels of the dream realm that God communicates to us through. The first way God communicates to us is through speech or His spoken word. God speaks (*dabar*) to people several times in many different figurative ways in order to communicate His eloquent messages. He will appoint others to speak His counsel to us. He will advise us in affairs of life. He will bid, command, and commune with us. He will declare truths to destroy harmful plans and give us clarity about His promises. He will sing over us, say loving words of encouragement, and be a spokesman who subdues our enemies. He talks to us, teaches us His truths, and tells us of His plans and purposes. He will speak the answers to our prayers while we sleep. He thinks of us night and day. He entreats us through utterance, and He works with us in varied manners to enable us to understand.

If we do not perceive or understand His speech, He will come to us when we are in slumber (*tenuwmah*). This is when we are drowsy or just starting to slip into sleep. If we don't comprehend His ways during slumber, He will speak again during the next phase called deep sleep. Deep sleep (*tardemah*) is during times of lethargy or, by implication, a trance state. When we are in this trance state, God often moves us into the next realm, which is the vision (*chizzay-own*) realm. God will show Himself to us in this phase of sleep. This phase of deep sleep brings forth an expectation of revelation through a dream or vision. The last level of the dream realm mentioned in this passage is called the dream phase (*chalom*). In this dream phase, God reveals His plans and purposes to us.

Seeing the future is the most difficult for us to handle because we are not wise or mature enough to come to grips with it yet. This is why God hides things from us to keep us from pride. He uses symbolism so we do not fully know or recognize the magnitude of what He reveals. If we knew certain things about the future, we would not be fully prepared to embrace them at our present level of spiritual development. This is one reason why God seals the things He shows us in dreams.

Once His plans are revealed to our spirits, the Holy Spirit then begins to make us into the people of God we need to be by developing our faith, trust, and character. We don't recall the dream until we have developed our lives to the point where we are able to handle the great blessings God has shown us. Once we reach maturity or a specific point of development or we gain the needed wisdom, the dream is recalled or unsealed, and we remember the dream in detail.

Concealed truth protects people from being accountable to the truth that they are not able to comprehend yet. It is the glory of God to conceal a matter until we are able to dig it out, comprehend it, and walk in the weighty truth it reveals (see Prov. 25:2). God desires to bring a greater weight of glory, so He is developing our faith muscles. Without faith, it is impossible to please God (see Heb. 11:6).

Job heard God speak to him, and he gained a revelation about God. Job said, "*...I spoke of things I did not understand,* *things too wonderful for me to know. …My ears had heard of You but now my eyes have seen You"* (Job 42:3,5 NIV). At another time, Job said, *"After my skin has been destroyed, yet in my flesh I will see God"* (Job 19:26 NIV). The Bible tells us no man can see God and live. Our flesh is not compatible with a holy God. During Job's trial his flesh hung on his bones. His body was being destroyed by painful boils, grief, and fasting. As his flesh become weaker Job's spirit man became stronger. In a sense Job's flesh died and his spirit awakened to see God. Job knew even in his physical death his spiritual eyes would still have the ability to see God.

When we die to our fleshly nature and its carnal desires we will see visions of God in Spirit and in Truth. God made His visible presence real to Job. When we die to ourselves God applies eye salve to our eyes so that we can see in the realm of the Spirit. Those that know their God through the spirit shall perform great exploits (see Dan. 11:32). Matthew 5:8 declares, *"Blessed are the pure in heart, for they shall see God."*

God inhabits us when we offer Him a pure heart as a dwelling and resting place. Job's obedience broke him into the realm of double. We are in a much better place. We live in the time of fullness or spirit without measure.

When Job humbled himself and prayed for his friends, the process of his restoration to greater prosperity began (see Job 42:10). God restored Job's fortunes and gave him back double for his trouble. The Lord blessed and increased Job more in his old age than He had formerly. Job knew the importance of forgiving those who did him wrong. Job was long-suffering, merciful, and gracious, and he treated his friends with goodness. Job was a man who always spoke the truth. The spirit of truth will lead and guide us into all truth (see John 16:13).

A LIFE OF LOVE

We can learn a lot about life from following Job's example. Life is about learning how to love. Life is also about seeing others through the eyes of love. We come to love not by finding the perfect person, but by seeing an imperfect person perfectly through God's eyes of love. The best things in life are experienced with an open, loving heart.

Things of true beauty in this world cannot be held or even seen. They must be felt in our hearts and experienced in our dreams in order to remove the impossibilities. Life is full of adventure, triumph, tragedy, and challenging changes that enable us to grow in love and mature in Christ-likeness. Our goal in life is to be love, like Jesus.

TESTING BRINGS PROMOTION

Tests and trials are designed to help develop our character and integrity. Clean hands and a pure heart enable us to step into and successfully handle the powerful destiny God has waiting for us. Tests align us with the future plans, hope, and purposes that God has chosen for us (see Jer. 29:11). Tests are given for the purpose of promotion, increased blessings, and friendship with God coming into our lives. Their fire forges a purity and holiness within so that God's pure light can shine through everything we do in life. Purity releases God's power. Those with clean hands and a pure heart will see God! Trials enable us to develop our spiritual muscles so we can win the race that is set before us with grace and stamina.

ENDNOTES

1. Strong, *Strong's Exhaustive Concordance*, Hebrew #2472.

2. Breathitt, *When Will My Dreams Come True?*

Chapter 7

NOTHING IS IMPOSSIBLE WITH GOD

God's plan is for us to succeed—to be the head, not the tail—to be overcomers, not those who are overcome. We are light-bearers in this dark world. We bring the hope of God into life's situations when we act with the faith of God in our hearts. Every hard or difficult challenge we overcome through the great grace and faith of God in our hearts enables us to move closer to God's heart and into the "greater works" (see John 5:20, John 14:12). The thorny trials of today prepare us to be winners tomorrow and champions in the future. The challenges in life enable us to accomplish the impossible through knowing the God in whom nothing is impossible.

GOD KNOWS YOUR NAME!

It is comforting to know that God knew each of us by name before we ever existed in this earthly realm. Our lives are set apart and appointed for purpose and destiny. His plans for us were completed in Him, even before we were formed in our mother's wombs.

NATHANAEL

We find a wonderful illustration of this fact in John 1:45-51. Philip found Nathanael and informed him, *"We have found Him of whom Moses in the Law and also the Prophets wrote—Jesus of Nazareth, the son of Joseph"* (John 1:45).

A discouraged Nathanael cynically questioned Philip, *"Can anything good come out of Nazareth?"* (John 1:46).

Philip answered, *"Come and see"* (John 1:46).

When Jesus looked upon Nathanael, He saw him as a true Israelite, one who could be trusted. In response, Nathanael inquired, *"How do you know me?"* (John 1:48).

Jesus answered, *"Before Philip called you, when you were under the fig tree, I saw you"* (John 1:48). In other words, He was saying, "I looked into the realm of the Spirit and saw you questioning things and pondering life when you were sitting under the fig tree, before Philip told you about me."

Nathanael was amazed and said, *"Rabbi [Teacher], You are the Son of God; You are the King of Israel"* (John 1:49).

Jesus replied to Nathanael, *"Because I said to you that I saw you under the fig tree, do you believe? You will see greater things than these"* (John 1:50). Then Jesus said, *"Truly, truly, I say to you, you will see the heavens opened and the angels of God ascending and descending on the Son of Man"* (John 1:51).

By coming into contact with Jesus, Nathanael was given the promise of having his spiritual eyes opened to see angels and the invisible realms of Heaven. He would be able to observe the coming and going of angels through spiritual gateways. Jesus is the gateway to the Father. In Jacob's vision, Jesus is positioned standing at the top of the ladder. In order to reach Jesus, each consecutive rung of the ladder must be ascended. Similar to the ladder of success, the higher one climbs the closer they are to obtaining their goal. Jesus is the goal. Everything has its being and existence in Him. Spiritual disciplines such as communing and fellowshipping with the Lord in times of prayer and fasting, praise and thanksgiving, sowing and reaping, binding and loosing enable us to ascend this heavenly ladder to reach the heart of Jesus.

JACOB'S PRAYER LADDER

Jacob's eyes were opened to see a heavenly ladder descending to earth. Prayer opens our eyes, and it creates possibilities in the realm of the spirit. To be blessed of God, we must pray. Prayer attaches or bonds itself to people, situations, or nations. The Bible tells us we have the ability to bind and loose things on earth as they are in heaven. The words we pray have substance when they are mixed with faith. Faith-filled words have the ability to open a way of escape; remove curses, sickness, and disease; loose chains of opposition; and set the prisoners free.

When John the Baptist recognized Jesus coming to the Jordan River to be baptized he spoke these anointed words, "Behold the Lamb who takes away the sins of the world." The heavens opened and the Holy Spirit descended and came to rest on Jesus. The Bible tells us the dove remained upon Him. The words we pray have an ability to open and shut heaven. The more we pray and spend time in the presence of God, the higher we climb on a spiritual ladder. Prayer removes natural and spiritual limitation. When we pray correctly, according to God's will, plans, and character, the Holy Spirit enables us to move higher in power and authority as we ascend into the higher spiritual realms.

If we prayed without ceasing, we would be like Enoch, who walked with God. He was able to ascend into the heavenly heights and become "no more" because the Lord took him (see Gen. 5:24). Enoch was able to navigate the ladders, gates, and doorways of Heaven. Jesus is the door that leads to the Father and every dimension of the spirit realm. He is the one who gives us the keys to access these higher dimensions. It all comes through intimate times spent in the presence of a holy God.

We need to daily walk with God in prayer. We must pray before troubles mount up or overwhelm us. If we are unable to pray for an hour, we must pray several times a day for a few minutes until the time we spend with God expands.

JACOB'S DREAM

As we follow Jacob's life we can see how he began to develop a prayer life and became spiritually aware of God's presence watching over him. As Jacob journeyed from his safe home in and through the wilderness, he discovered the God of his father Isaac was real. His eyes were opened to see a heavenly ladder (the beginning of the ladder disappeared into the heavens and its end rested on earth). Jacob saw the angels of God moving freely upon this mystical ladder. Jesus gave Jacob many wonderful promises at the beginning of his journey. Then God took Jacob full circle through the process to develop Jacob's character into the type of man who could possess and walk in those weighty promises. If we believe in Christ Jesus, we are heirs to the same promises that were given to Abraham, Isaac, and Jacob.

All of the different types of angelic beings are ministering spirits who serve God. They are sent to help those who will receive salvation (see Heb. 1:14). Angels are like sentinels around our hearts. They guard and protect us from harm until we are able to come to the knowledge of Christ. Once we are saved, they begin to make themselves known to us. They bring us messages, wisdom, and revelation from the gates of Heaven.

When the Holy Spirit commissions angels, they can release anointings and ignite our spiritual gifts, bringing them to a new level in God. Jacob started his journey with a certain band of angels when he left his safe, secure home. These angels returned to glory and ascended up the ladder. As Jacob's life transitioned, he needed different angels to help him continue on his worldly journey. Jacob would need to know how to handle a schemer like him, how to gain wealth, and how to acquire a wife to love. The angels ascending up and down the ladder were a picture of the changing of the angelic guard in his life.

The ladder can represent prayer and the power of God that is manifested when our souls connect with God. We see Jesus at the top of this heavenly ladder. But the Bible exhorts us by saying, *"Do not say… 'Who will ascend into heaven?'"* The kingdom of Heaven is within you; it is not up in the sky somewhere.

> *But the righteousness based on faith speaks as follows: "Do not say in your heart, 'Who will ascend into heaven?' (that is, to bring Christ down), or 'Who will descend into the abyss?' (that is, to bring Christ up from the dead)." But what does it say? "The word is near you, in your mouth and in your heart"—that is, the word of faith which we are preaching* (Rom. 10:6-8).

Jacob knew that God would fulfill His promises. He saw the ladder at Bethel, (the house of God); the place of prayer, a place of changing conditions on earth. Here the angels began on earth and traveled to Heaven. This represented the earthly ascending into a heavenly place of understanding.

Genesis 28 tells the story:

> *Then Jacob departed from Beersheba and went toward Haran. He came to a certain place and spent the night there, because the sun had set. He took one of the stones of the place and put it under his head, and lay down in that place. He had a dream, and behold, a ladder was set on the earth with its top reaching to heaven; and behold; the angels of God were ascending and descending on it. And behold, the Lord stood above it and said, "I am the Lord, the God of your father Abraham and the God of Isaac; the land on which you lie, I will give it to you and to your descendants. Your descendants will also be like the dust of the earth, and you will spread out to the west and to the*

east and to the north and to the south; and in you and in your descendants shall all the families of the earth be blessed. Behold, I am with you and will keep you wherever you go, and will bring you back to this land; for I will not leave you until I have done what I have promised you."

Then Jacob awoke from his sleep and said, "Surely the Lord is in this place, and I did not know it." He was afraid and said, "How awesome is this place! This is none other than the house of God, and this is the gate of heaven." So Jacob rose early in the morning, and took the stone that he had put under his head and set it up as a pillar and poured oil on its top. He called the name of that place Bethel; however, previously the name of the city had been Luz. Then Jacob made a vow, saying, "If God will be with me and will keep me on this journey that I take, and will give me food to eat and garments to wear, and I return to my father's house in safety, then the Lord will be my God. This stone, which I have set up as a pillar, will be God's house, and of all that You give me I will surely give a tenth to You" (Gen. 28:10-22).

Years later, God brought Jacob back to Bethel, but he was still the same man who wrestled and held on until he got what he wanted. He was still holding onto the ways of the world until the angel's touch wounded him and forever changed his walk and ways. Jacob was confronted by God at the brook Jabbok, where his name changed from Jacob, the deceiver, to Israel, the prince of God:

Then Jacob was left alone, and a man wrestled with him until daybreak. When he saw that he had not prevailed against him, he touched the socket of his thigh; so the socket of Jacob's thigh was dislocated while he wrestled with him. Then he said, "Let me go, for the dawn is breaking." But he said, "I will not let you go unless you bless me." So he said to him, "What is your name?" And he said, "Jacob."

He said, "Your name shall no longer be Jacob, but Israel; for you have striven with God and with men and have prevailed." Then Jacob asked him and said, "Please tell me your name." But he said, "Why is it that you ask my name?" And he blessed him there. So Jacob named the place Peniel, for he said, "I have seen God face to face, yet my life has been preserved." Now the sun rose upon him just as he crossed over Penuel, and he was limping on his thigh (Gen. 32:24-31).

God has called each of us to be world-changers; but first, God has to change us. We can influence the world around us! All we have to do is recall what God said, hear what God is saying and, in obedience, do what He speaks in order to change the world.

When God was building Job into the man to hold a double portion, his friends came to accuse and offer their opinions and judgments. Job protested, "What kind of help did you come to offer a weak helpless hurting friend? Did you come to rescue me or to accuse me when I have no strength left in my arm? What kind of wisdom or mixed up advice is this counsel? Where did you get these helpful insights that you so abundantly provide? Do you know whose spirit has caused you to utter these inspired words?"

Job wisely shared with his friends about the greatness of God. He told how man was in God when He created the earth and spread the skies over the unformed space of the heavens above. While Job was still in God's loins, he marveled when he saw God hang the world on nothing. *"He stretches out the north over empty space and hangs the earth on nothing"* (Job 26:7). The Lord spoke to Job out of the whirlwind in Job 38:1-7. God asked, "Who are you, Job, to darken My counsel with words that do not have knowledge? If you think you know so much gird up your loins with truth. I will ask you some questions so you can instruct Me!"

Where were you when I laid the foundation of the earth? Tell Me, if you have understanding, who set its measurements? Since you know. Or who stretched the line on it? On what were its bases sunk? Or who laid its cornerstone, when the morning stars sang together and all the sons of God shouted for joy? (Job 38:4-7)

God was encouraging Job to remember who he was and where Job was before his life began on earth. Job was in God. We were all in God from the beginning. We were each given a blueprint, a God strategy and plan for our life. All we need to do is remember, enter back into God, stay connected, and follow His leading. When we discover the plans God has given us for life, we become the world changers God designed us to be from before time began. There is a specific time and season for everything to be accomplished in our life. God lovingly opens millions of beautiful flowers without forcing a single bud. This serves to remind us to be patient and not to force anything, for things happen at the right time.

GATEWAYS TO HEAVEN

God is the One who knows the fullness of time. God knows when something needs to be revealed or remain concealed. God knows when each of us reaches our maturation process. He knows when we are ready to come into perfect alignment. God is able to take time past, remove the pain and failures, and redeem it for good. God stewards time present and causes it to properly align so it connects to a future time. God knows the beginning from the end. He understands the cycles of the seasons, tides, and the orbiting paths of the planets and how they affect our world. In God there is always a perfect timing. He is never late. If God begins a work, He will also complete it.

When God spoke to the prophets and seers in the Old Testament, He would tell them to travel to specific geographic locations. These locations often housed the school of the prophets because they were located at heavenly gateways, like we see with Jacob's ladder. When Jacob entered into a restful sleep state under the open heaven that was spiritually charged with God's presence, he saw visions. His eyes were opened to see a gateway flooded with angelic beings. He beheld God's presence and heard the voice of Jesus. Jacob gained promise, clarity, and direction for his life under this heavenly portal of revelation.

The heavens and the earth were aligned for destiny and purpose beyond our natural vision. When we agree with and step into the syncopated rhythm God created for His universe we enter into destiny, the realms of blessing, and prosperity.

There is an appointed time for every person and event under God's great heaven. We are born at a specific time and we die when that time has expired. Jacob threw stones at his brother Esau and ran into the wilderness to escape his wrath. There Jacob reached the time to gather stones as a pillow, and then he erected a pillar of stones to commemorate seeing God at the place of visitation (Eccl. 3:5).

There is an appointed time and season for everything under Heaven. Nothing in God is random or takes place in happenstance, but everything is exact and precise. God lovingly controls His world. We have the ability to think and reason, but we will never totally understand the ways of God. Yet God accomplishes His purposes at the correct time. Whatever God does will continue forever; because God is eternal we cannot add to it or subtract anything from it. The past is the past; whatever was, is. Whatever will be is what will happen in the future, because time and destiny totally depend upon God. Therefore, we are called to respect and fear God. God has created the planets of the universe to rotate at a determined rate of speed on their exact orbital paths.

The earth rotates at a precise speed, in a specific orbital path. The first heaven, the sky above us, rotates at a certain speed. In addition, there is the second heaven, the place where Satan reigns. The third Heaven is where God Almighty rules. Each of these three heavenly places rotates at a designated speed. If we view these three different layers of the heavens as a separate disc or plate, we begin to get the picture. Each of these layers contains openings, gateways, or portals. These various gates have to be aligned so they are stacked on top of each other so a clear open channel of communication is established from Heaven to earth.

When these various heavenly gates align at certain times and come into a perfect sequence over a specific geographic location, they form a clear linear conduit, much like a megaphone, through which Heaven is able to communicate to earth. When the three heavens align, they form a shaft or audio tube through which God can communicate to people in an amazingly clear manner. The windows of Heaven are opened, and revelation is poured out upon those who have positioned themselves to be touched by God's presence, to hear and see that which God reveals.

The Lord began speaking to a prophet or seer while they were at a certain location. They could hear His voice at a certain level of clarity and understanding. God would admonish the seer to go to Bethel, Ramah, Jericho, Gilgal or Jerusalem, or one of the other schools of the prophets. By the time the prophetic seer had journeyed from the place where God first spoke to them to the designated geographic location, the three heavens would have aligned and the windows of revelation were opened. The prophet or seer was then able to receive revelation from God under an open heaven on a grand scale. The seer could then hear the audible voice of God more than the still small voice or impressions he heard previously. Under the gateway of Heaven the spiritual ladder of revelation was extended to earth enabling the seer to receive a heavenly download of vision. Jesus is at the top of the ladder with angelic messengers ascending and descending upon this ladder.

As it was in the past for the ancient prophets and seers to receive revelation it is the same for us today. Israel is the largest portal of revelation in the world. Thousands make the pilgrimage to Israel every year to hear from and encounter God.

Today seers are able to step into a dimension of understanding revelation knowledge that has never been received before because it has never been the fullness of time until now. In obedience to God's voice, we walk the process out. We come into the window of opportunity that has been opened for us. We step into the portal to receive the download from Heaven. Our eyes and ears are opened. We receive the anointing of prosperity, the blessings of God's wisdom, and abundant provision comes to us. We step into a realm of the impossible with the grace and favor of God resting upon us to make all things possible. With God we can do all things. He chose each one of us to come to this earth for a specific purpose.

Have you ever asked yourself, "Why am I here?" What am I called to do? What is the probability of me being born? What are the chances of one egg being penetrated by one sperm out of the millions that attempted to make the journey? Only one sperm reaches its goal to bring forth life. You are extremely special and unique. Each of us was in the loins of God before time began because God had an eternal plan. Yet He knew us before we were born. He planned the magnitude of the calling and destiny that is resting upon us for such a time as this. When we try to grasp the concept of eternity, it is very difficult. When God created the earth and all the galaxies in the universe, He said, "Let light be!" Still to this day, the universe is expanding and crashing through barriers of nothingness at the speed of light. The universe is still expanding and will continue to spread out through all the eons of time and eternity because God's Word is creative and progressive. The dimensions of space are still being rolled out like a carpet.

HEAVENLY LADDERS

During Chuck Pierce's 2011 Passover celebration in Texas, I saw a vision of two heavenly ladders coming down to earth. The angels who helped us during the last season of our lives ascended up one ladder. Angels have certain assignments and abilities that assist us during certain eras or time periods. Once their commission has been fulfilled, their job is complete, so they return to Heaven for their next assignment. I then saw God release a new host of angels that have an increased level of power, authority and revelation knowledge to help us in the new season we are entering. The angels are sent to help us move in areas of anointing so we can reach levels of spiritual understanding and realms of creative power that we have never entered before. These angels held the keys to unlock the miracle realm and to bring healing to incurable diseases like diabetes and cancer. It is not business as usual.

We get used to walking in ankle deep water, so God releases the next level. We trudge through the river at knee level until that becomes comfortable. Then water is released to our loins, so we have to work harder to navigate that level of anointing, but we are still given our footing. God has released a river of anointing for us to step into that is over our heads. It functions like the wheel within the wheel that moves with the Spirit of God wherever He leads.

We will move with God wherever the river leads because the waters of God's Spirit will totally consume us. As we surrender, the Spirit will be over our heads. We will not have any footing to stop ourselves from going into the rapids of God.

God will carry us along in His River until we accomplish that which we are called to accomplish. It will not be by our might or by our power, but it will be by the Spirit of the Lord. We will step into that flow that is over-our-head knowledge. We will move in complete trust of what God is doing in the Spirit realm by removing human-made limitations.

The eyes of the Lord are searching for those who have dedicated their whole lives—body, soul, and spirit—to His purposes on the earth. *"For the eyes of the Lord move to and fro throughout the earth that He may strongly support those whose heart is completely His..."* (2 Chron. 16:9).

Chapter 8

CALLED TO BE CHAMPIONS

It's time to run the race as champions to win! What is a champion? A champion is a warrior, a fighter who defies a challenge and wins. Their eyes are singularly focused on Jesus and His cross! No matter how many times a champion is knocked down or beaten unfairly he always stands up again. Champions hold first place because they overcome every obstacle that is erected. They can run through a hoop and leap over a wall. They always rise to the top and succeed against all odds. A champion is an advocate, a defender of a cause, or one who supports and carries the weak. The champion's love and grace exceeds all others, yet they remain humble.

Who are the Dread Champions of God? Who is called? Who is chosen? And, how do we qualify? What does it take to become a champion? It will take everything we were, everything we are, and everything God has destined us to become to be one of His dread champions.

We are all called, but few are chosen. Most step out of the race because of the weight or magnitude of the grueling training process. God uses our past failures to qualify us. God fashions our present trials and our future triumphs to increase our character to promote us in spiritual power, influence, and great compassion. Every situation, person, difficulty, pressure, test, tragedy, disappointment, and betrayal is part of the tools that are necessary to sculpt a champion.

The champions that have gone before us have forged a narrow path for us to follow. They are the great cloud of witnesses who watch and cheer us on from their heavenly surroundings. They encourage us to keep a forward motion, leaving every encumbrance, distraction, and entanglement by the side of the track.

> *Therefore, since we have so great a cloud of witnesses surrounding us, let us also lay aside every encumbrance and the sin which so easily entangles us, and let us run with endurance the race that is set before us, fixing our eyes on Jesus, the author and perfecter of faith, who for the joy set before Him endured the Cross, despising the shame, and has sat down at the right hand of the throne of God* (Heb. 12:1-2).

God is removing the limitations from us so we can be the champions that He has called us to be.

RACETRACK VISION

When I moved to Texas, the Lord told me He was sending me to enable the wild horses to run because they had been corralled and kept locked up in a religious stall or system.

Years later, in October, 2010, I had a dream of a beautiful white thoroughbred. She was being brought to the starting gates at the race track. She was going to be released to run in the race of champions. This dream came during the same time when the movie, *Secretariat*, about the 1973 Triple Crown winner, was released in the cinemas. I try to gain spiritual insights from things that happen in the natural because God is always communicating to us.

When I was a child, I read every book I could find on Secretariat. I discovered some interesting facts about the making of a champion. Secretariat's mother's name was 'Something Royal' and his fathers name was 'Bold Ruler.' He came from a bloodline of royal rulers. (We are called to rule and reign in the kingdom of God here on earth.) When he was born, he sprang to his feet faster than any of the other colts the trainers had seen before. *"My steps have held fast to Your paths. My feet have not slipped"* (Ps. 17:5). They first called Secretariat "Big Red." Red is the color that represents power.

Secretariat would lean back and rest in perfect peace against the starting gate. (Rest in the Lord, wait patiently for Him. Lean not unto your own understandings but acknowledge God in all your ways and He will cause your path to prosper.) Secretariat's owner used to say, "Let him run his race!" because he always came from behind to win.

This year's 2012, Derby winner, I'll Have Another, won by coming from the nineteenth position to overtake the first place horse. (The number nineteen means faith that removes lack and barrenness. This type of faith brings perfection of divine order through judgment.) I'll Have Another, is on his way to becoming a contender for the Triple Crown.

Secretariat would start the race slow but steadily increase his pace until he exploded like a locomotive train, crossing the finish line in first place. (We are not to despise small beginnings but realize that the work God has begun in us He will finish.) Secretariat's owner lived by this philosophy, "Life is ahead of you and you don't know how far you can go unless you run!"

Secretariat had a ravenous appetite. He ate more grain than other horses. (We need to consume large amounts of spiritual food. Unless a grain falls to the ground and dies it remains alone.)

When Secretariat died, an autopsy was performed. They found that his heart was two and a half times larger than a normal horse. God had given Secretariat a grand heart. Secretariat had a massive heart that beat like a real champion. This enabled him to run every race as a champion. He devastated the competition. He won his races thirty-one lengths ahead of the next horse. (The number thirty-one means offspring of divine perfection or deity.) We are the spiritual offspring of Jesus, who is the firstborn of many brethren. Jesus is our Dread Champion, the one we are called to pattern our lives after. Divine perfection is the dimension of spiritual power that God is taking us into. I believe Secretariat was a sign to us then, and he still is today.

In my dream, I watched as the trainers were loading the white horse into the starting gates. I looked, and saw her dry, shattered, cracked, chipped, split hooves. I could see an x-ray that revealed the inner condition of the hooves. Her hooves were in desperate need of repair. They were not in any condition to run the race. I knew if the horse was pushed to race, she would go lame. She needed to rest and recuperate from her last race season. She needed new shoes before she entered the race of champions.

The horse represented the power anointing that God desires to release. Yet we must shod our feet with the preparation of the kingdom's gospel of peace in order for us to successfully run the race. We must prepare to run at the level of power and speed that God desires. This is the race that we are called to win. God doesn't want us to fall short or pull up lame.

God is moving us into a season of resting in Him. As we allow the Holy Spirit to move through us, we will not be seen any more. We will be in the cleft of the rock. When we have the proper shoes on, we will walk out the demonstration of the powerful gospel of the kingdom. When the gospel of the kingdom is preached to the world, it will give a witness. God is calling all of Heaven and earth together to be a witness of what He is doing during our time.

The horse I saw in my dream was stalled for months to allow her hooves to be treated, healed, and repaired. As the months progressed, I had other dreams that showed her hooves growing sound. In the final dream, I saw her being loaded back into the starting gates. But this time she had on

High-Tec performance shoes with rubber padding to cushion and protect her hooves as she ran. Every time her hooves struck the earth like thunder, these new shoes gave support and protection.

Horses are being shod with the shoes of champions. Everything up to this point has been training and practice to run the race of champions. The race track is formed in an oval. The horses make one complete lap returning to the same starting point. We have been on the track running in circles. But God is going to give us the breakthrough as He opens up the starting gate. We are going to have a new start. He is going to make a way where there seems to be no way. Instead of running around and around at breakneck speeds without making progress, I watched as the horses burst through the starting gate. They ran neck and neck to the first curve in the track. But instead of the horses making the loop, the fence opened up as a gate. The horses didn't run around the crooked, winding track; but they ran straight into destiny on a straight and narrow path. No more excuses! It's time to run the race to win. God has released His champion horses out of the starting gate to set world records.

We are being shod with the gospel of the preparation of peace (see Eph. 6:15). It is the peace of God that is able to crush Satan under our feet. It is peace that releases revelation. If we are not in peace, we cannot hear God. We can't come into understanding because we have stepped out of faith and into fear. If we are in fear, we can't hear God's voice.

God is releasing the gospel of peace because peace releases revelation knowledge. Revelation is what reveals God. We see and understand God through the realm of the spirit. God is able to make every crooked, curved path in life straight. The mountains come down and the valleys come up as God releases the highway of holiness. When we move in the spirit of holiness, we are able to speak to a disease and see it bow before the name of Jesus.

THE PROCEEDING CREATIVE WORD

When God's word goes forth, it will accomplish what it has been sent forth to accomplish. The Word of God comes to test and try us. It determines where our character is weak. The living Word of God measures the depth of our integrity. If we are found lacking in any area, the Word of God, which is immediate, prevailing, authoritative, and spiritually alive, has the power to change and transform us into the image of the living Word, Jesus. If we allow the Holy Spirit to write God's words on the tablets of our hearts, we will fulfill our destinies as God's champions. Isaiah 55:11-12 says:

> *So is my word that goes out from my mouth—it will not return to me unfulfilled; but it will accomplish what I intend, and cause to succeed what I sent it to do. Yes, you will go out with joy, you will be led forth in peace...* (CJB).

God's Word is truth; it is a shield, and the light that continually guides us in our lives. The Word of God has a creative dimension that opens possibilities we have never seen or dreamed of before.

Doors of opportunity bring the joy of the Lord into our lives to strengthen us. We know we have chosen the right path because the Holy Spirit leads us by the peace of God that passes all natural understanding. Peace triumphs over difficulties by producing revelation knowledge that solves life's problems. No one and nothing can steal our peace or destiny unless we willingly surrender it into their hands.

We were created by God's eternal spoken word, and His word is quick, sharp, and powerful. His word is able to renew us in the spirit of our minds so that we begin to see clearly, think higher thoughts, and walk in higher ways. Kingdom purpose is activated by faith. Our faith gives permission for an unseen destiny (that which we already are) to come forth out of the invisible spiritual realm and manifest in its fullness.

Believers live and prosper by every word that proceeds out of the mouth of God. Proverbs 30:5 tells us that *"every word of God is tested; He is a shield to those who take refuge in Him."* In Deuteronomy 8:3, it further states,

> *He humbled you and let you be hungry, and fed you with manna which you did not know, nor did your fathers know, that He might make you understand that man does not live by bread alone, but man lives by everything that proceeds out of the mouth of the Lord.*

Moses did not cause the manna to fall from heaven to feed the Israelites in the wilderness—it was God the Father. They ate of that bread and still died. God the Father gave us the true living bread (Jesus' flesh) which came down from Heaven and brought eternal life to everyone who would eat of His flesh and drink of His blood. Jesus came to save the whole world.

The Apostles saw Jesus multiply the five loaves of bread for the five thousand to eat. After everyone was fed they had twelve baskets left over. Jesus broke the seven loaves to feed the four thousand and they had seven baskets remaining. Jesus allowed His body to be broken to feed the masses throughout all eternity so man can find eternal life in Him. Jesus heard the disciples discussing the fact that they had no bread. In Mark 8:16-21, Jesus asked, "Do you remember the multiplication of the loaves? Are you not able to see or understand I am more than enough? You have eyes yet they do not see beyond the surface? You have ears yet they do not hear the words of eternal life I speak. Are your hearts dull or hardened? He who comes to Me I will satisfy. He will not hunger or thirst."

OVERCOME TEMPTATION

Jesus the Living Word overcame temptation and wilderness testing by using the written Word, so we can too. The

Holy Spirit led Jesus into the desert to be tempted by the devil. Jesus didn't eat anything for forty days and nights, and He became very hungry. The tempter then came, questioning whether Jesus was the Son of God. If Jesus had power, would He abuse that power and command stones to become bread? Jesus answered his taunts with Scriptures, *"It is written."* It is not only bread that keeps people alive; their lives depend on every word that proceeds from the mouth of God (see Matt. 4:1-4).

Jesus knew His Father was well-pleased with Him. God's pleasure did not depend on Jesus doing miracles or any great works, but simply on Him being Himself, enjoying communion with God, and remaining continually in God's presence through intimate prayer. It is the same for us. God wants relationship.

THE TRANSFIGURATION OF JESUS

The sudden emanation of heavenly radiance from Jesus' body and clothing took place in Matthew 17:9. Jesus and the disciples were overshadowed by a bright cloud. God's audible voice silenced people's voices as He thundered His heavenly endorsement of Jesus to earth. The Transfiguration that took place on the mountain was to give us a visual picture of the glory we are called to carry. Jesus is our example. If the glory in the Old Testament is fading, the glory we are called to carry is permanent. God's eyes are continually looking for a people to be His resting place, a habitation where He can lay His head.

Jesus led a remnant—Peter, James, and John—up to a private place on the mountain to be alone with Him. There in that quiet place, Jesus revealed His glory and its transforming power to them. The disciples were being trained to look to the Lord, to seek His face and His strength. As they intently watched, His appearance changed from the inside out. Jesus' face became as bright as the noonday sun. His clothes were filled with a white luminous light. Moses and Elijah—part of the great cloud of witnesses—came from Heaven to have a deep conversation with Jesus about His upcoming death.

A bright radiant cloud enveloped them, and the voice of God sounded from deep within the cloud. The disciples fell to the ground in great fear. God's voice trumpeted, "This is my Son, the one I have marked with My love. He is my focus and delight. I am very pleased with Him. Listen to and obey Him." Jesus then came and touched His friends. He said, "Stand up. Don't be afraid." When his followers opened their eyes to look around, Elijah and Moses had ascended into Heaven; they saw *only Jesus.* (See Matthew 17:5-8.)

If our eyes are focused to see Jesus and constantly remain on Jesus, He is all we need to see. As we gaze upon Him, we will be transfigured into His image. The glory of the Lord will shine out of us, and we will become carriers of His glory. The Christ in us will begin to manifest. God is our beginning and eternal source of glory. God created us with hearts of flesh. The Word of God will try and test the heart until it removes every stony part. The Word of God will tear down everything that exalts itself against the knowledge of God to replace it with God's truth. This new heart will feel the pleasures and favor of God resting upon its every beat. God's heart beats for the souls of people. The Word of God provides avenues of change that enable us to become fishers of people's souls.

Jesus poured His life into His disciples so they would be prepared to stand and continue preaching the kingdom once He was crucified. Jesus warned Peter and the disciples that Satan had demanded permission to sift them like wheat. "I have prayed for you, that you will not lose your faith. Please help your friends to be strong once you repent and come back to Me." Peter erupted, "I am ready to go to prison and death with You." Jesus said, "Peter before the rooster crows, you will have denied Me three times today" (see Luke 22:31-34).

THE RESTORATION OF PETER

Even though Peter had seen the transfiguration of Jesus on the mountain and many miraculous signs, he still fell away from the Lord. Spiritual encounters do not prevent us from falling short of the mark or failing. Before we are able to step into a greater level of glory in our lives, we must experience a breaking. This breaking allows an opening in our hearts for the focused light of God's glory and love to shine through us like a fine-tuned laser.

Peter denied three times that he even knew Jesus. Peter was impetuous, always intent on speaking and not listening. Peter was so busy denying Christ that he wasn't even aware that the roosters had crowed twice, until the third rooster shattered the silence, releasing the final blow. When the Lord came to restore Peter back to his first love, and into his place as a friend and soul winner, Jesus asked Peter three times, *"Peter, do you love me?"*

> *Jesus said to Simon Peter, "Simon, son of John, do you love me more than these other men love me?" Peter answered, "Yes, Lord, you know that I love you." Then Jesus said to him, "Take care of my lambs." Again Jesus said to him, "Simon, son of John, do you love me?" Peter answered, "Yes, Lord, you know that I love you." Then Jesus said, "Take care of my sheep." A third time Jesus said, "Simon, son of John, do you love me?" Peter was sad because Jesus asked him three times, "Do you love me?" He said, "Lord, you know everything. You know that I love you!" Jesus said to him, "Take care of my sheep"* (John 21:15-17 ERV).

Love covers a multitude of sins (see Prov.10:12; 1 Peter 4:8). Jesus knew that if Peter was not restored to his first love, in his discouragement, he would return to and lead the other disciples back into their previous secular life callings. Jesus had called each of the disciples, both past and present, to be lovers of God and fishers of people's souls. When Jesus died on the cross and before His resurrection, the disciples were left to their ways, talents, natural abilities, and giftings. In his fallen state, Peter decided to go back to what came naturally to him: fishing. He returned to his comfort zone. Sadly, Peter took the other disciples with him. They worked and toiled all night, applying their natural skills and talents, but caught nothing. It is the same with us today. If we forget to seek the Lord for His direction, but follow human ways and traditional programs, we remain barren and unfruitful.

Jesus called to the disciples from the shoreline. Jesus saw their situation from a different heavenly perspective. His presence always brought in abundance, success, and prosperity. Jesus said, *"Cast the net on the right-hand side of the boat and you will find a catch"* (John 21:6). When the disciples followed Jesus' directions and did things the "right" way, they caught so many fish they were not able to pull the net full of fish back into the boats. Their boats had to drag the net full of 153 fish back to the shore. Peter was so energized that he wrapped his coat around himself, jumped into the water, and swam to shore (see John 21:6-11). Do you get that excited when you hear the Lord's voice calling you?

The number 153 represents the nations of the world that are waiting for the "sons of God" to arise. The sons of God are both men and women. They are the Dread Champions of God who have been tried and tested and not found wanting for any good thing. The sons of God will move in the spirit and power of God to accomplish great exploits. When the sons of God cast their nets on the right side, they will bring in the largest harvest of souls ever. The 153 fish also symbolically represents revival, harvest, the ingathering, kingdom multiplication, and evangelism, because of the different kinds of fish that were saved in the nets, a full yield, and it represents the number of the elect, the children of God. The harvest will not come in by our might or by our power, but by seeing and following the direction of the Spirit of the Lord (see Zech. 4:6; 1 Sam. 2:9).

The whole world is groaning and the earth is quaking as it is waiting for the sons of God to arise into their place of restoration (see Rom. 8:19). When the sons of God arise, walk with God in friendship, and move in obedience to the Spirit of God, the greatest harvest of souls that the world has ever seen will come to pass. Romans 8:19-22 says,

> *For the earnest expectation of the creation eagerly waits for the revealing of the sons of God. For the creation was subjected to futility, not willingly, but because of Him who subjected it in hope; because the creation itself also will be delivered from the bondage of corruption into the glorious liberty of the children of God. For we know that the whole creation groans and labors with birth pangs together until now* (NKJV).

God sees us saved, healed, whole, and complete in Him. He knows us completely. He sees us in our now, but more importantly, He sees the end product—what we are destined to be in the future. When we hear and receive His written and spoken words in our hearts, they release the needed power for us to become the people we are in the future.

Faith enables us to see our future. Prayer, worship, praise, and decrees enable us to bring the future into our now. God's words go before us to prepare the way, to open the double doors, and to establish spiritual gateways so that His presence can accelerate the transformation process. This process is demonstrated in Isaiah's prophecy to Cyrus:

> *Thus says the Lord to His anointed* [that's you], *To Cyrus, whose right hand I have held—to subdue nations before him and loose the armor of kings, to open before him the double doors, so that the gates will not be shut: "I will*

go before you and make the crooked places straight; I will
break in pieces the gates of bronze and cut the bars of iron.
I will give you the treasures of darkness and hidden riches
of secret places, that you may know that I, the Lord, Who
call you by your name, Am the God of Israel" (Isa. 45:1-3
NKJV).

The presence of God resting on our lives changes us.
Learning to sit at His feet, receiving His love, and giving
Him our love, is all God asks of us. Jesus says, "Come to Me
with all your struggles and burdens, seek My face, and I will
give you rest. Learn of Me I am gentle and humble in heart"
(see Matt. 11:28).

Let's learn to *ask* largely and correctly so that our joy may
be full (see John 15:11; 16:24). When we *A*sk, *S*eek, and *K*nock
in times of intimate fellowship in God's powerful presence,
our requests will be given to us. Matthew 7:7 encourages us
to keep asking, to continue seeking, and to knock until the
door is open to us. We need to ask until we see what we have
asked for manifested in our lives.

Did your mother ever tell you, "If you meet your Father
at the door when he comes home, and you ask him nicely, he
will give you what you want?" Sometimes we ask our heavenly
Father for things, but in the wrong way or for our own lust
or selfish gain (see James 4:3). We must learn to ask without
self pity, manipulation, or complaining. When we continue
to ask in a more appropriate manner, with the correct words
and the proper attitudes in our hearts, then our requests will
be given to us.

JABEZ ASKED FOR ENLARGEMENT

Jabez was a man who was more honorable than his
brothers. But his mother named him Jabez, which means,
"affliction," because she bore him in pain. Maybe she named
him Jabez because she wanted him to overcome a painful

birth. Names often speak of destiny. Imagine being called affliction your whole life. What kind of destiny would that be? No one wants a life of affliction and pain. Jabez didn't want to be known as an affliction, or one who caused pain, so he called out to God. God is the only one who can transform us. Jabez asked to be blessed, with an enlarged measure of God's presence resting upon his life. He asked for God's hand to be upon him. *"Be near me and don't let anyone hurt me"* (1 Chron. 4:9-10 ERV). God granted his request.

Jabez asked for his territory and his borders to be enlarged. When I meditated on this passage, I saw a vision of God's presence. It was like God's giant hand, formed out of a glory cloud, came to rest over Jabez and everything he owned. The light of God came to rest over his property and sealed Jabez in an invisible canopy or an enclosed protected zone. If we surrender all and allow the territory or magnitude of God's presence to increase in our lives, like it did in Jabez's life, the level of pain we experience and the level of pain we cause others will decrease.

More of God in our lives means more of every good thing will rest upon us. Jabez realized it was God's hand and presence that brought forth the increased measure of blessing, favor, and prosperity in every area of his life. He hungered for and desired more of God. The prayers Jabez uttered enabled God to bless him indeed. The prayers we offer will allow God to bless our lives, too!

Chapter 9

KNOWN BY GOD

MOSES

Moses was raised in the Pharaoh's palace; there he developed a belief that anything imagined or desired is possible. Moses knew he had the authority and power to accomplish any feat. He saw gigantic pyramids and a vast kingdom built through the use of the Jewish slaves. He thought out of the box. His thoughts were not confined to the narrow ways of slavery. His thoughts were ones of freedom, liberty, creativity, education, authority, ruling, and reigning. Everything Egypt did was large. Moses knew the ways of the Pharaohs; he knew the ways of the Egyptian world.

After Moses murdered the Egyptian, God took him out of Egypt into the desert wilderness to train him to move in the Spirit. It was through this process that Moses learned to pull aside to see the miraculous and hear God's voice in the burning bush. The angel of the Lord (a Theophany of Christ) appeared to Moses in a blazing fire from the midst of a bush (see Exod. 3:1-6). Moses was able to turn aside to see the burning bush. First Moses looked, and then he looked again for a second time and beheld—the bush was burning with fire, yet the bush was not consumed. Moses said, *"I must turn aside now and see this marvelous sight, why the bush is not burned up"* (Exod. 3:3). When the Lord saw that he had turned aside to look, God called to him from the midst of the bush and said, *"Moses, Moses"* (Exod. 3:4).

Moses made the shift from just hearing the word of God to seeing the plans of God manifest in his life. Moses was dwelling in the wilderness and pasturing his sheep there. This is the same place we have found ourselves in the past. But Moses' wanderings finally brought him to Horeb, the mountain of God. It is encouraging to know that in God we continue to cycle from wilderness experiences of isolation into the valley, where we confront our weaknesses, and finally to the mountain top, where our lives are transformed from the inside out when we encounter God.

God was able to redeem and use Moses' visionary upbringing and training by applying them to godly kingdom principles. Moses was called to free Israel. He led the two million Jewish slaves from Egypt. When he stood before Pharaoh, his cry was God's cry: "Let My people go!" (see Exod. 9:1). Moses was born to lead a nation back to God. He had a humble birth as a slave. He was fished out of a river, and schooled in kingly palace protocol. Moses learned that favor with God and learning His ways was more important than the favor of an earthly Pharaoh.

This was Moses's prayer:

> *Now therefore, I pray You, if I have found favor in Your sight, let me know Your ways that I may know You, so that I may find favor in Your sight. Consider too, that this nation is Your people* (Exod. 33:13).

When God's presence comes to us, everything is made known. Our prayer should be: *Lord reveal Your form to me in a vision. Show me Your face in a dream. Speak to me mouth to mouth. Teach me Your loving ways, laws, and kingdom principles.* Moses was born with a leadership gift; but it took many years to train and develop before he was ready to step into the fullness of his call.

Prophets and seers of today also go through an extensive training process to understand how their revelatory gifts operate. They must become intimate with the Lord like Moses was so that God can lead and direct them through their own burning bush experience and wilderness journey. Moses had an intimate relationship with God so he knew God face to face, and God communicated to Moses plainly. The Lord said of Moses:

Hear now My words: If there is a prophet among you, I, the Lord, shall make Myself known to him in a vision. I shall speak with him in a dream. Not so, with My servant Moses, He is faithful in all My household; With him I speak mouth to mouth, Even openly, and not in dark sayings, And he beholds [sees] *the form of the Lord...* (Num. 12:6-8).

Israel was forty years in the wilderness, and they didn't know God's ways, but they still received His blessings. Therefore, God swore that that generation should not enter into His rest in the Promised Land or God's presence. *"For forty years I loathed that generation, and said they are a people who err in their heart, and they do not know My ways"* (Ps. 95:10).

The Bible tells us that if we hear God's words and do them, we are wise; we will be like a person built upon a rock. Jesus is the Rock. All the epistles are built upon what Jesus taught. When we focus on the Word of God it will come alive in us to shape and mold us into the image of Jesus, the Living Word. What we focus on we empower in our life. We remember things that are important to us. The things we value are easy for us to learn and appropriate in our lives.

Learning to hear the voice of the Lord is vital if we want our lives to be fulfilled, happy, and successful. The Bible tells us that our treasure dwells where our heart resides (see Matt. 6:21, Luke 12:34). Where is your heart? What is your number one priority or desire in life? We have two ears—we have the equipment, but do we have the desire and the dedication to develop our spiritual abilities to hear God's voice and observe what is going on in the Spirit realm? *"He who has an ear let him hear what the Spirit is saying to the churches..."* (Rev. 2:11). When we have ears to hear what the Spirit of God is saying we will be able to make the necessary changes to please the Lord.

The first thing the Holy Spirit modifies when He leads us through a season of change is our spiritual climate or atmosphere. He creates a spiritual expectancy within us. When Moses went up on the mount, the atmosphere was charged with God's presence. In this new location, He saw God and received a fresh message and impartation from God.

Just like the men and women of old, our vision will change when our location changes. The pillar of fire and the cloud appeared to lead the children of Israel when they left Egypt. God wants to change our vision. We can only receive a new vision when we can see it. We have to see it to apprehend it! How can we receive the promises of God if we are blind to what God is doing? If we are in an old or wrong location or with the wrong people, we can lose what God is trying to do in and through us. Abraham had to get out of the tent to see the heavenly stars (see Gen. 15:5). Elijah had to get out of the cave to see the Lord passing by (see 1 Kings 19:11-13). The apostles had to leave the fiery upper room to win the souls in the street (see Acts 1:5-16). Change begins within, not from outside pressures.

We have been through the fires of refining for years. The fires consumed the wood, hay, and stubble in our lives (see 1 Cor. 3:12). The fires also purified our hearts and cleaned our hands so that we can receive and carry the glory and blessings of the Lord. We find ourselves warming our outstretched hands around a burning bush. Many find themselves in the fiery furnace that has been heated up seven times hotter by their enemies. This furnace of affliction destroys the strongmen in our lives, but leaves us with the image of the fourth man, Jesus, imprinted on our spirits. We learn that the hatred and persecutions of our enemies are really working on our behalf. It is time to thank and bless our enemies for their help in perfecting us. The fire causes the scales to fall from our eyes so we see as Jesus sees.

God is calling each of us by name. He is tuning our ears to hear His voice. Now the Holy Spirit is going to focus our eyes to see God in the invisible realms of the Spirit. *"And then Moses said, 'Here I am'"* (Exod. 3:4). Be encouraged! You have not been forgotten. As with Moses, God knows exactly where you are, and He has a great plan for your life.

> *Then He* [God] *said, "Do not come near here; remove your sandals from your feet, for the place on which you are standing is holy ground"* (Exod. 3:5).

Moses understood that he was just being introduced to the fire and who God is. God said also,

> *"I am the God of your father, the God of Abraham, the God of Isaac, and the God of Jacob." Then Moses hid his face, for he was afraid to look at God* (Exod. 3:6).

When Moses first encountered God, before the fire had done its work, he was afraid to look into God's beautiful face. Moses hid his face in shame in the presence of a holy God. After the fire had refined Moses and God had completed the cleansing process, God met with Moses face to face and called him a friend. Each of us must go through the process of spiritual refinement so we can boldly approach a holy God. Developing an intimate friendship with God or man requires an open heart of trust and an ability to share secrets. We must be transparent. We are a needy people. We need God in every area of our life not just in some.

God is always reaching out to man for relationship. God shares His secrets and mysteries with His friends, the prophets and seers. God is the best at show and tell. Everything that God has told Jesus, the Holy Spirit makes known to us.

Before we are able to clearly discern the voice of God, we will hear the sound of north, south, east, and west winds as they blow through our life. The rain of the Spirit will come to water the seeds we have sown. The fire will come to burn up everything that is not of God so that what remains will be as pure as gold. When we hear His voice and obey it, we will become His voice (see John 10:4-5; Acts 4:29-30).

GOD CALLED MOSES BY NAME

Moses found favor in the sight of the Lord, and he delivered his people from Egypt. Years later, as they were beginning their journey to the Promised Land, Moses said to the Lord:

> *See, You say to me, "Bring up this people!" But You Yourself have not let me know whom You will send with me. Moreover, You have said, "I have known you by name, and you have also found favor in My sight." Now therefore, I pray You, if I have found favor in Your sight, let me know Your ways that I may know You, so that I may find favor in Your sight. Consider too, that this nation is Your people* (Exod. 33:12-13).

The Lord then answered Moses, *"My presence shall go with you, and I will give you rest"* (Exod. 33:14).

However, Moses responded:

> *If Your presence does not go with us, do not lead us up from here. For how then can it be known that I have found favor in Your sight, I and Your people? Is it not by Your going with us, so that we, I and Your people, may be distinguished from all the other people who are upon the face of the earth?* (Exod. 33:15-16).

The Lord told Moses, *"I will also do this thing of which you have spoken; for you have found favor in My sight and I have known you by name"* (Exod. 33:17).

Then Moses prayed again. He asked the Lord to show him His glory! Moses was not satisfied with an unfulfilled promise, even though he had experienced the presence of the Lord. He wanted more. He hungered for the glory realm where God manifested His goodness when He passed by. The Lord said,

> *"I Myself will make all My goodness pass before you, and will proclaim the name of the Lord before you; and I will be gracious to whom I will be gracious, and will show compassion on whom I will show compassion." But He said, "You cannot see My face, for no man can see Me and live!" Then the Lord said, "Behold, there is a place by Me, and you shall stand there on the rock; and it will come about, while My glory is passing by, that I will put you in the cleft of the rock and cover you with My hand until I have passed by. Then I will take My hand away and you shall see My back, but My face shall not be seen* (Exod. 33:19-23).

Here is my paraphrase of God's words to Moses:

I will show my favor, love, and mercy to anyone I choose. I will make my perfect goodness pass before you. I will be gracious and proclaim My character and attributes before you. You will know Me and hear My name as Lord! I will show you My compassion. But you cannot fully see My face, for no person can see Me in all of My glory and continue to live! I will open your spirit eyes to see or behold. There is a place by Me in the Spirit where you can stand upon the Rock, Jesus. When you are able to see Jesus, you will see My glory. I will place you securely in Jesus, in the cleft of the rock, and safely cover you with My hand. No one will see you, but they will see My glory resting on you. I will hide you from their view and manifest Myself through you. When I take My hand away, all you will see is the cross and My Son's scarred, bloody back, but not My face.

I fully believe that Moses saw the stripes that Jesus bore on His back and that the blood that Jesus shed released the glory. The glory of God is in the cross of Jesus Christ.

Moses told God He wanted to see His glory. God placed Moses beside Him on a rock. We know that the rock symbolizes Jesus. There God showed Moses His goodness, His nature, and the attributes of His names. God pressed Moses into the cleft of the rock and covered him with His hand while He passed by.

When the hand of God covers us, we are no longer seen, but other people see God's image shining through us. When we are covered by God's hand, the five dimensions of ministry begin to flow. People see who Christ is because we are positioned beside Him. He is covering us and leading us. We are on the rock. We are pressed into the shape or image of the Rock, where we surrender to Him and take on His image. When we get pressed into a form, we take on that form. It is no longer we who are living, but Christ comes forth in us. We have been crucified with Christ; nevertheless, we live. The resurrection power of Jesus now manifests through our lives.

TURN ASIDE TO SEE YOUR FUTURE

We must prepare the eyes of our hearts to turn aside to see the future. When we *say* what we *see* in prayer, we will experience destiny in our own fiery, burning-bush God-encounter. The fire of God's glory comes to cleanse and purify. He is an awesome, jealous God who defends His beloved, and He is to be reverenced. His holy fire releases the baptism of fire to bring us into the Spirit of holiness. God's presence is a consuming fire that produces righteousness, peace, and spiritual understanding. The righteous and just are able to live with the appearance of His continual burning, consuming fire.

> ..."*Who among us can live with the consuming fire? Who among us can live with continual burning?*" *He who walks righteously and speaks with sincerity, he who rejects unjust gain and shakes his hands so that they hold no bribe; he who stops his ears from hearing about bloodshed and shuts his eyes from looking upon evil...* (Isa. 33:14-15).

God will cause these people to dwell in the high places of favor with Jesus as their rock and fortress (see Isa. 33:16).

How do we survive and prosper when we walk through the firestorms of life? We must learn to adhere to God's truth, live right before Him, despise exploitation, refuse to take bribes, reject all forms of violence, and avoid evil amusements. Because of our obedience, God will increase the standard of our living. We will be nourished in safety and stable in all our ways. We will see the King of Kings in His colorful, vibrant beauty. If we honor God in all we say and do, our needs will be met according to His riches in glory even if He has to bring it to us from a foreign land. The more we know God the more we honor, revere, fear, and see His hand in every situation of life.

The Spirit of the Lord rested on Jesus when He walked the earth. He was able to flow in whatever dimension of the Spirit He needed to accomplish His Father's will. We are able to walk in the fullness of the sevenfold Spirit of God while we minister here on earth. If Jesus, the perfect One, needed the fullness of the Spirit, how much more do we?

> *The Spirit of the Lord will rest on Him, the spirit of wisdom and understanding, the spirit of counsel and strength, the spirit of knowledge and the fear of the Lord* (Isa. 11:2).

As the seven fiery Spirits of God ignite our lives with the holy presence of the Lord, we will delight in the fear of the

Lord. We will stop judging circumstances and people by what our natural eyes see. We will begin to see into the invisible realm. We will no longer continue to make decisions by what we want or desire. We will not make decisions based on what we hear people saying, but will tune our ears to hear what the Spirit is saying.

As we are clothed in a robe of righteousness and the belt of faithfulness, we will give grace to the poor and make fair decisions for those who are less fortunate and afflicted. Then our encouraging words of love will carry authority that will convict the wicked of their wrong ways (see Isa. 11:3-4).

WAIT IN GOD'S PRESENCE

God is our defense and source. His love shapes our life for success. As we wait upon the Lord He renews our strength and cuts off those who do evil so we can inherit the earth. The Bible is full of God-given revelation knowledge that came through dreams, visions, and prophecy. We must study to show ourselves approved so that we can operate in the Spirit of understanding. We need to be spiritually fruitful in today's age of increasing spiritual awareness—which is both good and evil. We must learn from the Holy Spirit to discern between the two and have the character to reject the evil and embrace the true. This is what Paul prayed for the believers in Ephesus:

> That the God of our Lord Jesus Christ, the Father of glory, may give to you the spirit of wisdom and revelation in the knowledge of Him, the eyes of your understanding being enlightened... (Eph. 1:17-18 NKJV).

Pray that God will open your eyes to see His miracles and wonders. The tangible presence of God residing in our lives, enabling us to do the impossible, is more important now than ever before in history. We do well to adopt the prayer of Moses in Exodus 33:13-16 (below). God builds us up through His Word and graces us with clear understanding of revelation. Moses asked God to show him His ways. This involves the spiritual realm of vision and God training us in His deep wisdom. If we are able to see our future and understand the ways in which God wants us to walk, we will prosper. God gives us insight so we can do what He tells us to do. It is time to see the grace and favor of God resting upon us in the realms of glory. Part of knowing God is recognizing His truth and glory manifested in and through our lives. Do we really know God if we are not walking in the strength of His power and doing great exploits?

> *"Now therefore, I pray, if I have found grace* [favor] *in Your sight, show me Your way, that I may know You and that I may find grace in Your sight. And consider that this nation is Your people." And He said, "My Presence will go with you, and I will give you rest." Then he said to Him, "If Your Presence does not go with us, do not bring us up from here. For how then will it be known that Your people and I have found grace in Your sight, except You go with us? So we shall be separate, Your people and I, from all the people who are upon the face of the earth"* (Exod. 33:13-16 NKJV).

ABRAHAM WAS KNOWN BY GOD

Abraham found great favor with God because he trusted God. He left everything that was safe and familiar to follow God into the unknown. The Bible tells us that Abraham was known by God (see Gen. 17). The Lord trained Abraham to live by the counsel of His word. Abraham recognized the sound of God's voice. God's word became a beam of light that showed Abraham where the Lord was leading him. God gave Abraham great spiritual insight and common sense. God breathed His wisdom over Abraham so he could understand the ways of God. Abraham saw the Lord and His angels. The Lord appeared to His friend Abraham in his tent (see Gen. 18:1).

While the Lord was already present with Abraham, He sent three (the number three represents the Trinity) of His angels to communicate His plans and share His purposes with Abraham. When Abraham looked up, and saw the angels, he ran into the presence of the Lord, bowed down, and greeted them with, *""My Lord, if I have now found favor in Your sight, do not pass on by Your servant"* (Gen. 18:3 NKJV). Abraham knew that the presence of angels meant God's favor and increase were present. God's Theophany was adding to him. The angels came to deliver God's message and release the fulfillment of God's promises to Abraham by sharing in a covenant meal.

> *"Please let a little water be brought, and wash your feet, and rest yourselves under the tree. And I will bring a morsel of bread, that you may refresh your hearts. After that you may pass by, inasmuch as you have come to your servant." They said, "Do as you have said." So Abraham hurried into the tent to Sarah and said, "Quickly, make ready three measures of fine meal; knead it and make cakes." And Abraham ran to the herd, took a tender and good calf, gave it to a young man, and he hastened to prepare it. So he took butter and milk and the calf which he had prepared, and set it before them; and he stood by them under the tree as they ate* (Gen. 18:4-8 NKJV).

The angels asked Abraham for Sarah his wife. They had come to bring the promise of a son to life in her womb. Their words brought laughter and joy into her heart, which opened her womb to receive the promised seed. Joy is healing like medicine. Sarah laughed within herself, saying, *"After I have grown old, shall I have pleasure, my lord being old also?"* (Gen. 18:12 NKJV).

And the LORD said to Abraham, "Why did Sarah laugh, saying, 'Shall I surely bear a child, since I am old?' Is anything too hard for the Lord? At the appointed time I will return to you, according to the time of life, and Sarah shall have a son" (Gen. 18:13-14 NKJV).

The angel let Abraham know that God had sent His words of joy to open Sarah's womb to fulfill His promise of a son to Abraham. The angels would return in nine months to observe the miraculous birth of Abraham's son.

Then the men rose from there and looked toward Sodom, and Abraham went with them to send them on the way. And the Lord said, "Shall I hide from Abraham what I am doing, since Abraham shall surely become a great and mighty nation, and all the nations of the earth shall be blessed in him? For I have known him, in order that he may command his children and his household after him, that they keep the way of the Lord, to do righteousness and justice, that the Lord may bring to Abraham what He has spoken to him." ...Then the men turned away from there and went toward Sodom, but Abraham still stood before the Lord (Gen. 18:16-19, 22 NKJV).

God visited Abraham in his tent; He walked with him, and talked with him in daily times of intimacy. God shared His secrets and plans with Abraham. Abraham shared his disappointments, heart's desires, hopes, and plans with the Lord. Abraham patiently waited years for his promise of a son born to Sarah to be fulfilled. Over the years they developed an intimate relationship which required an open trusting heart and face-to-face dialogue. God blessed Abraham with wealth and great influence but none of those things meant anything to Abraham without a son, an heir to leave with his inheritance. The word of the Lord came to Abram in a vision, saying "Do not fear, Abram, I am a shield and friend to you; your reward shall be very great." Abram said, "O Lord

God, what will You give me to take away my sorrow, since I am childless. Sarah and I have no offspring of our own. The only heir to my house is a slave born in my house named Eliezer of Damascus?" (see Gen. 15:1-2).

God granted Abraham his heart's desire for an heir, but the promise was fulfilled only after it seemed impossible. The Lord appeared to Abraham in a Theophany and shared a covenant meal of communion with him. In Scripture, a meal is shared to bring forth or seal the covenant agreement between two parties. God appeared and shared a meal with Abraham to release his promised heir.

Abraham was the father of faith. Abraham's faith in God caused him to receive the promises of God in the fullness of time. His faith enabled him to be a friend of God. We too will become intimate friends of God as we develop our love and faith through overcoming the trials and tests of this life.

We must remember that God is always present. He is all powerful so nothing is impossible. If we will hide His word in our hearts and seek God's face, we will be able to continually abide in His presence. It is the presence of God in us that empowers us to bear eternal fruit. If we live our lives apart from God, we will not be able to do anything. The Bible says it like this: *"...Apart from Me you can do nothing"* (John 15:5). Abiding in God's presence will ensure that the dreams of destiny that God has sown in each of our hearts will come to pass.

WHAT DO YOU SEE FOR THE FUTURE?

As long as there is a future there is always a hope. What are the God-given dreams that you hold dear in your heart? Are you holding onto them or have you relinquished them because of past pain and disappointments. What do you see for your future? Do you see hope or despair, faith or fear? Have the painful things in life caused your dreams of tomorrow to dim? Have the destroyers removed the hope that once inspired you to greatness? Are you focusing on past losses and failures or releasing your regrets and moving forward knowing that things will be better tomorrow. Remember a simple truth—what we gaze upon we become like. Be encouraged. Joel 2:25-27 gives us a promise of restoration,

> *I'll make up for the years of the locust, the great locust devastation—locusts savage, locusts deadly, fierce locusts, locusts of doom, that great locust invasion I sent your way. You'll eat your fill of good food. You'll be full of praises to your God, the God who has set you back on your heels in wonder. Never again will my people be despised. You'll know without question that I'm in the thick of life with Israel, that I'm your God, yes, your God, the one and only real God. Never again will my people be despised* (MSG).

Are you tired of the enemy stealing from you and plundering your hopes and dreams?

> *But this is a people pillaged and plundered, all trapped in holes and sequestered in prisons. They are there to be plundered, with no one to rescue them; there to be pillaged, and no one says, "Return them!" Which of you will listen to this? Who will hear and give heed in the times to come?* (Isa. 42:22-23 CJB).

God is calling us to repent once again and to listen to His healing voice of love, deliverance, and salvation. He wants to give us understanding in everything as we prepare our minds for service, exercising self-control and placing our hope in the grace of Jesus Christ. We are not to pattern ourselves after the people of this world, but to let God change us from the inside out so we have a new way of thinking. Then we will be able to decide and accept what God wants for us. We will be able to know what is good and pleasing to Him and what His perfect will is.

We must be made new in our hearts in order to see God. The pure in heart shall see God (see Matt. 5:8). When our thinking is renewed, we will become that new person who was made to be like God, truly good and pleasing to Him. We cannot hide what we are thinking from an all-knowing God. God already knows our deepest hidden thoughts. He understands our weaknesses, that we are only made of dust. The Holy Spirit speaks to people in the way that agrees with what God wants. He brings a clear picture of who we are to be in Christ. We are called to think of ourselves as servants to God and slaves to mankind—the same way Christ Jesus humbly thought of Himself. Jesus came to seek and save the lost.

> *But Jesus called them to Himself and said, "You know that the rulers of the Gentiles lord it over them, and their great men exercise authority over them. It is not this way among you, but whoever wishes to become great among you shall be your servant, and whoever wishes to be first among you shall be your slave; just as the Son of Man did not come to be served, but to serve, and to give His life a ransom for many"* (Matt. 20:25-28).

We have good news that will set the captives free and open the prison doors. God is gathering the prodigals, healing the brokenhearted, restoring hope, and planting vision in the heart of His bride. We need to see the Lord walking in, through, and by us along life's journey. He is there when the rivers rage and the fire roars. We belong to the Lord. Jesus saved us for Himself. He has a grand plan for each of us. He walks with us in times of triumph and trouble. His love for us is without measure; there is no cost too great to pay for our redemption.

> *Jacob, the Lord created you. Israel, he made you, and now he says, "Don't be afraid. I saved you. I named you. You are mine. When you have troubles, I am with you. When you cross rivers, you will not be hurt. When you walk*

through fire, you will not be burned; the flames will not hurt you. That's because I, the Lord, am your God. I, the Holy One of Israel, am your Savior. I gave Egypt to pay for you. I gave Ethiopia and Seba to make you mine. You are precious to Me, and I have given you a special place of honor. I love you. That's why I am willing to trade others, to give up whole nations, to save your life. So don't be afraid, because I am with you. I will gather your children and bring them to you..." (Isa. 43:1-5 ERV).

Friends, it is essential that our focus returns to and remains on Jesus as our first love so that we are encouraged in the midst of change, transition, and the shaking of the earth. God has a divine plan that will allow us to discover our successful future (see Jer. 29:11). In order to leave the past—with all its failures, pains, and disappointments—and enter into our prosperous future, we must take steps to cross the threshold into the new. Let's leave the old season and advance into a new season with God.

YELLOW CAR DREAM

Recently, I had a dream in response to my request that the Holy Spirit would help me understand where we are in the timetable of transition and change.

I dreamt of a yellow car full of people. The vehicle represented people's lives—their careers, families, churches, businesses, and decisions. We are all in the middle of the process of making life-changing decisions that will align us so that we may reach our greatest potential and destiny in God.

The car was yellow because everyone was used to using their minds, their intelligence, and the powers of carnal reasoning to make decisions. No one was seeking God's face or asking Him for His wisdom in order to make the transition successfully.

The car was at the halfway point on a major highway. It had come to rest in the middle of a key crossroad or intersection. As the oncoming traffic passed back and forth on either side of the car, I could feel the force of the wind from the oncoming vehicles shaking the car.

It was not possible to continue forward because the windshield was fogged over. There was no clear vision or ability to see where to go next or how to turn. It was too risky to go in reverse. I knew that would mean we would be losing ground. The Holy Spirit said, "We need to wait on Him and the leading of His Spirit for our next move, or our next step, no matter how scary and uncomfortable it feels right now." He said, "He is going to give strategy and new vision, and He is going to lead us in a new way where we have never been before." He wanted us to be totally absorbed in His love, dependent upon His voice and His vision, and obedient to His leading.

Isaiah 43:18-21 says,

> *Do not remember the former things, nor consider the things of old. Behold, I will do a new thing, now it shall spring forth; shall you not know it? I will even make a road in the wilderness and rivers in the desert. The beast of the field will honor Me, the jackals and the ostriches, because I give waters in the wilderness and rivers in the desert, to give drink to My people, My chosen. This people I have formed for Myself; they shall declare My praise* (NKJV).

God is giving us prophetic insight to see our new season, but we must wait until our eyes are given clear vision and our ears hear His voice saying, *"This is the way walk in it!"*

> *O people in Zion, inhabitant in Jerusalem, you will weep no longer. He will surely be gracious to you at the sound of your cry; when He hears it, He will answer you. Although the Lord has given you bread of privation and water of oppression, He, your Teacher will no longer hide Himself,*

but your eyes will behold your Teacher. Your ears will hear a word behind you, "This is the way, walk in it," whenever you turn to the right or to the left. And you will defile your graven images overlaid with silver, and your molten images plated with gold. You will scatter them as an impure thing, and say to them, "Be gone" (Isa. 30:19-22).

God's ears are tuned to hear and answer the cries of His children. He will make Himself obvious as He comes out of His hiding place to deliver us from our past depravity and oppression. We will see Him and hear His voice leading us every step of the way upon the new path He has chosen for our success.

JEREMIAH WAS GIVEN EYES TO SEE

A good example of the Lord revealing Himself to a man and teaching him to see is found in the prophet Jeremiah. The Lord came and revealed the next steps Jeremiah was to take to enter into his new season to achieve his future. At first Jeremiah was not able to see his future clearly because all he saw was his barrenness, great need, and malfunction. His boldness to move forward into visual clarity didn't come until God removed his fear, doubt, and excuses.

We are always so eager to make excuses regarding why we are not qualified to accept God's love and the call He has placed on our lives for greatness. We point out our sin, our weaknesses, our lack of training and skills, and our failures. We are full of reasons why we can't do something or why we are not the right ones for our assignments. We offer God excuses when He comes to send us forth into our calling. Jeremiah did this, too. God was establishing Jeremiah as a prophet, but Jeremiah could only focus on his past weaknesses because he couldn't see his bright future.

Now the word of the Lord came to me saying, "Before I formed you in the womb I knew you, and before you were born I consecrated you; I have appointed you a prophet to the nations." Then I said, "Alas, Lord God Behold, I do not know how to speak, because I am a youth." But the Lord said to me, "Do not say, 'I am a youth,' because everywhere I send you, you shall go, and all that I command you, you shall speak. Do not be afraid of them, for I am with you to deliver you," declares the Lord. Then the Lord stretched out His hand and touched my mouth, and the Lord said to me, "Behold, I have put My words in your mouth. See, I have appointed you this day over the nations and over the kingdoms, to pluck up and to break down, to destroy and to overthrow, to build and to plant" (Jer. 1:4-10).

The Lord assured Jeremiah that His presence would go with him to deliver him everywhere He sent him. God knew Jeremiah and had called him as a prophet to the nation before he was even born. The Lord touched his mouth to enable Jeremiah to speak as the oracle of God. God's loving persistence abode with Jeremiah to give him skill and understanding to develop his prophetic eyes to see vision and his ears to hear the word of the Lord.

The word of the Lord came to me saying, "What do you see, Jeremiah?" And I said, "I see a rod of an almond tree." Then the Lord said to me, "You have seen well, for I am watching over My word to perform it" (Jer. 1:11-12).

Jeremiah successfully described the vision of the almond tree to the Lord. God continued to confirm Jeremiah's success, "You have seen well," as the Lord articulated Jeremiah's potential and refused to allow Jeremiah to focus on his excuses, fears, or failures.

God also speaks to the positives of what His Word says we are and what His Word says we can become, rather than emphasizing the negatives. For example, God does not speak to our sickness and disease; He speaks to our health and healing. He does not verbalize our poverty or lack; He addresses our wealth and abundance. He does not talk to our failure or mistakes, but He proclaims our triumphs and celebrates our successes. He does not focus on the past; He speaks to the present and to our future.

Our yesterdays cannot hold us back from reaching our tomorrows unless we allow them to. Our past does not dictate or mirror the future unless we refuse to embrace God's directions and change. God speaks the language of hope to encourage each of us to succeed. We do not like to be left in the dark, so God brings us into the light. He wants us to know the wonderful plans He has for the future as much as we want Him to reveal them to us.

JEREMIAH WAS TRAINED TO SEE

Jeremiah told God that his lack of maturity and eloquence of speech would prohibit him from speaking for Him. Therefore, by touching Jeremiah's weak areas, God imparted a divine grace that overrode Jeremiah's weakness. God believes in us. He promises that if we will have faith in Him and in His divine empowerment, He will provide what is needed for us to fulfill our future. An impartation of Christ's nature empowers us to overcome:

> *Grace and peace be multiplied to you in the knowledge of God and of Jesus our Lord, as His divine power has given to us all things that pertain to life and godliness, through the knowledge of Him who called us by glory and virtue, by which have been given to us exceedingly great and precious promises, that through these you may be partakers of the divine nature, having escaped the corruption that is in the world through lust* (2 Peter 1:2-4 NKJV).

We are not alone on life's journey. God promises to go before us and to defeat our enemies. He lives largely within us, and He daily walks beside us—constantly encouraging us.

Each new day is fresh, and we receive fresh grace and mercy. Satan's lies scream, "You are not loved, called, equipped, or anointed!" If we listen to or agree with his lies, we won't believe that God's grace can take the place of our greatest weakness. Every night the Holy Spirit comes to hover over us with His loving embrace to overshadow us with dreams and visions so that we will conceive and see our potential.

Mary was overshadowed by the presence of the Holy Spirit, and she conceived Jesus, the Savior of the world and the Son of the living God. When Gabriel announced that she was to birth the Son of God, she said, "*…May it be done to me according to your word*" (Luke 1:38). God's touch resolved any questions or fear with which Mary may have been struggling. The Virgin Mary knew that being pregnant outside of wedlock could end in her being stoned to death. In Mary's moment of belief and faith, God imparted a supernatural grace to her that empowered her to envision the giver of eternal life and receive her amazing future.

Later, at the wedding, when they ran out of wine, Mary told the servants to do whatever Jesus said. Jesus told Mary "It is not yet My time to move in miracles" (see John 2:1-5). However, Mary knew the creative power of God's word. As she prophesied, Jesus saw His heavenly Father move to release Jesus' first miracle by turning the water into wine (see John 2:6-11).

The Holy Spirit guides and teaches us as we step into every new season. God's promises are true. The word He speaks to us prepares us to see our future.

God fulfilled His promises to Abraham, Mary, and Jeremiah. And He will faithfully fulfill His promises to you. You are His beloved! The word *watch* (*shaqad*) means "to be alert, i.e. sleepless; the awakening one; hence to be on the lookout (whether for good or ill) to hasten, remain awake, to keep watch of, watch for, and be wakeful over."[1] The same word can be translated into "almond-shaped, to make like (unto, after the fashion of almonds), or almond blossoms." Many people would agree our eyes are almond shaped. When our eyes are focused on the Lord we will see the awakening of the spring season in our life.

Once the Lord had placed His words in Jeremiah's mouth, He inquired once more of Jeremiah, "What do you see?" This time, Jeremiah did not answer with another defense, reason, or justification for his lack or weakness. Instead, Jeremiah responded properly as prophetic vision was given to him, *"I see a branch* [or shoot] *of an almond tree* [the emblem of alertness and activity, blossoming in late winter]*"* (Jer. 1:11).

The almond tree is the first to bud or awaken in a new season with blossom cups that are shaped like almonds. On my Nutrition, Plants, and Flowers dream symbol cards, the almond also represents virginity, hope, watchfulness and fruitfulness, health, gifts, authority, happiness, and offering your best (see Gen. 43:11).[2] Diligence and hard work will result in increased production, harvest, and profits, resulting in wealth, God's choice, success, and financial gain (see Num. 17:8).

When Jeremiah received God's grace, his eyes were opened to see from God's perspective. God's vision enabled Jeremiah to overcome his weakness and boldly step into his destiny and near future. When we receive God's great grace in every season of transition in our lives, our eyes will also be opened to see from God's perspective concerning our destiny. The prophet Jeremiah was awakened to see his new season and future. He received grace to fulfill his divine destiny call.

Each morning we awake from a new dream; it is a new day, a new beginning, a new awakening. We open our eyes to see by the dawn's early light. God is pouring out fresh grace, enlightenment, and spiritual dreams and visions that will awaken us to new possibilities. Heaven is drawing near to empower us to fulfill our destiny. The Lord sends His angels to watch over, guide, and protect each of us, to ensure His word comes to pass in our lives. God is a protector and a defender of the weak, so He continues to speak to our potential. God is the only one who knows the future! It is time to draw close to God. Then we will see our divine destiny and future.

ENDNOTES

1. Strong, *Strong's Exhaustive Concordance*, Hebrew #8245.

2. Barbie L. Breathitt, *Dream Encounter Symbol Book*, Volume II, (Self-published, 2008).

Chapter 10

FRIENDS WITH ANGELS

Angels help to train and equip seers to understand what they are seeing and hearing in the spiritual realms of eternity. Once seers are fully trained, they are able to gaze into the heavenly realms of beauty and glory. After studying the training process of seers, the lives of prophets seem almost non-eventful or common in comparison.

Seers are acquainted with the angelic realm. They are accustomed to seeing these beings of light. To seers, an angel is a messenger or a teacher sent by God to bring more understanding to the realms of the spirit. Angels give added clarity to visions so seers will know what they have seen and heard.

Angels instruct seers on heavenly protocol and procedures as their prayers carry them through heavenly places. Seers' ears are tuned to the frequencies of the tongues of angels. They hear the still small whispers of the Holy Spirit and obediently follow the slight impressions He gives. Seers stand in the presence of angels to receive power, divine counsel, insight, understanding, and skill. The angelic realms of messengers are also used to bring us into revelation knowledge and spiritual insights. We must learn to discern the different angelic realms and messengers because not every "angel" spirit or messenger is sent from God.

ANGELS FROM PAKISTAN VISIT

The mystery of angels and their connections in our lives, along with their many functions and facets, have long fascinated mankind. The realms of the supernatural draw our spirits like a magnet. Many times the divine connections we have with people can open the doors for angels to visit us. Oftentimes, angels are assigned to bring a message to us from the heavenly realms. Our prayers act as doorways or avenues for angels to soar on, invading the earthly realm with their heavenly glory.

One of those heavenly connections happened to me several years ago. I had promised Marion and Joy, two friends of mine, that I would serve as their intermediary to Heaven while they traveled the country of Pakistan as missionary evangelists.

Faithfully, I would remember them in times of prayer as they made their way through the hot arid country; stopping in little villages and connecting with the beautiful people of Pakistan.

I retired to my bedchamber early one evening and drifted off into a deep sleep. I was suddenly awakened by a brilliant light that filled my room. Out of a billowy white cloud filled with gold flecks of glory two persons appeared. Their presence startled me. It was fearful yet exciting and exhilarating at the same time. I gathered my wits about me and sat up in bed. I found my bedroom completely filled with the radiant glory of the eternal realm. It was like waking into an electric field of light and energy. The countenances of the two angelic beings were exactly like my two girlfriends. I knew it couldn't really be them as they were on the other side of the world in a foreign country. Yet somehow they had come to visit, standing an arm's length away from me. I asked why they had come and their reply was direct and to the point.

"Marion and Joy's lives are endangered." "There are those that are seeking to kill Americans in Pakistan." "Contact their host and get them out of the country." Then as quickly as they appeared the angels vanished as they stepped back into the golden misty cloud. The light, that only moments before had filled my room, returned to the darkness of midnight; but the atmosphere had changed. My prayers had connected to the realms of heaven and paved a way for the angels to deliver their warning.

Upon awaking the next morning, I began the process of making the necessary phone contacts to alert my friends of the impending dangers. That night on the news I witnessed a report that told the gruesome story of six American men being machine gunned to death in their car on the streets of Pakistan.

Joy and Marion were holding an open-air meeting in front of a multitude of people that evening. An old tattered car sped onto the dusty scene. Men wheeling machine guns piled out of the car and pressed their way through the crowd. Upon receiving the urgent warning from America, the host of the meeting grabbed the ladies and threw them to the ground. Pushing them under the stage, they motioned for them to crawl to the back of the stage where a car was awaiting to carry them to safety. It was a narrow escape; but the angels' warning the night before had saved their lives. They returned to the United States, safe to tell their story of a miraculous escape.

ACCOMPANIED BY ANGELS

Jesus loved God and all of His creation, including the cosmos. Jesus was constantly aware of the angelic realm that accompanied Him. The angels were with Jesus every step of His journey. The angels were in Heaven with the Father, the Son, and the Holy Spirit when the godhead decided Jesus would be the Savior of the world.

Angels were there to guide the interpretation of Joseph's dreams and Mary's engagement. The angels announced Jesus' birth to the lowly shepherds who tended their flocks by night. The heavenly host sang and rejoiced that the Son had been born, Jesus, the Savior of all humankind. They were there with Jesus at His earthly beginning. They talked with Jesus and watched over Him in His dreams at night. The angels walked with Jesus every day of His life. They assisted in all the healings and miracles Jesus performed.

They were there with Him at His betrayal in the Garden of Gethsemane. They saw when the soldiers drew back and fell to the ground, slain from the power of His Spirit, when Jesus lovingly said, "I AM He!" The angels were there with Jesus during His mock trial. They saw Him turned over to the jealous religious rulers. The angels helplessly watched the vicious beating and malicious stripes that maimed His body and marred His beautiful face beyond recognition. They watched as Jesus kept turning His cheeks to absorb another blow from the Roman soldiers. With each stripe Jesus took, His blood covered and healed human depravity, sickness, and disease.

The angels walked along the blood-strewn Golgotha road, watching the hatred in people's hearts tear their beloved Jesus apart. They were there when the cruel Roman soldiers stripped Him naked and drove nails into His gentle healing hands and feet. The angels where there when Jesus hung on the shameful cross, suspended between Heaven and earth. They watched Him bear the sins of every man, woman, boy, and girl who ever had or would live. The angels gazed at the Son of Man as He struggled for each breath, having to press His torn, bruised flesh against an old rugged cross until He breathed His last. The angels heard Him cry out, "Father, forgive them! They know not what they do! Into Your loving hands I commit my Spirit! It is done! It is finished!"

The angels were there when the soldiers took His dead, mangled body from the cross. Their celestial tears helped to wash His bloodstained body as He was prepared for burial in a borrowed tomb. They stayed with Jesus for three long days while He descended into hell to lead captivity captive and gave gifts unto people.

Then the powerful Resurrection angels descended from Heaven with lightning, and an earthquake shook the earth as the angel said, "Jesus has conquered death, hell, and the grave! To fulfill Scripture, it is time for Jesus to arise from the dead!" The power of God resurrected Jesus from the dead. The angels rejoiced at the resurrection of Jesus. There was so much power released that hundreds of people were also resurrected from the dead.

The angels saw Jesus present himself to his disciples for forty days after His suffering with many convincing proofs concerning the kingdom of God. The angels watched as Jesus walked through walls to appear to His disciples. They looked on as doubting Thomas stuck his hand in Jesus' side. The angels were present when Jesus commanded the disciples not to leave Jerusalem. Jesus told them, "Wait for the Father's promise of the Holy Spirit's baptism of fire and power to be My witnesses throughout the earth!" After Jesus said these things, the angels lifted Jesus up. While His disciples intently watched, Jesus was received in a cloud, rising out of their sight. As the disciples continued to gaze into the sky, two angels dressed in white stood beside them saying,

> *Men of Galilee, why do you stand looking into the sky? This Jesus, who has been taken up from you into heaven, will come in just the same way as you have watched Him go into heaven* (Acts 1:11).

Jesus understood how powerful the realm of vision is to success in the kingdom of God. Most of us are more concerned about our ability to see in the natural realm because we are so blind to the invisible, spiritual realm. However, we don't walk by our physical sight, but by faith or spiritual vision. The physical realm is a mere shadow of the reality of life behind what we see with our eyes. What is to come in the spiritual realm is far more glorious than what we now see. The substance of the spirit realm belongs to Christ, who will reveal all things to us at the fullness of time.

When Jesus and His disciples were leaving Jericho, a large crowd was following Him. When the blind men heard that Jesus of Nazareth was passing by, they cried out, "Jesus! Have mercy on us, Son of David!"

The crowd sternly rebuked the beggars, saying, "Be quiet!"

But they cried out all the more. "Jesus! Son of David, have mercy!"

When Jesus heard their cries, He stopped and answered them with compassion, "What do you want Me to do for you?"

Throwing their beggars' cloaks aside, they jumped up and came to Jesus. "Rabboni, we want to regain our sight!"

And Jesus touched them and said, "Go! Your faith has made you well." Immediately their sight was regained and they followed Jesus on the road. (See Matt. 20:29-34; Mark 10:46-52.) When the Bride of Christ regains her vision, she will once again follow Jesus on the Kingdom road.

Jesus told the Pharisee, Nicodemus, that a person must be born again to see the kingdom of God. He told him:

> ...*Unless one is born of water and of the Spirit he cannot enter into the kingdom of God. That which is born of the flesh is flesh, and that which is born of the Spirit is spirit. The wind blows where it wishes and you hear the sound of it, but do not know where it comes from and where it is going; so is everyone who is born of the Spirit* (John 3:5-6).

We are born of flesh, but transformed into living spiritual beings when we accept the Holy Spirit. Our spiritual eyes open; the eyes of our hearts are enlightened to see when they are born of the Spirit of God. We have to learn how to look in order to see, to behold, and to perceive the invisible realm of faith. From the creation of the world, God's invisible image and attributes, His eternal power and divine nature, have been clearly seen. He is the only glorious God, the eternal, immortal invisible King who is worthy of all honor. Nicodemus was a religious leader and teacher when Jesus walked the earth yet he had very little spiritual understanding. Jesus told him, if you don't understand these simple earthly truths that I am sharing with you, how can you possibly understand the mysteries of heaven?

Nicodemus said to Him, "How can these things be?"

Jesus answered and said to him, "Are you the teacher of Israel and do not understand these things? Truly, truly, I say to you, we speak of what we know and testify of what we have seen, and you do not accept our testimony. If I told you earthly things and you do not believe, how will you believe if I tell you heavenly things? No one has ascended into heaven, but He who descended from heaven: the Son of Man. As Moses lifted up the serpent in the wilderness, even so must the Son of Man be lifted up; so that whoever believes will in Him have eternal life. For God so loved the world, that He gave His only begotten Son, that whoever believes in Him shall not perish, but have eternal life. For God did not send the Son into the world to judge the world, but that the world might be saved through Him. He who believes in Him is not judged; he who does not believe has been judged already, because he has not believed in the name of the only begotten Son of God. This is the judgment, that the Light has come into the world, and men loved the darkness rather than the Light, for their deeds were evil. For everyone who does evil hates the Light, and does not come to the Light for fear that his deeds will be exposed. But he who practices the truth comes to the Light, so that his deeds may be manifested as having been wrought in God" (John 3:9-21).

The Bible tells us we are to observe those who walk according to a heavenly pattern. They are the ones who love light. But the enemies of God dwell in continual darkness; they run from the light. The enemies of the cross of Christ will end in destruction. They worship ungodly appetites and set their minds on earthly things.

> *Brethren, join in following my example, and observe those who walk according to the pattern you have in us. For many walk, of whom I often told you, and now tell you even weeping, that they are enemies of the cross of Christ, whose end is destruction, whose god is their appetite, and whose glory is in their shame, who set their minds on earthly things. For our citizenship is in heaven, from which also we eagerly wait for a Savior, the Lord Jesus Christ; who will transform the body of our humble state into conformity with the body of His glory, by the exertion of the power that He has even to subject all things to Himself* (Phil. 3:17-21).

Christ's eternal DNA gives us the power to create eternity through faith and belief or the temporal through doubt and unbelief. God has hidden destiny and eternity in our hearts. Discovering these hidden mysteries opens the door to abundant life. Life does not exist in beginning and ending, but in a continuous flow that grows and brings forth new life. Life is a continuous journey in which our destination is never reached. The secret things concealed in our hearts belong to the Lord; but the things revealed belong to us and our children, so the cycle of life and revelation continues from generation to generation.

Everything God does will endure forever; nothing can be added to it and nothing taken from it. God acts so that people will revere Him. All life comes from Him and through Him, and to Him it returns. The depths and paths of the wisdom and knowledge of God are beyond tracing because they are always expanding and unfolding to reveal His perfect will. Eternity is represented by an unending circle. God is giving us an invitation to partake of the eternal and break out of the temporal realm of the natural. As Paul wrote, *"So we fix our eyes not on what is seen, but on what is unseen. For what is seen is temporary, but what is unseen is eternal"* (2 Cor. 4:18 NIV).

Often, we live our lives in toil and worry, thinking and being aware of the natural realm. Our goal should be kingdom power, which exists in the fruits of the Spirit. Kingdom power is manifested in love and peace that passes all understanding, which is obtained on a higher spiritual plain. This leaves us with little room to worry about temporal encumbrances. Believers should seek first the kingdom of God.

ANGELIC PRESENCE

The Bible tells us that Jesus is an ever present help in our time of need, but at times we do not discern His presence. Jesus discerned the presence of angels in the Garden of Gethsemane when they came to strengthen Him.

> *Now an angel from heaven appeared to Him, strengthening Him. And being in agony He was praying very fervently; and His sweat became like drops of blood, falling down upon the ground* (Luke 22:43-44).

Mary Magdalene saw and heard the angels speak to her at the Garden tomb, but she didn't recognize Jesus in His resurrection body.

> *And she saw two angels in white sitting, one at the head and one at the feet, where the body of Jesus had been lying. And they said to her, "Woman, why are you weeping?" She said to them, "Because they have taken away my Lord, and I do not know where they have laid Him." When she had said this, she turned around and saw Jesus*

standing there, and did not know that it was Jesus (John 20:12-14).

Mary Magdalene came, announcing to the disciples, "I have seen the Lord," and that He had said these things to her (John 20:18).

But the manifestation [shining appearance] *of the Spirit is given to each one for the profit of all* (1 Cor. 12:7 NKJV).

Manifestation in the Greek is *phanerosis,* meaning "shining appearance," and it implies a bringing into the light and making a public exhibition.[1]

Mary Magdalene went to the garden tomb to visit Jesus' body while it was still dark. She saw that the chiseled stone had been rolled away from the entrance. Jesus' body was no longer in the grave. The tomb was empty. Mary ran and told Peter and the other disciples that someone had taken Jesus away. Simon Peter and John ran to the tomb. Looking in, John saw the linen wrapping. Peter impetuously entered the tomb and saw the linen face-cloth and wrappings rolled up in their place. They saw and believed, yet they did not understand the Scripture, telling that Jesus must rise again from the dead; so they left the tomb.

Mary remained standing outside the tomb, weeping. When the disciples left, she stooped down and looked into the tomb. She saw two angels dressed in white sitting where Jesus had lain. The angels spoke to her, "Woman, why are you weeping?"

Mary replied, "I weep because they have taken Jesus and I don't know where they have laid Him." As she turned, she saw Jesus standing before her. She did not recognize Him in His new resurrected form.

Jesus repeated the same question to her, "Woman, why are you weeping?" but Jesus followed that question with one of more importance, "Whom are you seeking?" Jesus asked Mary, "Who do your eyes desire to see?" Like all of us, Mary wanted to see her Lord.

Mary was able to discern, hear, and see the angelic realm. But her spiritual sight had not been developed to a high enough degree to rightly discern Jesus, her Savior and Lord, who stood before her in His new form. Supposing Jesus was the gardener, Mary replied, "Sir, if you have moved Him to another place please tell me where you have laid Him, and I will take Him away."

Mary's eyes did not recognize Jesus, but when He spoke her name, "Mary!" her ears recognized His voice. She turned and cried "Rabboni!" or teacher. Mary clung to Jesus.

He said to her, "Stop clinging to Me, for I have not yet ascended to My Father. Now go and tell the disciples that you have seen the Lord. Tell them that I ascend to My Father and your Father, and My God and your God." (See John 20:11-17.) Mary's ears recognized Jesus' voice, and then her eyes were also opened to see Him on a higher, ascending level. The peace of God will help us ascend into the realms of revelation knowledge and obtain new spiritual insights.

THE POWER OF PEACE

Peace is a powerful force, atmosphere, or substance that releases revelation knowledge. We are told if a home is worthy, to leave a blessing of peace (see Matt. 10:13). Here we see that the blessing of peace enabled Jesus to manifest through closed, locked doors in the presence of His disciples. When Jesus released peace in the room, it drove out fear. Jesus revealed His hands and side to His disciples. The peaceful presence of Jesus released joy to the disciples. A second time, Jesus blessed them with peace by saying, "Peace comes to you; as the Father has sent Me, I also send you." Jesus blessed the disciples with a spirit of peace twice. He breathed the

Holy Spirit upon them. He said, "If you forgive sins, they will be forgiven; but if you retain anyone's sins, they will be retained." (See John 20:19-23.)

Doubting Thomas was not with the twelve when Jesus came to visit. The other disciples told him, "We have seen the Lord!"

Thomas responded, "I won't believe unless I see the nail prints in his hands. I won't believe unless I can touch Him and place my fingers in the nail prints and into His side" (see John 20:24-25).

Eight (meaning "resurrection, new beginnings") days later, Jesus reappeared, walking through the closed, locked door. Jesus stood in the disciples' midst and released the atmosphere of peace. Knowing Thomas' thoughts, Jesus encouraged him to see His hands and to reach his hand into His side. "Do not be unbelieving, but believing."

Thomas said, "You are my Lord and my God!"

Jesus said to him, "Thomas, because you have seen Me, you have believed. Blessed are those who have not seen and yet have believed" (John 20:29 NKJV).

ANGELS AND DEMONS

The Bible lists several angels by name, one of which is Lucifer, or Satan. He is a fallen archangel who operates through a network of evil spirits and demonic powers. Fallen angels are of a higher rank than demons or evil spirits. Demons have no body of their own so they seek out a human or animal body as their host vessel. Demons will manifest their personality, power, and agenda through that person's mind, will, and emotions (see Matt. 12:43-45). The job description of demons is to cause sickness and disease—to hurt, kill, steal, lie, deceive, and destroy. A large portion of Jesus' ministry was healing the sick and casting out demons.

Angels maintain their spiritual bodies so they do not seek to enter the bodies of humankind. Fallen angels reside and rule from thrones in the second heaven realm located above earth and below God's heavens (see Dan. 10:12-13; Rev. 12:9). Angels are called sons of God; they are created beings with spiritual bodies. Angels vary in operations, power, and size. Seraphim and cherubim have wings, while other common angels mostly appear in human form. The functions of angels are multiple in that they assist us as ministering spirits, protect us from evil, and come as messengers from God (see Ezek. 10:3-22; Isa. 6:1-6; Mark 16:5-7; Heb. 12:22). At times angels also help to train prophets and seers understand the revelatory realms.

ANGELS TAUGHT ZECHARIAH TO SEE

Zechariah was taught by heavenly angels. Zechariah was a prophet and priest in the days of Ezra. He authored the book of Zechariah. He is named as a grandson of Iddo the priest and seer. Zechariah was a contemporary of the prophet Haggai and the high priest Joshua. Following the captivity of Israel, Zechariah helped lead his community of Judah in the land of Israel in the restoration process. Zechariah 1:1 tells us he began his seer ministry in October or November of 520 BC as a young man, just two months after Haggai started his prophetic ministry.

Zechariah, whose name means "Jehovah is renowned or remembered and God remembers," was trained to see and understand the vision realm by an angel. Although Zechariah was highly trained and educated in the ministry, he knew to ask the angel to explain what he was seeing in the ten visions that are recorded in the Bible. He didn't presume to know or understand anything he was seeing, even though the visions he saw looked familiar to him.

He asked questions. It is always necessary to look and continue looking to see, staying focused until the vision disappears. Don't assume you know or understand the depths of what you are seeing in a vision. Always prayerfully ask the Holy Spirit or the angel that is present for clarity and insight. Let them teach and assist you in gaining Scriptural understanding in receiving revelation. It is so important that we remain humble and teachable at all times.

VISION OF THE FOUR HORSES

God sent a message to the prophet Zechariah. He saw a man astride a red horse (horses of ten represent wisdom or strength) in the shadows of a birch grove. He was accompanied by three other horses, a red, a chestnut, and a white horse. Zechariah asked the angel why the men and horses had appeared. The angelic messenger replied, "These are the riders sent by God to observe things that are happening in the earth. They report to the angel over God's armies. They have been observing the earth for seventy years. They want to know how long God is going to stay angry with Jerusalem and the cities of Judah. God assured them saying, 'I am very possessive over, compassionate toward, and care deeply for Jerusalem and Zion. But, I am going to take action against the godless nations that act as if they own the whole world because My anger has been aroused. I will rebuild My temple, release prosperity, and comfort to Zion and Jerusalem. They will be favored again with My mercy and help to move ahead and prosper'" (see Zech. 1:7-17).

THE FOUR HORNS

Zechariah looked up and saw four horns in a vision. He asked the messenger angel who was training him, "What do these four horns represent?"

The messenger replied "These are the horns that represent the power of the curse behind the nations that attacked and forced the people of Israel, Judah, and Jerusalem to scatter and go to foreign countries without showing any mercy. They have robbed them of their prosperity."

Then Zechariah said, "The Lord has shown me four workers. What are these four workers coming to do?"

"These four workers have come to remove the curses and frighten the horns and throw them away" (see Zech. 1:18-21).

THE MEASURING LINE

Sometimes we do not measure up to someone's expectations of us in life. But if we keep looking up, the Lord will send us the answers we need. When Zechariah looked up he saw an angel with a measuring rod. "Then I looked up and was surprised when I saw a man holding a rope for measuring things. I asked him, 'Where are you going with that measuring tape?'"

He answered, "I am going to measure and survey Jerusalem, to see its width and length."

The messenger angel on assignment was met by another angel coming in who said, "Run! Tell the Surveyor, 'Jerusalem will burst and not be able to contain all the people and animals within its walls. God is going to release a decree that will cause fire to dwell around and protect the unwalled city. He will dwell there with His radiant glorious presence within her walls'" (see Zech. 2:1-5).

THE GOLDEN LAMPSTAND
AND OLIVE TREES

In another vision, the angel spoke to Zechariah and roused him, as a man who is awakened from a deep sleep. The angel asked "What do you see?"

Zechariah said, "I see a golden lampstand with bowls on the top, of seven lamps, with seven spouts. There are two olive trees by the lampstand. I see one tree on the right side and one on its left side."

Zechariah then asked the angel to explain what he saw; "What are these?" The angel replied, "You don't know what these are?"

"No, my lord I don't know!"

So the angel said:

> *This is the word of the Lord to Zerubbabel saying, "Not by might nor by power, but by My Spirit," says the Lord of hosts. "What are you, O great mountain? Before Zerubbabel you will become a plain; and he will bring forth the top stone with shouts of 'Grace, grace to it!'" ...The hands of Zerubbabel have laid the foundation of this house, and his hands will finish it. Then you will know that the Lord of hosts has sent me to you. For who has despised the day of small things? But these seven will be glad when they see the plumb line in the hand of Zerubbabel—these are the eyes of the Lord which range to and fro throughout the earth (Zech. 4:6-10).*

It would have been easy for Zechariah to assume he knew what he perceived. After all, the lampstand would have been a familiar image to someone in the priesthood. Even if the temple and its implements were not available during the exile, Zechariah would have known about them, their uses, and their appearance. But instead of presuming to understand what his traditions taught, Zechariah remained humble and allowed the angel to describe and define the images he perceived in the vision. We practice this when we pray asking God to open (even familiar) Scriptures to us and, then we will also receive revelation, by reading and studying God's Word.

Next Zechariah asked the angel, "What are the two olive trees on the right and left of the lampstand which empty the golden oil from themselves?"

The angel replied, "You don't know what these are?"

"No, my lord!"

The angel said, "They are the two anointed men [Jew and Gentile nations] who have been chosen to stand by the Lord of the whole earth. *The blended oil of this light will empower spiritual vision for the future*" (see Zech. 4:11-14).

THE FLYING SCROLL

Then Zechariah lifted up my eyes to look and he saw another vision. This time when he looked, he beheld a flying scroll. The angel asked him, "What do you see?"

He said, "I see a flying scroll that is thirty feet long and fifteen feet wide."

The angel told him, "There is a curse written on both sides of the scroll. One side is a curse against thieves that steal, and on the other is a curse against people who lie and break promises. God Almighty will send that scroll to thieves and liars when they use His name to make promises. The scroll is so powerful it will even destroy the stones and consume the wooden post of their homes." This scroll deals with dishonesty that comes against us (see Zech. 5:1-4).

THE WOMAN AND THE BUCKET

Next, the angel took Zechariah outside and asked him to look. "What do you see coming?"

Zechariah replied, "I don't know! What am I seeing?"

The angel said, "You are seeing a measuring bucket to measure peoples' sin."

Zechariah watched as a lead lid was lifted from the bucket so he could view a woman. The angel told him, "The woman represents evil. That which has been covered up will be revealed like removing a rotten apple before it can ruin the whole barrel. Look! Do you see her?"

"Yes!"

Then the angel pushed the evil woman back into the bucket and covered her again. As Zechariah continued to watch, he saw two winged women. They flew with the wind in their stork-like wings. He watched them pick up the bucket. They flew through the sky carrying the bucket of evil. Zechariah asked the angel, "Where are they carrying the evil?"

The angel replied, "They will build a house for the bucket in Shinar" (see Zech 5:5-11). Shinar consisted of several cities, one of which was Babylon. The humanistic murderer, Nimrod, set up his kingdom in Shinar. The Tower of Babel was also located in Shinar. Around 606 BC, King Nebuchadnezzar took the temple vessels from Jerusalem to Shinar (see Dan. 1:2). It was after the prophet Isaiah prophesied that the Jews would return from captivity (see Isa. 11:11) that the prophet Zechariah saw a vision of the removal of the great harlot, "Babylon the Great," a symbol of imperial Rome (see Rev. 17:5).

THE FOUR CHARIOTS

The angel continued to teach Zechariah to understand the vision realm. When he turned around and looked up, Zechariah saw four chariots going between two bronze mountains. The first chariot was pulled by red horses. The second was pulled by black horses, and white horses were pulling the third chariot. Horses with red spots were pulling the fourth chariot. Zechariah asked the angel, "Sir, what does this mean?"

"These chariots and horses represent the four winds. They will execute judgment in the heavenly realms beyond what is known by natural means. They have just come from the Lord of the whole world. The black horses will go north;

the red horses will go east. They are anxious to go look at their part of the earth."

The angel told them, "Go walk through the earth."

"The white horses will go west, and the horses with red spots will go south." Then the angel shouted at Zechariah and said, "Look, the northern horses have finished their job in Babylon. My spirit is calm; I am no longer angry" (see Zech. 6:1-9).

VISION OF JOSHUA

Finally, the angel took Zechariah to a heavenly place and showed Zechariah a vision of Joshua the high priest standing in front of the Angel of the Lord. Satan was standing by Joshua's right side to accuse Joshua of doing wrong in the past and to oppose him in the future.

Then the angel of the Lord said to Satan, "The Lord rebukes you, Satan! What you do is evil and wrong. God will continue to correct you! The Lord has chosen and saved Jerusalem to be His special city. He pulled Jerusalem from the fire. God plucked her like a brand."

Zechariah saw that Joshua was clothed in dirty, filthy garments, as he stood in front of the angel. The angel spoke to the other angels that stood near, "Take away the filthy clothes and remove the iniquity and guilt from Joshua." The angel said, "I am going to give him new clean clothes and a rich robe. I will crown the priesthood with a crown of favor and a robe of authority. I will remove the effects of the mistakes they have made in the past and cleanse them. They will begin to see themselves in a new light through God's eyes of mercy and grace."

Zechariah said, "Let the angels put a clean turban on Joshua's head."

Then the Lord's angel spoke to Joshua: "If you do what the all-powerful God says, and live the way I tell you and do everything I say, you will be in charge of God's temple. You will be given care of its courtyard. You will be free to go anywhere in the temple, just like these angels standing here. Listen to all I tell you, Joshua, and you fellow priests seated before him" (see Zech. 3:1-7).

Angels have always been used to train prophets and seers to understand dreams and visions. The Holy Spirit sends angels to come to teach God's people how to know, see, and understand the invisible realm where angels dwell. Holy Spirit is our Comforter and He is also our teacher. Sometimes He chooses to send angels on assignment with spiritual lessons or parabolic messages to help us learn valuable lessons in life.

ENDNOTE

1. Strong, *Strong's Exhaustive Concordance*, Greek #5321.

Chapter 11

VISIONS

Seers are visionaries. To develop one's seer's gift it is essential to understand the realm of spiritual vision. A *vision* is defined as "the faculty of sight; (good vision) something that is or has been seen; unusual capability in discernment or perception; intelligent foresight; the way in which one sees or conceives of something." Visions are mental images created by the imagination. Visions are the mystical experience of seeing as if with the supernatural eyes. Spiritual beings from the supernatural realm often appear in visions.

Visions can also be defined as a view, a shape, an appearance, or a sequence of colorful images, symbols, vivid sounds, and strong emotions that come to us through a trance or dream. Visions give us an unusual capability to perceive or discern through intelligent foresight. They are mental images created through the imagination, a mystical experience of seeing a supernatural reality with either the spiritual or the natural eyes.

Visions can be experienced again just by reciting the visual experience, recalling the pictures, and reliving the feelings, sensations, and emotions of the event.

Revelation from the spiritual realm often comes to us through our spiritual visual perception in visions. We can receive visions when we are awake or asleep. Visions reveal images, pictures, or short dreams that are introduced into the conscious mind. Visions can also appear when we are in a trance-like state. Visions reveal that which is not actually present at the current time or place. Visions are the expression of spiritual things to the five senses; they open the natural eyes and ears to see and hear clearly. Through visions, we see the manifestation of that which is normally invisible and inaudible and comes from the supernatural, coexisting spiritual realm.

The vision realm connects the natural realms of reality, knowledge, and physical sensations to the spiritual realms of revelatory knowledge and spiritual sensations. We possess five natural senses of sight, touch, taste, smell, and hearing. These natural senses can be engaged with our spiritual senses to allow us to feel and experience spiritual visions. During a vision, the five natural senses are usually engaged or heightened. This allows us to physically experience what we are seeing or beholding in the realm of vision. Our bodies can experience many varied combinations of impartations, revelation, wisdom, and knowledge. We can experience angelic visitations, physical or emotional healing, or deliverance. We can also gain strength, feel weakness, and obtain spiritual gifts through the vision realm. For these reasons, visions are easier to remember than dreams.

We can recall visions more easily because our physical body, emotions, and senses are engaged in what we see. When our emotions are involved with the learning process, we more readily remember the information that is shared. Visions are imprinted on the soul; they are more literal than symbolic dreams. Most of the time, visions do not require extensive interpretation because what we see often will manifest or become a reality in our waking lives.

Visions usually concern a time or event that is yet to come or to be experienced. Visions give us the ability to see and know things that will literally happen in the coming days or years of our lives. For this reason alone, it is important to pay close attention to visions. God also often uses visions to show us the enemy's intrusive plans of destruction. This allows us the foresight and benefit of canceling the enemy's harmful plans. Then we can establish the opposite by releasing God's power and presence into a situation through prayer and intercession. We are never to come into agreement with a vision that shows any type of negative outcomes.

OPEN VISIONS

Open visions are seen with our natural or spiritual eyes—also called the eyes of our understanding (see Eph. 1:18-19). In an open vision, we may observe the spiritual or heavenly vision realm being opened and revealed. When this type of vision occurs, the natural world seems to fade from reality for a short time. The person experiencing an open vision may be caught up in observing the vivid, colorful, visual pictures as if watching motion pictures of another world unfold. Open visions allow us to gaze into the spiritual gates of Heaven to observe what is transpiring in a higher realm while we remain here on the earth.

The prophet Isaiah experienced an open vision while he was standing on the earth. His natural eyes were opened to see visions of the Lord seated on a throne in the realms of Heaven. Isaiah's vision revealed his own desperate need and lack and he cried out, *"Woe is me, for I am undone"* (Isa. 6:5 NKJV). The New Testament stoning of Stephen also gives us another example of an open vision. Stephen saw the Lord stand up in Heaven to welcome him home (see Acts 7:55-56).

Saul's conversion into the apostle Paul involved the realm of vision and the audible voice of the Lord (Acts 9:3-9). Ananias, the believer who was used to restore Saul's sight, also had a vision (see Acts 9:10-19). Visions have the ability to strategically lead and guide us in the way we should go.

PAUL AND THE MACEDONIAN MAN

The life and ministry of the Apostle Paul was led by prayer and visionary experiences. When Paul sought the Lord for new direction He would answer him in different ways to shed light upon his path.

> *And a vision appeared to Paul in the night. A man of Macedonia stood and pleaded with him, saying, "Come over to Macedonia and help us." Now after he had seen the vision, immediately we sought to go to Macedonia, concluding that the Lord had called us to preach the gospel to them* (Acts 16:9-10 NKJV).

This vision appears to be an example of a man being caught up in the coexisting spiritual realm. He may have been caught up by the spirit of the Lord who transported him from one geographical location to another in order to extend an invitation to Paul in a vision. This man was chosen to be sent on assignment to implore Paul to come help the Macedonians. However, when Paul journeyed to this land, he connected with a woman named Lydia instead of the man in his vision. This indicates that not all visions are literal; otherwise, Paul would have physically met the man in his vision that extended the invitation to Macedonia.

It is important to discern the message as well as what is being viewed in the vision. But never place the interpretation of God's vision in a box of absolute. God is a Spirit that continues to flow and unfold revelation knowledge when we seek Him for understanding. God brings forth clarity as He desires.

THE HEAVENS OPENED

Another example of an open vision took place at the Jordan River when Jesus was baptized. Although Jesus was perfect in all His ways He submitted to John's baptism to fulfill all righteousness. John the Baptist was sent by God to prepare the way of the Lord in the wilderness. His message was one of repentance (see Matt. 3:2). The kingdom of God is always ushered in through repentant hearts. Jesus' baptism in the Jordan River opened the heavens, ushering in a new era. Both Jesus and John saw the Holy Spirit as a dove descending from on high to rest on Jesus. They also heard the audible voice of God lovingly acknowledge and validate His pleasure in His son, Jesus (see Matt. 3:16-17). This took place before Jesus had done any great signs, wonders, or miracles. In the time of testing and trial, Jesus stood on the heavenly words His Father's voice had spoken over Him at His baptism, *"This is My beloved Son, in whom I am well pleased"* (Matt. 3:17). God is pleased with us, too!

When John the Baptist was beheaded, his mantle passed to Jesus, who continued the same clarion call, *"Repent, for the kingdom of heaven is at hand"* (Matt. 4:17). When Jesus ascended, I believe the mantle passed to John the Revelator, who saw the Lord and received revelation of Christ on the Isle of Patmos. When we pull aside and spend time alone with Jesus He will also give us revelation about His love for us.

What loving words has God spoken to you recently in your dreams or in times of prayer? God's words are true; they release life, hope, and purpose. What creative ideas has the Holy Spirit given you? Have you developed a plan for pleasing God? Are you energetically pursuing God's purposes in your life?

The scriptural words that are spoken over our lives and the dreams we receive form righteous pathways for us to walk upon. The steep paths are not always easy because they lead us upward toward God and the high call on our lives. The difficult paths enable us to forge a forward path, step by step, in obedience to the confirming words of God's favor. God watches over His word to perform it.

When the word of God comes to us, it will try us to determine whether we are able to carry it. If we choose to carry His word, it will change us into His image. The proceeding words of God are living, powerful, and creative. The words of God will fashion us into the vessels of honor He has called us to be. The word of God is perfect. We are called to be perfect as well. It is the word of God that changes us and transforms us from one level of glory to another higher and greater level.

JESUS' TRIBUTE TO JOHN THE BAPTIST

Jesus was always about His Father's business. He loved people. Jesus even loved His enemies with the same passion with which He loved His family and friends. Jesus was always trying to communicate the kingdom of God and the love of His Father to the people. He often asked them questions to provoke positive thoughts or to break them out of harmful traditions. Jesus asked the people three times, "What did you go out into the wilderness to see?" The disciples of John reported to him about all these things. Summoning two of his disciples, John sent them to the Lord, saying, *"Are You the Expected One, or do we look for someone else?"* (Luke 7:19).

When John's disciples arrived they witnessed the many signs, wonders, and miracles done by Jesus. They saw Jesus cure many people of diseases, sicknesses, and afflictions. He had cast out evil spirits with a word. Jesus restored sight to the many blind that now followed fast after Him. When John's disciples asked Jesus if He were the Expected One, Jesus answered John's disciples by saying,

> *Go and report to John what you have seen and heard: the blind receive sight, the lame walk, the lepers are cleansed, and the deaf hear, the dead are raised up, the poor have the gospel preached to them. Blessed is he who does not take offense at Me* (Luke 7:22-23).

When the messengers of John had left, He began to speak to the crowds about John and the great work he had done for the kingdom.

What did you go out into the wilderness to see? A reed shaken by the wind? But what did you go out to see? A man dressed in soft clothing? Those who are splendidly clothed and live in luxury are found in royal palaces! But what did you go out to see? A prophet? Yes, I say to you, and one who is more than a prophet. This is the one about whom it is written, "Behold, I send My messenger ahead of You, who will prepare Your way before You." I say to you, among those born of women there is no one greater than John; yet he who is least in the kingdom of God is greater than he (Luke 7:24-28).

In Luke 7:21-22, six of the seven signs of the Messiah are listed. Isaiah 61:1 states that the Messiah would have the Spirit of the Lord God upon Him, that the Lord would anoint Him to bring good news to the afflicted; He would be sent to bind up the brokenhearted and to proclaim liberty to captives and freedom to prisoners. John the Baptist sent his disciples to ask Jesus, "Are you going to set me free from the prison, or am I going to die in captivity?" Jesus mentioned all of the signs of the Messiah but the last one. Jesus did not mention the captives being set free. Jesus' response to John let him know that he was going to die in prison. *"Blessed is he who does not take offense at Me"* (Luke 7:23).

John the Baptist had seen the Holy Spirit ascend as a dove and remain upon Jesus at His baptism. But even after a heavenly sign of that magnitude, John the Baptist still needed affirmation that Jesus really was the promised Messiah. John realized Jesus was the Messiah, but that his life was going to be that of a martyr. Jesus was not going to set John free. He had to love not his life even unto the death.

EXTERNAL VISIONS

Most people who operate in a seer's gift see visions from within their imagination but mature seers also move in external visions. External visions can be seen with our spiritual or natural eyes as they are projected from Heaven into the natural realm in front of us.

The Old Testament prophet Elisha prayed that the Lord would open the eyes of his servant to behold those who were for them because their numbers far outweighed those against them. Thus, the servant was given an external vision to see the greater number of horses and chariots driven by fiery angels surrounding their enemies on the hills. Elisha's second prayer was to strike their enemies with blindness. In this one passage, we see God open eyes to the spiritual realm while blinding eyes in the natural realm. Later Elisha prayed that God would reopen his enemy's eyes, and their sight was restored. (See 2 Kings 6:17-20.)

INTERNAL VISIONS

Internal visions are viewed within the spirit by our spiritual eyes (or mind's eye) as the pictures are displayed on the screens of our hearts' imagination or internal image center. Our conscience interacts and dialogues with the voice of the Holy Spirit as He leads, guides, and directs the course of our lives.

THE APOSTLE JOHN

John the Beloved was banished to the island of Patmos because of his passion for the word of God and the testimony of Jesus, which is the spirit of prophecy (see Rev. 1:9). Instead of sinking into depression, his heart rejoiced. He gladly separated himself to focus on the Lord. His isolation positioned him to receive the revelation of Jesus Christ. All of creation expectantly waits for the light of illumination to reveal the mystery of Christ, who is seated on the heavenly throne and the throne of every believer's heart.

Through many times of quiet contemplations, John had learned to still his soul, surrender to the presence of God, and to enter into the spirit realm to receive vision and revelation. John heard the voice of the Lord as clearly as he had when he walked and talked with Jesus on a daily basis. To John, the voice of the Lord was like a clear, piercing trumpet that released an obvious sound. John was obedient to the voice of God who stood behind him.

John wrote the details of what he was shown. He sent the revelation of Jesus to the seven churches. Have you ever wondered what a voice looks like? The Bible says John turned to see the voice of the One who spoke like the voice of many waters. Today we are able to measure and record visual sound waves; but I believe John was given eyes to see the beautiful colors that flowed from the mouth of the Lord as He spoke to John. John saw seven golden lampstands, which are the seven churches. In the middle of the lampstands, he saw Jesus, the son of man, clothed in a beautiful robe that girded His chest with a golden sash. His hair was white with the wisdom of the ages, and His eyes were blue like the hottest flame of fire.

Jesus' feet were like burnished bronze that had been tried in the fires of adversity, yet overcame. He held seven stars, which are the angels to the seven churches, in His right hand. Jesus had a sharp two-edged sword that pierced out of His mouth to bring judgment and justice to the nations. John saw Jesus' face like the bright and morning sun shining in all its strength. John saw the voice of God, who is the first and the last, and he fell at His feet like a dead man (see Rev. 1:9-20).

Jesus lifted John up with His strong right hand and reassured him by saying,

> *Do not be afraid I am the first and the last, and the living*
> *One; and I was dead, and behold, I am alive forevermore,*

*and I have the keys of death and of Hades. Therefore write
the things which you have seen, and the things which are,
and the things which will take place after these things*
(Rev. 1:17-19).

John's great love and admiration for Jesus, his spiritual
ability to hear and see enabled God to visit him. John was
entrusted with the revelation of Jesus.

NEW VISION

Often a new vision is given in our darkest hour and at
the crossroads of life. When one vision is coming to an end
or completion, a season is ending and a new one is beginning; a new strategy is formulated. Visions, like a photo, are
developed in a dark room in a dim or mysterious space. If we
carry that vision through the whole process of development,
we will exit the darkness with clarity, hope, and a new plan
for success and true godly prosperity. God's plan is for us to
prosper in every way and in every area of our lives.

When we capture a picture of light and God's goodness
for our lives in the midst of the dark place of our existence,
we have vision. Vision releases hope. Hope enables us to
change. Change releases destiny. Destiny drives us out of
the now and propels us into the future. Once we catch a
glimpse of who we are in the future, we are able to bring it
into the reality of today. This is one of the major ways God
is able to accelerate good in our lives through dreams and
visions. If our spiritual eyes remain dark (or bad) our bodies
will be filled with darkness and doubt. If the light that is in
us is darkness, how great is that darkness (see Matt. 6:23).
The more of God's light we can see and believe, the more
enlightened and full of faith we can become. We must see
the revelation of God in order to be it! God births dreams
and visions in us in order to bring revelation, illumination,
and inspiration.

Revelation is God's revealed light or the discovery of hidden, unsearchable truth. *Illumination* is the spiritual reflection or the intellectual enlightenment we experience in response to God's revelation. Inspiration is communicating the revelation—the understood, discovered truth—to others. To *inspire* means "to inhale, or breathe in the Spirit to stimulate the mind, to create or to activate the emotions to a higher level of feeling."[1] To spiritually inspire is to guide, affect, or arouse by the divine influence of the Holy Spirit. Through revelation, illumination, and inspiration, the Spirit of the Lord is calling to the Holy Spirit within us as He allows us to see the deep things, secrets, and mysteries of God.

Psalm 42:7-8 reads:

Deep calls to deep in the roar of your waterfalls; all your waves and breakers have swept over me. By day the Lord directs His love, at night His song is with me—a prayer to the God of my life (NIV).

WIDEN YOUR VISION

There is a depth in God that many may never experience because of the great cost and pain that is associated with total surrender. Many are not able to drink of the same cup Jesus drank from in the Garden. Few are able to say as Jesus said, "Not my will but Your will be done in my life." To transition from the shallow waters where we enter at salvation into the unfathomable things that are hidden in God, we must embrace the breaking that comes to widen our spirit to receive more of God's presence in our life. It is time to widen our vision and advance God's kingdom. Those who surrender all, including the pain and disappointments of the past, will receive God's promotion and an increased measure of love in their heart. But if we focus on the difficulties of the past season instead of the potential of our promising future, fear will stop us from making the necessary changes in order to see a future hope. God has big hopes and dreams for all of us.

> *Make your tent bigger. Open your doors wide. Don't think small! Make your tent large and strong, because you will grow in all directions. Your children will take over many nations and live in the cities that were destroyed. Don't be afraid! You will not be disappointed. People will not say bad things against you. You will not be embarrassed. When you were young, you felt shame. But you will forget that shame now. You will not remember the shame you felt when you lost your husband. Your real husband is the one who made you. His name is the Lord All-Powerful. The Holy One of Israel is your Protector, and He is the God of all the earth! Like a woman whose husband has left her, you were very sad. You were like a young wife left all alone. But the Lord has called you back to him. This is what your God says. "For a short time I turned away from you, but with all my love I will welcome you again. I was so angry that for a while I did not want to see you. But now I want to comfort you with kindness forever." The Lord your Savior said this* (Isa. 54:2-8 ERV).

The past is over; it cannot dictate our potential, expectations, or hopes unless we give it permission to rule our present and future. God has promised to remove the shame, embarrassment, and reproach that causes fear. God is calling us back to our first love with all of His love. It is time to return to the basics of seeking Jesus with our whole heart. The Lord is exalted and dwells upon the heights of heaven to execute righteousness and justice; yet He brings forth stability in our times of need. He is a wealth of salvation, wisdom, and knowledge. The fear of the Lord is our precious treasure that resides in our heart. We have a rich treasure in the greatness of a powerful God, who lives in earthen vessels. Let the words of our lips and the meditations of our heart always praise His excellent greatness.

Deuteronomy 30:11-14 tells us that success is in our mouths:

> *For this commandment which I command you this day is not too difficult for you, nor is it far off. It is not [a secret laid up] in heaven, that you should say, Who shall go up for us to heaven and bring it to us, that we may hear and do it? Neither is it beyond the sea, that you should say, Who shall go over the sea for us and bring it to us, that we may hear and do it? But the word is very near you, in your mouth, and in your mind and in your heart, so that you can do it* (AMP).

God wants us to receive His love. God wants us to decree His Word to release favor, breakthrough, strategic alignment, and prosperity. The decrees of the Lord place an iron-like strength in our soul. When we decide the past is over and it is time to step into a new day, in a new way, God's light will shine brightly on the new path.

> *You shall also decide and decree a thing, and it shall be established for you; and the light [of God's favor] shall shine upon your ways. When they make [you] low, you will say, [There is] a lifting up; and the humble person He lifts up and saves. He will even deliver the one [for whom you intercede] who is not innocent; yes, he will be delivered through the cleanness of your hands* (Job 22:28-30 AMP).

This is a powerful Scripture that demonstrates the power of the prayers of the righteous. When we boldly decree kingdom principles, God will establish them for us. The light of His favor will show us the way to pray. If we (or a friend) slip or fall, God will lift us up. God will also deliver people from the enemies' snare, even if they are guilty, if we will pray for them. Persistent prayer enables us to enter the heart of God's plans and purposes.

The fire of God touched the mouths of Isaiah and Jeremiah with a supernatural bestowment of grace so they would speak forth His words of life concerning the future. Now God is placing His powerful words within the mouths of His anointed bride—you and me. We will confess that God's kingdom has come and that His will be done on earth, in each earthen vessel, as it is in heaven (see Matt. 6:10). The Lord desires that we have the God kind of faith—which is faith like God! It is time to have the faith of God manifesting in our lives!

His supernatural empowerment is opening double doors to our future. Like a true gentleman, He goes before His bride to keep the gates open. He is making the crooked places straight, and revealing the treasures that have been hidden in secret places of darkness (see Isa. 45:1-3). To move forward into our new season will require that we develop a greater measure of trust and faith for more of His grace. God imparts *grace* to remove and overcome our every weakness and empower us to move forward.

The Holy Spirit speaks to each of us through dreams and visions of the night. To receive these dreams of the night, all we have to do is ask God for them. God speaks to us through this wonderful picture language to communicate His plans, purposes, and desires to us. The Word of God declares that the Spirit of God will be poured out upon all flesh in the last days:

> *But this is what was spoken by the prophet Joel: "And it shall come to pass in the last days, says God, that I will pour out of My Spirit on all flesh; your sons and your daughters shall prophesy, your young men shall see visions, your old men shall dream dreams. And on My menservants and on My maidservants I will pour out*

My Spirit in those days; and they shall prophesy. I will show wonders in heaven above and signs in the earth beneath: blood and fire and vapor of smoke. The sun shall be turned into darkness, and the moon into blood, before the coming of the great and awesome day of the Lord. And it shall come to pass that whoever calls on the name of the Lord shall be saved" (Acts 2:16-21 NKJV).

Were you aware that God has always spoken through dreams and visions? This passage of Scripture makes it clear that one of the manifestations of the outpouring of the Holy Spirit upon people is dreams and visions. God communicates His purposes and plans to us through dreams, but He reveals Himself through visions.

The Bible says, *"Your young men shall see visions."* Visions are much easier to understand than dreams because they are more realistic or literal. Even the spiritually immature or young in the Lord can understand what God is communicating to them in a vision. Visions are sealed upon the tablets of the heart so we can remember their message and recall the experience. Do you understand what the Lord is saying or showing you in the symbolic dreams and beautiful visions of the night? To gain understanding of the images God is giving you, simply ask the Lord for wisdom and clarity. Holy Spirit will interpret the meaning of each symbol and how they relate to a collective whole, so you are able to apply the visionary message to your life.

ABRAM'S VISIONARY DREAM ENCOUNTER

Abram's dream describes the ancient method of establishing covenant between people in his day. A covenant is the giving of one's self totally to another. Abram walked between the sacrifice and the fire (see Gen. 15:9-19). The Almighty perfectly fulfilled His covenant. God had no desire from within or pressure from without, yet He spoke to and established a covenant with Abram through the visionary dream realm. God is everlasting love. For love to be true, it must be shared. A true love story never ends. God gave us Jesus as our covenant heir (see Isa. 49:8).

> *For when God made the promise to Abraham, since He could swear by no one greater, He swore by Himself, saying, "I will surely bless you and I will surely multiply you." And so, having patiently waited, he obtained the promise. For men swear by one greater than themselves, and with them an oath given as confirmation is an end of every dispute. In the same way God, desiring even more to show to the heirs of the promise the unchangeableness of His purpose, interposed with an oath, so that by two unchangeable things in which it is impossible for God to lie, we who have taken refuge would have strong encouragement to take hold of the hope set before us. This hope we have as an anchor of the soul, a hope both sure and steadfast and one which enters within the veil, where Jesus has entered as a forerunner for us, having become a high priest forever according to the order of Melchizedek* (Heb. 6:13-20).

Abram cried to God for insight from His Word. His cries came into the presence of God who gave Abram His personal attention. Abram asked God to rescue and keep His promises to him. Abram's dream and visionary encounter are the first to be recorded in the Bible. We can gain a lot of spiritual insights and understanding from studying Abram's encounters with God. For example, we will discover the differences between a dream and a vision. How can we correctly discern the differences? Some say the only difference between a dream and vision is that one happens while the person is asleep and the other happens when the person is awake. This is only partly true. In Genesis 15:1-12, Abram experienced both a vision and a dream:

*After these things **the word of the Lord came to Abram in a vision, saying, "Do not fear, Abram, I am a shield to you; your reward shall be very great."** [God revealed Himself to Abram.]* ***Abram said,*** *"O Lord God, what will You give me, since I am childless, and the heir of my house is Eliezer of Damascus?" And **Abram said,** "Since You have given no offspring to me, one born in my house is my heir." **Then behold, the word of the Lord came to him, saying,** "This man will not be your heir; but one who will come forth from your own body, he shall be your heir." And He took him outside and said, "Now look toward the heavens, and count the stars, if you are able to count them." **And He said to him,** "So shall your descendants be." **Then he believed in the Lord;** and He reckoned it to him as righteousness. **And He said to him,** "I am the Lord who brought you out of Ur of the Chaldeans, to give you this land to possess it." **He said,** "O Lord God, how may I know that I will possess it?" **So He said to him,** "Bring Me a three year old heifer, and a three year old female goat, and a three year old ram, and a turtledove, and a young pigeon." Then he brought all these to Him and cut them in two, and laid each half opposite the other; but he did not cut the birds. The birds of prey came down upon the carcasses, and Abram drove them away. Now when the sun was going down, **a deep sleep fell upon Abram;** [Abram is having a dream] **and behold, terror and great darkness fell upon him. God said to Abram,** "Know for certain that your descendants will be strangers in a land that is not theirs, where they will be enslaved and oppressed four hundred years"* (Gen. 15:1-13).

In verse one, Abram had a vision in which God revealed Himself. So we discover that God reveals Himself in visions. In verse two, Abram began to converse with God. In the vision, Abram asked God if He would give him a son, an heir, to inherit his wealth instead of allowing his estate to pass to his servant, Eliezer. The Word of the Lord came to answer Abram in verse four. God assured Abram he would have an heir from his own body who would produce descendents as vast as the stars in Heaven. Visionary experiences allow the person to dialogue and converse with God so they awake with a clear understanding

In verse twelve, Abram fell into a deep sleep. He was terrorized by the dream God gave him. Abram saw a cloud of great darkness fall upon him, and God spoke to Abram out of this ominous cloud. As God communed with Abram, He revealed His divine plan for his descendants during the next four hundred years.

The language of dreams and visions is a very diverse and complex subject. There is too much to learn about the diversity and differences between a dream and vision in a few pages. For an in-depth study, I suggest you purchase my book "Dream Encounters Seeing Your Destiny from God's Perspective." But simply put in a nugget, God determines whether He wants to speak His plans and strategies to us through dreams or reveal Himself through visions. He gives each of them to us for different reasons.

> *He said, "Hear now My words: If there is a prophet among you, I, the Lord, shall make Myself known to him in a vision. I shall speak with him in a dream. Not so, with My servant Moses, He is faithful in all My household; with him I speak mouth to mouth, even openly, and not in dark sayings, and he beholds the form of the Lord. Why then were you not afraid to speak against My servant, against Moses?"* (Num. 12:6-8).

DARK SPEECH

The Bible tells us that God spoke to His friend Moses openly, face to face, and not through dark speech. But it never mentions God speaking to Moses or Elijah in a dream. Those who continually commune with God in deep, personal ways keep their ears tuned to God's heartbeat. He is able to direct their paths by simply redirecting the gaze of His beautiful eyes. He does not have to grab their attention through a puzzling dream or nightmare.

God did not hide His plans or purposes from Moses through veiled mysteries. Moses ascended the mountain, entered into the mist of the glory cloud. There Moses communed with and spoke with the Lord for forty days and nights. Moses was given the exact pattern for the Tabernacle. Not many people have been successful in developing such a close, trusted relationship with the Lord that He can speak to them clearly, face to face as a friend. Some are able to boldly behold God while others only know Him through a veil, through His Word, or by what they have heard expressed by others. The call has gone forth for us to see and know Him in all His glorious beauty. Allow God to remove the scales from your eyes and behold the beautiful One.

Job 4:12-17 is an example of the Lord speaking stealthily or in dark sayings. Dark speech comes in a hidden veiled manner. When people experience dark speech, their bodies will discern the presence of spirits in the room. People often become paralyzed with fear. We all have two sets of senses. One is natural and the other one is spiritual; but they both mirror each other. The difference is, our spiritual senses are our real senses that communicate truth and a higher heavenly perception.

Sometimes it is difficult to discern whether it is the natural, spiritual, or both dimensions that are receiving a faint whisper. They receive a soft voice, hear a voice pose a riddle, a parable, or ask a question. The spirit messenger takes on a visionary form or appearance that is difficult to fully discern. It comes to interrupt the silence of the night. The eyes do not fully see the form of the messenger, but see an apparition floating on the wind of the spirit. To understand the mysteries of dark speech, one must seek God for the interpretation.

Now a word was secretly brought to me, and my ear received a whisper of it. In disquieting thoughts from the visions of the night, when deep sleep falls on men, fear came upon me, and trembling, which made all my bones shake. Then a spirit passed before my face; the hair on my body stood up. It stood still, but I could not discern its appearance. A form was before my eyes; there was silence; then I heard a voice saying: "Can a mortal be more righteous than God? Can a man be more pure than his Maker?" (Job 4:12-17 NKJV).

During an episode of dark speech, one's thoughts are disquieted and run rampant. They try to discern the origin of the spirit. Is this presence from God, a demonic source, or a human spirit? The person attempts to decipher what is happening or the reason for the spirit's visit. Their body will sense and respond to the movement of the spirit. The more power the spirit carries, the greater the manifestation will be upon the person's body. Their pulse will quicken. Their hair stands up on their body, goose bumps may rise as a cool or warm breeze blows against their skin. The level of light may increase or diminish in the room. The person may fall into a trance-like state, or their body may tremble or shake.

DREAMS REVEAL GOD'S PLANS

Dreams reveal God's plans, strategies, and purposes to us. God chooses the dream symbols and colors that appear in the parabolic stories of the night. The context and the setting of these symbols represent the procedures God wants us to follow. We must interpret the symbolism in the dream to know the plan of God and His heart's desire toward us.

VISIONS REVEAL GOD'S NATURE

Visions reveal the nature, character, personality, or attributes of God. Visions reveal God's goodness, righteousness, and the judgments of God. He makes Himself real to us through visionary encounters. True visions are infrequent. Visions come to break and remake us. When we are at the crossroads of life, visions change our destiny.

We hear God's voice in a vision. We can commune there with Him face to face. *God reveals who He is to us in a vision.* Visions usually deal with things that will take place in the future. We can be awake when a vision comes, or we will awaken out of sleep during our visionary encounter.

Prayer is always the key to receiving what we need from God. He knows what we need before we ask. But asking and seeking His face is always part of the process. The Lord gave Ezekiel the interpretation of his visions of the four figures, divine glory, and many others when he prayed. The hand of the Lord would come upon Ezekiel, the Spirit would enter him and stand him on his feet, or carry him to a new location, or suspend him in mid-air. He was given heavenly scrolls to eat so the Word of the Lord would dwell within him. Ezekiel was continually surrounded by the spirit realm. Ezekiel is the most mystical character in the Bible. We can learn much by studying the various visions and spiritual encounters he had with heavenly beings and creatures. He saw and experienced more supernatural events than the other prophets.

Daniel was a prophet who moved in internal and external (or open) visions where he beheld spiritual beings with his natural eyes. Daniel learned to look and keep looking while the visions played out their visual message. The enemy's plans were shown but he continued watching until he saw the Lord's plans prevail before him in the visions of the night (Dan. 7:2-14). This is a key for us to remember: stay focused and keep looking beyond the different layered scenes to see everything that is being communicated. In Daniel 8:15-16, the Bible tells us that Gabriel gave Daniel skill, timing, and understanding of the visions he was given. God is not a respecter of persons—if an angel came to assist Daniel, they will also come to assist us in gaining skill to understand the timing of the dreams and visions we experience.

A vision can come as a spectacular dream of the night, called a "vision of the night." The dreamer usually awakes during a vision of the night. Their physical and spiritual senses are engaged and heightened because the encounter feels real or as if it is literally happening. When our senses are involved, the visionary experience is recorded by our body as an actual happening or memorable event that has already taken place. During the vision, there is often a preparation process that takes place to change the dreamer. God never changes; He always remains the same and consistent. So that means, for us to move into a higher realm of revelation or understanding, we are the ones who must repent, change, and increase or develop new skills.

Before God can reveal Himself to us in a vision He must first reveal to us our sinful nature and true desperation. Brokenness comes when we realize our desolate, undone state of existence. We repent, like Isaiah, who cried out in woeful sorrow for God to save and cleanse him. A vision will cause us to stand in awe of God's love, might, and holiness. The reverential fear of the Lord comes upon us during a true vision. We will never forget a true vision of God because it is imprinted upon the tablet of our heart.

The vision realm allows us to see the King, the Lord of Hosts and His glory. We can observe the angels and hear the cries of the seraphim, who abide in the heavenly throne room of God. The Prophet Isaiah told of gazing up from earth to see the gates of heaven open. He saw a vision of the Lord seated upon His throne surrounded by seraphim and glory. He heard an audible voice cry out as smoke filled the temple.

In the year that King Uzziah died, I saw the Lord sitting on a throne, high and lifted up, and the train of His robe filled the temple. Above it stood seraphim; each one had six wings: with two he covered his face, with two he covered his feet, and with two he flew. And one cried to another and said: "Holy, holy, holy is the Lord of hosts; the whole earth is full of His glory!" And the posts of the door were shaken by the voice of him who cried out, and the house was filled with smoke. So I said: "Woe is me, for I am undone! Because I am a man of unclean lips, and I dwell in the midst of a people of unclean lips; for my eyes have seen the King, the Lord of hosts" (Isa. 6:1-5 NKJV).

We know that the prophet Habakkuk moved in the vision realm because in Habakkuk 2:1-3 he offers us some insightful keys to help us interpret visions. Habakkuk, like Daniel, watched and continued to watch until he both heard and saw the Lord's answer. He waited for God's precision to come. Then he wrote the vision out to make it plain. If the vision was delayed, Habakkuk continued to pray until it came to pass.

I will stand my watch and set myself on the rampart, and watch to see what He will say to me, and what I will answer when I am corrected. Then the Lord answered me and said: "Write the vision and make it plain on tablets, that he may run who reads it. For the vision is yet for an appointed time; But at the end it will speak, and it will not lie. Though it tarries, wait for it; because it will surely come, it will not tarry" (NKJV).

Watch, look, and see what God shows in the vision. Then listen to hear what God says. Wait upon the Lord in prayer and meditation until He brings clarity to the revelation. Write down the steps of the vision so it is plain. Read, contemplate, and reflect on the vision. Constantly pray that God will bring the revelation of the vision to pass; keep it before you. Take the necessary steps of action to accomplish the vision. Do not become discouraged or weary if the vision is delayed. Keep the faith and remain hopeful. Do not let unbelief or doubts enter your heart; they will destroy the vision. Sin separates us from God. Sin will delay and then destroy a vision. Be persistent and prayerfully prepare to be successful. God will fulfill the vision in His perfect time. Prayer and following God's word will help fulfill visions. As it says in Proverbs, *"Where there is no* [revelation] *vision, the people perish: but he that keepeth the law, happy is he"* (Prov. 29:18 KJV).

The Lord told Joshua that, in order for him to see God's plans unfold in their fullness, to obtain a spiritual vision or to observe what God was doing, he must do according to all that was written in God's Book of the Law; then he would obtain good success. The more of God's Word we have in our hearts and minds, the more vision God will give us.

> *This Book of the Law shall not depart from your mouth, but you shall meditate* [focus] *in it day and night, that you may observe* [have vision] *to do according to all that is written in it. For then you will make your way prosperous, and then you will have good success* (Josh. 1:8 NKJV).

GOD SPEAKS TO THE UNGODLY

God speaks to every saved and unsaved person on the earth past, present, and future through the realms of dreams. When God speaks to everyone through dreams, it has always amazed me that so few people seek to gain an understanding of their dreams. Kings retained wise men and dream interpreters who constantly stood in their courts to interpret the king's dreams. There are several examples of God giving ungodly kings extrinsic dreams that forewarned of things that would happen in their nations. God came to warn Abimelech, an ungodly, yet truthful king in a dream:

> *But God came to Abimelech in a dream of the night, and said to him, "Behold, you are a dead man because of the*

woman whom you have taken, for she is married." Now Abimelech had not come near her; and he said, "Lord, will You slay a nation, even though blameless? Did he not himself say to me, 'She is my sister'? And she herself said, 'He is my brother.' In the integrity of my heart and the innocence of my hands I have done this." Then God said to him in the dream, "Yes, I know that in the integrity of your heart you have done this, and I also kept you from sinning against Me; therefore I did not let you touch her. Now therefore, restore the man's wife, for he is a prophet, and he will pray for you and you will live. But if you do not restore her, know that you shall surely die, you and all who are yours" (Gen. 20:3-7).

God told Abimelech that he was a dead man if he touched Abraham's wife, Sarah. In God's grace and mercy, He allowed Abimelech to see and hear himself speak in the dream. If you observe yourself in a dream, the dream is about you. Abimelech heard himself dialoguing with God. Abimelech observed himself as he presented his defense and pled his case. Abimelech told God he had been misinformed by Sarah and Abraham. The king had given Abraham a large dowry to purchase Sarah to be his wife in the integrity of his heart. God released revelation knowledge to and through Abimelech to protect him from harm. Abimelech's dream revealed God's desired arrangement. He was shown that he must return Sarah to Abraham to revoke his death sentence. Abraham received his wife, Sarah, back. He then left Gerar with the wealth king Abimelech had given Abraham as a marriage dowry for Sarah, still in his possession.

TALK, LISTEN, AND PRAY

We can talk to and commune directly with God in visions. But in dreams, we are not able to speak to God directly. Dreams allow us to step out of the dream to observe ourselves as a third party having a conversation with God or others. The plans, wisdom, and strategies we see and the conversations we hear must be expressed back to God through prayer upon waking. Prayer will cause good dreams to come true and bad dreams to be destroyed. Dreams in which we dialogue with God enable us to gain wisdom. We are shown the actions to take and the words to pray to deliver us from destruction. Dreams reveal God's plans so we can cooperate with His purposes for our lives.

When the spirit of wisdom enters our heart it brings knowledge that is agreeable with our soul. Discretion becomes like a sentinel posted at our heart's gate. Spiritual understanding watches over us to deliver us from the schemes of enemies. When we gain wisdom she will love and watch over us to help us gain understanding. Wisdom originated on the earth, and understanding joined in to establish the heavens above. God's knowledge released a profound depth deeper than the heights of the sky. As long as we dwell in the presence of wisdom and discretion, our soul will enjoy abundance in life and our foot will not stumble. Wisdom and understanding joins Heaven and earth together by enabling us to accurately process revelation.

ENDNOTES

1. Barbie L. Breathitt, *Dream Encounters: Seeing Your Destiny from God's Perspective,* (DeLand: Holy Fire Publishing, 2009).

Chapter 12

GODLY WISDOM

When we love God, we will love His teachings. When we love His Word, we will talk about it all the time. We will keep His commandments and obey His instructions to gain understanding. His sweet words of wisdom often come to us in visions to enable us to know truth in our inner parts. Wisdom empowers us to be wiser than the ancient mystics, those who are older, our enemies, and also empowers us to confound the teachers of this world.

When wisdom enters the heart, it gives knowledge to the soul. Wisdom will direct our paths away from evil, temptations, and destruction. When our heads lovingly rest on our Beloved's chest, we will walk in the power that His wisdom brings. True godly wisdom will empower us to rule and reign over God's kingdom here on earth as it is in Heaven. But to do this we must become a people whose hearts follow the desires of the Lord.

DAVID

David was a man after God's own heart. David cried out for God to search every part of his life, even his very heart, to discover if there were wicked areas that didn't please God. *"Search me, O God, and know my heart; try me, and know my anxieties; and see if there is any wicked way in me, and lead me in the way everlasting"* (Ps. 139:23-24 NKJV).

David went through many testings and trials. He was rejected and misunderstood by his own family. David had great promise, yet his transformation process required him to run from Saul and hide in caves. God created a godly heart in an obscure shepherd boy who was destined to be the king. Our faith and trust are pleasing to God. Fear, doubt, and unbelief bring God's displeasure because He cannot look upon sin. Trials empty us of ourselves, making more room for the faith and love of God to reside within us. Faith opens and enlightens the eyes of our heart to see hope beyond present limitations.

DAVID TAUGHT SOUND WISDOM

God enjoys it when we place a demand upon His power! He is waiting for us to ask Him for things that are exceedingly, abundantly above our current ability to think or imagine. When we enter the realm of the impossible, we tap into the faith dimensions that God has reserved for those who trust and believe in His mighty power.

King David raised his son Solomon in the royal palace, where he was given sound teaching. Solomon was able to acquire the best instruction, the highest wisdom, and understanding from the wisest of men. David instructed Solomon to prize, love, and seek God's wisdom as she would watch over and guard him all the days of his life. David said, "Do not forget God's teachings and obey God's commandments so you will have a peaceful, long life of prosperity. Be kind and truthful in order to find favor and build a good reputation with God and man" (see Prov. 3:1-4). God is our guardian who stays by our side to protect us from every evil. God guards us when we leave, when we return, He guards us now and forever.

David taught Solomon not to be wise in his own eyes, but to acknowledge and trust in God to direct his paths. David instilled the fear of the Lord in Solomon at an early age so he would not rely on his own understanding, but would shun evil (see Mal. 3:16-18). David shared that the secret of overflow was in honoring the Lord first in everything to gain plenty, wealth, and health.

David delighted to make Solomon adhere to a higher standard of discipline, correction, and reproof than his other sons. David taught Solomon godly principles that directed his life to success. To be blessed, have riches and honor, a man must first find wisdom and understanding in the matters of life. Solomon discovered that wisdom is more valuable than silver, gold, or precious jewels, because nothing in this life can compare to her. Wisdom brings a long, pleasant life of peace along with riches and honor. Wisdom and discretion helps one tap into the Tree of Life, who is Jesus.

The Lord founded the earth through wisdom. He established the heavens with understanding and His profound knowledge broke the inner core of the earth to allow the deep seas to spring forth. Wisdom brings peace, security, and a steady path that keeps one's foot from slipping. When the Lord is one's confidence, their feet will not be caught in a snare. If a person embraces godly wisdom they will lie down and not be afraid, but enjoy sweet sleep. The upright person will enjoy intimacy with the Lord and his dwelling place will be blessed.

David taught his son to always be kind and to do good when it is in your power to help your neighbor. When you love wisdom, she will exalt, honor, and be a garland of grace and beauty that clothes you all the days of your life (see Prov. 3).

David directed Solomon in the ways of wisdom. He led him in upright paths. This is what insured his steps were not impeded. Solomon was able to run without stumbling because he took hold of instruction and didn't let go of understanding. Solomon guarded wisdom because he understood that she is life. When David passed away, Solomon established himself securely over the kingdom. God was with him and greatly exalted him. Solomon communicated his wishes and set up his leaders, commanders, and judges over Israel. Solomon embraced godly wisdom. He is known as the greatest man of wisdom that ever lived. God visited him in a dream and gave him eyes to see God's wisdom in every situation. Wisdom gave Solomon the ability to solve riddles and personal and national problems.

SOLOMON'S DREAM

An example of the Lord appearing in a dream to reveal His plan to a godly king is found in First Kings 3:5-15. Solomon and the assembly had gone to the high place at Gibeon. He sought out the brazen altar, which was at the tent of meeting. There Solomon offered a thousand burnt offerings on it. That night God appeared to Solomon in a dream. Solomon had been preparing for this visitation all of his life. Even when Solomon slept, his subconscious had been trained to know it was important to ask God for wisdom and understanding. The spirits of wisdom and understanding give our spiritual eyes the ability to see in the natural and in the supernatural realms of visitation.

Solomon learned to enter into God's presence with thanksgiving. God allowed Solomon to see himself engaged in a thankful dream dialogue. Solomon thanked God for fulfilling His promises to David and for demonstrating His great loving-kindness toward his reign. Solomon thanked God for making him king in David's place. After Solomon praised God for His loving-kindness and goodness, he asked God for wisdom and the knowledge to rule His people. Here's the record of Solomon's prayer and God's response:

> In Gibeon the Lord appeared to Solomon in a dream at night; and God said, "Ask what you wish Me to give you."

Solomon's Prayer

Then Solomon said, "You have shown great lovingkindness to Your servant David my father, according as he walked before You in truth and righteousness and uprightness of heart toward You; and You have reserved for him this great lovingkindness, that You have given him a son to sit on his throne, as it is this day. Now, O Lord my God, You have made Your servant king in place of my father David, yet I am but a little child; I do not know how to go out or come in. Your servant is in the midst of Your people which You have chosen, a great people who are too many to be numbered or counted. So give Your servant an understanding heart to judge Your people to discern between good and evil. For who is able to judge this great people of Yours?"

God's Answer

It was pleasing in the sight of the Lord that Solomon had asked this thing. God said to him, "Because you have asked this thing and have not asked for yourself long life, nor have asked riches for yourself, nor have you asked for the life of your enemies, but have asked for yourself discernment to understand justice, behold, I have done according to your words. Behold, I have given you a wise and discerning heart, so that there has been no one like you before you, nor shall one like you arise after you. I have also given you what you have not asked, both riches and honor, so that there will not be any among the kings like you all your days. If you walk in My ways, keeping My statutes and commandments, as your father David walked, then I will prolong your days."

Then Solomon awoke, and behold, it was a dream. And he came to Jerusalem and stood before the ark of the covenant of the Lord, and offered burnt offerings and made peace offerings, and made a feast for all his servants (1 Kings 3:5-15).

God gave Solomon what he asked for, along with great riches, honor, and favor. God also let Solomon know that his continued prosperity was contingent upon his obedience; *"If you walk in My ways, keeping My statutes and commandments"* (1 Kings 3:14).

God invited Solomon to watch himself dialogue with Him in the dream realm. In this dimension, Solomon was able to explore his own needs and desires and the scope of his influence to arrive at his destiny. God encouraged Solomon to see who God wanted him to become. God showed Solomon His plans and told him what to ask for in order to find success. God showed him how to step out from under David's limiting shadow to become his own man, to sculpt his personal legacy. We all live in someone's shadow until God comes to set us free. Solomon needed to discover his own identity in order to develop God's plan in life. What kind of a king would he be? How was he going to be known? David was known as a man of blood, a brave warrior, and as a man after God's own heart, a worshipper.

When God visited Solomon in his dream, the previous limited image Solomon had of himself had to expand to hold the greatness of God's vision for him. Solomon had to see himself in a new, broader place. God invited Solomon in his dream to enlarge his abilities and the way he saw himself. God came to overshadow Solomon and to enlarge him. God let Solomon know what he should ask for when he awoke. Solomon was no longer limited by David. In the place of visitation, Solomon received unlimited increase and possibilities. Here Solomon asked God for His divine wisdom to rule His people instead of relying on the earthly wisdom he had received from his father, King David.

Every God-given promise, dream, or vision is either a picture of who God is, what God has purposed for us to see, or what He wants us to be and to become. Visions speak of who we are in the future. Visions reveal who God is, His nature and His character. Dreams reveal God's plans and purposes for us.

God wants us to reinterpret the size and the dimensions of favor and grace that have been released to us. The intimate relationship we have with God enables Him to bring an increased measure of favor and abundance into our lives. God views us as having already reached the largeness of our potential. He proclaims who we are and what we are called to accomplish in life through the dreams He gives. God reveals the gifts He has given and shows us how to develop our skills to accomplish our destiny. Seeing our future clearly enables us to remove the obstacles that attempt to crowd in or hinder our progress or God-given vision. We are called to greatness and success.

When direction comes in a dream, continue to persevere to the best of your ability. It is important to defeat the enemy totally and completely so the enemy does not resurrect to steal destiny. To experience true success, we must be determined to wholeheartedly agree with God's plans and purposes in our lives now and in the future.

God created each one of us with a specific plan in mind. God is very intentional in everything He does. Nothing is left to chance or random happenings. God is objective. He is very industrious. God loves the cosmos and all that is within it completely and perfectly with His whole heart and being. To accomplish what God has called us to accomplish, we must love ourselves and the world in which we live. We must see who we are in Christ and be willing to make the necessary changes to grasp the purpose for which we were born.

God comes to us in dreams to empower Christ to walk in and through us. When we see and understand His plans, we will be successful. God has given us divine promises to enable us to be partakers of His divine nature. As we love and accept ourselves for who we are presently, we will continue to embrace the needed changes that enable us to become who we are destined to be in Christ.

Ask God for something grand or impossible. Ask, seek, knock—and continue asking until you receive it. Asking is the process of establishing a face-to-face, intimate relationship on a daily basis. Enter into the prayer realm of faith. Walk in it continually until you see it manifest in the earthly realm of your reality.

First, we see the impossible in the vision or the dream realm. The more we prayerfully consider all the possibilities, the more it begins to take formation. It is necessary to stretch and challenge the measure of faith and power in our lives. Ask God to increase your measure of wisdom, clarity, and knowledge of His ways. Biblical knowledge deals in the realms of experience, not just written or spoken facts. To know God is to walk in relationship with Him and to encounter Him day and night. The Bible tells us to pray without ceasing because prayer brings us into communion with God.

God intentionally focuses on the promises He has given to enable us to fulfill the passions and the desires of our lives. He promises to fulfill the desires of our hearts when those desires agree with His largeness. Ask largely so that your joy may be full. God has a heart to answer our prayer requests. The more we pray the more we see and develop the needed relationship and communication with God.

Joy is a key that empowers and strengthens us to walk in fullness. Thanksgiving multiplies God's plans and provision. Imagination is another key that will allow God to bring about restoration in our lives. The Lord turned again the captivity of Zion when they dreamed (see Ps. 126:1). Our captivity will turn when we ask largely and passionately and when we dream big! God wants us to obtain favor that is exceedingly and abundantly above all we can ask, think, or imagine (see Eph. 3:20).

We cannot passively wait and expect our dreams to come true. Dreams are God's visual aids that are embossed in our spirits. When the dream manifests, it is time to take some action on our part to bring it about. The dream calls us to take action by coming into agreement with the things God is showing us. Speak to yourself. Confess God's will for your life. Hear yourself agreeing with what you saw happen in the dream. Write the dream down and then implement the necessary changes to accomplish the dream. Then prayerfully begin the training process of letting go of the old and becoming the new person the dream revealed.

Appreciate the new element of favor and grace that has been released. Prayer is a vital part in fulfilling any dream. Pray for divine strategies and wisdom about the proper timing and resources. People are always necessary to fulfill a calling dream. People are the ones who will carry us to our next promotion. It is important to follow the message and the directions God gave in the dream. Look for the hidden keys to unlock doors of destiny.

One must realize that changes take place in our body, spirit, and soul in dreams. After a dream plays out, we are no longer the same person in God's eyes; we have been transformed. We must begin to act, think, and respond differently. We must take responsibility for becoming a new person in Christ; so our identity first changes in our dreams.

To interpret dreams, break the big picture down into smaller, manageable steps and segments. Make the essential connections; develop a passion to embrace what was shown. Gather the needed resources, and acquire the financial arrangements to accomplish the dream. When a dream is given, we are at the beginning phase where we learn to create the A-B-C, 1-2-3 dynamics. When the process is completed, we are at the X-Y-Z phase of walking out our inheritance.

A successful, positive identity always attracts more favor, finances, power, and influence. People and money will follow true leaders. Proclaim who you are to yourself and others. Celebrate a new beginning. Tell every negative or critical person who tries to release distractions, barriers, or complication to move off of your path. Decide you will complete what you start; never turn back or stop halfway through the process. Everyone will go through difficulties in life as God takes us through a metamorphosis. To reveal the beautiful butterfly that emerges from a caterpillar encased in a cocoon takes a long process of change. We learn God's symbolic dream language and interpret life experiences against the backdrop of the Bible.

JOSEPH INTERPRETED DREAMS

The Bible tells us that Joseph was a dreamer and an interpreter of dreams. Genesis 37:5-11 explains two dreams that Joseph told his jealous brothers and Jacob, his father. Jacob understood and pondered the symbolic language of Joseph's dreams. Because the dreams were repeated, it also meant that God was establishing His plans in Joseph's life. (Pharaoh's dream was also repeated in Genesis 41:32; the law of double meaning indicates that the dream is established and will take place soon.) Joseph shared his dream with his brothers, who scoffed at him. "Are you actually going to rule and reign over us?" And His father, Jacob, rebuked him. Joseph said, "Please listen to the dreams I have dreamt." His brothers willfully altered the correct interpretation and timing of the dreams' fulfillment through their jealous cursing and hatred of Joseph. Negative words that are sown bring forth a negative harvest. A dream follows its interpretation. The fulfillment of Joseph's dream was delayed. Biblical history documents the twenty-two year process Joseph went through to make him into a national leader.

Betrayal is often the factor that forces us to align with destiny. After Joseph was betrayed by Potiphar's wife and jailed, he interpreted the dreams of the king's butler and baker while they were in prison (see Gen. 40:5-11). Both men had and remembered a dream on the same night. Keep in mind, when God gives a dream, He speaks with color and clarity and people can recall what is said or shown in the dream. Joseph was able to give each of them a separate, accurate interpretation. He knew details about their professions, personal proximity to the king, and their circumstances from serving them in prison. Through many years of practice, Joseph had learned to interpret his dreams and the dreams of others.

Upon waking from a dream, always pray for clarity and discernment. If the dream is God's plan, the prayer will establish it on a firm foundation and enable it to come forth and be fulfilled at the proper time. If the dream reveals the plan of the enemy, the prayer will erase or thwart its success and stop it from happening. Never agree with a negative dark dream of destruction or its devastation will be empowered in your life. There is power in agreement, both for good and for evil. *"A prudent man sees evil and hides himself, the naive proceed and pay the penalty"* (Prov. 27:12). What we focus on we empower to become larger than life. That is why the Bible tells us to magnify the Lord. Warning dreams, night terrors, and nightmares need to be cancelled through intercession.

GOD SPEAKS TO THE RIGHTEOUS AND UNRIGHTEOUS

God is always speaking but we do not always perceive what He is saying. In our simplicity, we do not understand the many varied ways God communicates. In Judges 7:9-14, God spoke to a farmer of barley named Gideon. He saw himself as the least of the least. He felt inadequate. Gideon was ruled by fear. But, when Gideon learned to fear the word of the Lord, the fear of man disappeared. God told Gideon to go down and conquer the Midian camp with only 300 soldiers. God wanted Gideon to learn not to focus on the enemy. That if God is for you, it does not matter how many are against you, you will win! Gideon placed his trust in the Lord. He quickly obeyed and gained the victory. This was a turning point in Gideon's life. Gideon became the fearless leader that God had destined.

> *Now the same night it came about that the Lord said to him, "Arise, go down against the camp, for I have given it into your hands. But if you are afraid to go down, go with Purah your servant down to the camp, and you will hear what they say; and afterward your hands will be strength- ened that you may go down against the camp." So he went with Purah his servant down to the outposts of the army that was in the camp. Now the Midianites and the Ama- lekites and all the sons of the east were lying in the valley as numerous as locusts; and their camels were without number, as numerous as the sand on the seashore. When Gideon came, behold, a man was relating a dream to his friend. And he said, "Behold, I had a dream; a loaf of barley bread* [represented the people of Israel, who were sustained by bread, and specifically Gideon, who was a the son of a barley farmer] *was tumbling into the camp of Midian, and it came to the tent and struck it so that it fell, and turned it upside down so that the tent lay flat." His friend replied, "This is nothing less than the sword of Gideon the son of Joash, a man of Israel; God has given Midian and all the camp into his hand"* (Judges 7:9-14).

God gave a dream to an unrighteous Midianite soldier. The same night, as Gideon eavesdropped, God gave the interpretation to another pagan soldier. Gideon and his armor bearer listened intently to their enemy's conversation and realized that God had delivered their enemies into their hands through a dream and the words spoken in its interpretation. Words are powerful. Within the words we speak is found the power of life and death, success or failure, creation and destruction, blessing and cursing; so choose the words that release life and create abundance.

Chapter 13

PROPHESY LIFE

Living a prosperous, happy life is easy if you apply God's Word, speak positive faith-filled words of life, and adhere to the words of the prophets. Prophecy is formed by speaking forth the inspired words from the heart of God.

The river of God is getting ready to overflow its banks. The water of God's Spirit is going to rise to such a height and power that people will not be able to control the move of God. They will have to go with God's flow or move far away from it. God has visited before, but now God is going to take up residence in a body. He is the head that moves in great authority. There are many big, influential fish and small, insignificant fish that need to be harvested in the depths of this water. Some fish are undesirables, bottom dwellers, or scavengers. Some fish come from the top realms of society; they are golden because they possess the wealth of this world. They will transfer the wealth of the wicked to finance the kingdom of God. Some fish are big rainbow-colored parrot fish that come from the sea of humanity. Once they are caught and cleaned they will flow in the seven Spirits of God to evangelize others. They will help raise up the schools of the prophets and speak forth the words of the Lord. You can see fishermen, soul-winners, standing united, shoulder to shoulder by the river, throwing their nets and catching many kinds of fish. There are all kinds of animals that live where this river goes.

Churches will become stagnant like swamps and ministries will become like stinky marshes, if they do not bring in, save, and disciple the lost. They are hirelings, deaf and blind shepherds who grow fat and heap monies upon themselves. They will not be refreshed if they refuse to repent and flow with the new move of God. Their salt will become tasteless and never become salty again. It will not preserve the meat of the word, but tickle the ear of the simple. Their salt will be trampled underfoot and thrown out, nothing shall grow there. They have a form of godliness but deny the power thereof; so they will remain stagnant and eventually disappear completely.

But those who step into the river of God's presence will be empowered, refreshed, and revived in the glory. They will discover all kinds of fruit trees growing on both sides of the river banks. The water for the trees comes from the Sanctuary that is alive and powerful. The leaves of these fruit trees will never wither or fall but will be for healing of the nations. When these leaves are sent forth on the wind of the Spirit, they will cure every incurable sickness and disease. The crippled and lame bones shall leap as a heart as God releases creative power that restores twisted bodies. The fruit of these trees will be for food. They will never stop growing. They will produce fruit twelve months a year.

God's anointed word, like a river, is going to flow across this world to water the barren dry places. The windows of Heaven are open and a call has been issued for us to come up higher to see the Valley of Dry Bones from a heavenly perspective. By speaking words of salvation and life, first to ourselves and then to those who are spiritually dead or sleeping, we will raise souls from the dead and draw them to God's eternal life and truth.

> *The hand of the Lord came upon me and brought me out in the Spirit of the Lord, and set me down in the midst of*

the valley; and it was full of bones. Then He caused me to pass by them all around, and behold, there were very many in the open valley; and indeed they were very dry. And He said to me, "Son of man, can these bones live?" So I answered, "O Lord God, You know." Again He said to me, "Prophesy to these bones, and say to them, 'O dry bones, hear the word of the Lord. Thus says the Lord God to these bones: "Surely I will cause breath to enter into you, and you shall live. I will put sinews on you and bring flesh upon you, cover you with skin and put breath in you; and you shall live. Then you shall know that I am the Lord."" So I prophesied as I was commanded; and as I prophesied, there was a noise, and suddenly a rattling; and the bones came together, bone to bone. Indeed, as I looked, the sinews and the flesh came upon them, and the skin covered them over; but there was no breath in them. Also He said to me, "Prophesy to the breath, prophesy, son of man, and say to the breath, 'Thus says the Lord God: "Come from the four winds, O breath, and breathe on these slain, that they may live"" (Ezek. 37:1-9 NKJV).

It is a decisive time for many who are waiting in the valley of decision to enter into God's kingdom of life. Prophesy hope and life to their dry, dead bones. By faith, command God's breath to enter this scattered, disjointed army so that they will rise up and live. God's anointed word will not return void (see Isa. 55:11); simply be obedient to the leading of the Holy Spirit.

THE PROPHET

Prophets function in a vocal gift that operates on a governmental level of anointing; but every individual can be used to exhort and comfort those that walk along the river.

Prophets are called *nabiy'*, which is "an inspired hearer and spokesman, prophet, or communicator on behalf of

God." They often hear audibly and spontaneously, and they activate their gift by faith. *Prophecy* is defined as "God communicating His mind, will, and thoughts to people at the proper time through a vocal expression, demonstration, action, symbol, picture, or miracle." God speaks through prophecy.

Prophets (male) and prophetesses (female) have the ability to hear God's voice. They learn God's ways, counsel, and thoughts through the Holy Spirit releasing the Spirit of revelation. They are able to use various forms such as the spoken or written word or dramatic actions to communicate God's message by allowing the revelation they have received to flow like a river or bubble forth like a fresh spring. As God's spokespeople, prophets can teach the supernatural realms of God beyond the obvious and superficial. They deal with issues of the past, present, and future. The symbols they employ are more literal than the symbolic realm used by the seer.

Prophets usually obtain greater favor than seers because they have developed their communication skills and are easier to understand. Prophets are inspired spokespeople, assigned by the Holy Spirit to speak to people on God's behalf. They are called to strengthen, build up, edify, encourage, exhort, comfort, and love the body of Christ. Prophets understand the governmental workings of the church. Many are service oriented in nature and achieve high levels of leadership.

Everyone who is an actual seer is also able to function as a prophet; but not every prophet is called to operate in the giftings of a seer. *"For the Lord has poured over you a spirit of deep sleep, He has shut your eyes, the prophets; and He has covered your heads, the seers"* (Isa. 29:10). If the prophets are the eyes, the seers are the eyes, ears, mouth, nose, and sensory feeler—the five spiritual senses and the ministry gifts represented by the head. That is why God has to cover the whole head of the seers to keep them from receiving revelation through one of the five senses.

The Bible only mentions the seer twenty-two times; so the seer is rarer than the prophet. It takes so much longer to train and develop the entire seer and the diversity of gifting. But the Bible mentions the prophets 491 times. This is more than any of the other ministry offices. God used the prophets to speak to His people. They wrote twenty-nine of the thirty-nine Old Testament books, and they wrote over 300 messianic prophecies that prepared the way for Jesus. God told and still tells His secrets and mysteries to the prophets and seers. As it says in Acts 3:18, *"But the things which God announced beforehand by the mouth of all the prophets, that His Christ would suffer, He has thus fulfilled."*

The Church is built upon the joint ministries of the apostle (masculine overseer leader) and the prophet (sensitive feminine perceptive intuitive leader). Just as it takes a husband and wife to be fruitful and multiply to bring forth children in a marriage, it takes both the prophet and the apostle for the Church to function properly and be fruitful and multiply. *"Having been built on the foundation of the apostles and prophets, Christ Jesus Himself being the corner stone"* (Eph. 2:20). The New Testament lists the five-fold offices of apostle, prophet, evangelist, pastor, and teacher in Ephesians 4:11. As part of this list, prophets are called to bring the restoration of all things back to the Body of Christ (see Acts 3:21). The prophetic voice is creative and speaks forth life and blessing upon those they contact. God utilizes prophets in order to mature, perfect, equip, activate, and impart to people, while birthing spiritual gifts and talents in them.

We know how important prophesy is because in Revelation 19:10, it says, *"For the testimony of Jesus is the spirit of prophecy."* Many have wrongly believed that, due to the canonization of the Scriptures, there is no need for the office of the prophet or seer in our day. However, prophets are mentioned as a ministry gift by Paul, and the prophets existed in the New Testament after Jesus' resurrection (see 1 Cor. 12:28).

For an indepth study of how God speaks, I suggest reading *Surprised by the Voice of God*, by Jack Deere. [1]

PROPHETIC GALLERY LISTED IN SCRIPTURE

Did you know that Abel was the first prophet mentioned in the Bible?

> *That the blood of all the prophets which was shed from the foundation of the world may be required of this generation, from the blood of Abel to the blood of Zechariah who perished between the altar and the temple. Yes, I say to you, it shall be required of this generation* (Luke 11:50-51 NKJV).

Did you know that Adam uttered the first prophecy in the Bible?

> *And Adam said: "This is now bone of my bones and flesh of my flesh; she shall be called Woman, because she was taken out of Man." Therefore a man shall leave his father and mother and be joined to his wife, and they shall become one flesh* (Gen. 2:23-24 NKJV).

Amos was a herdsman who rebuked Israel for idolatry (see Amos 7:12-15). Daniel was gifted to function as a seer. He was an Israeli captive endowed with great wisdom, understanding, and discernment. He had the ability to interpret dreams, visions, and mysteries. He trained with the Chaldeans and predicted the death of kings and the fall of kingdoms to come and the approximate time when the Messiah would come. Elijah was fed by angels and birds (ravens). He raised the dead, worked eight miracles, and called down fire (see 1 Kings 17). Elisha received a double portion of Elijah's spirit (2 Kings 2:15) and did twice the miracles. Elisha's bones even resurrected a dead man who touched his bones when he was thrown into Elisha's grave (see 2 Kings 13:21). Jude called Enoch a prophet: *"Now Enoch, the seventh from Adam, prophesied about these men also, saying, 'Behold, the Lord comes with ten thousands of His saints'"* (Jude 1:14 NKJV).

Ezekiel functioned as a seer. He was a powerful preacher who was both a priest and a prophet. He received many unusual visions and spiritual experiences. He demonstrated the prophetic in unusual ways. Ezekiel saw an angel with a measuring tape who walked east to measure one-third of a mile. Then the angel told Ezekiel to walk through the ankle deep water. The angel measured another one-third of a mile with his hand. There the water came up to Ezekiel's knees. At another place the water was waist deep. He measured another 1,000 cubits, but there the water was too deep to cross or wade through. It had become a river deep enough to swim in. Then the angel said to Ezekiel, "Human being, did you pay close attention to the things you saw?" (see Ezek. 40:4).

Habakkuk prophesied using a lyrical form; he was possibly a Levitical musician. Haggai proclaimed that Elijah would come before the great and terrible day of the Lord. Haggai prophesied about the rebuilding of God's temple (see Hag. 1:8). Isaiah foretold the coming of the Messiah. He was a very fruitful evangelist of the Old Testament. Jeremiah is known as the "weeping prophet" (see Jer. 31:15-16). He was very compassionate. Joel prophesied the future outpouring of God's Spirit of prophecy, dreams, and visions upon all flesh, which was fulfilled on the day of Pentecost (see Joel 2:28-29).

John the Baptist was filled with the Holy Spirit in the womb. He prepared the way of the Lord and looked for the "Promise of the Father" to be manifested (see Luke 24:49). Jesus declared him the greatest prophet that ever lived (see Luke 1:5-80; Matt. 11:11). Jonah's prophetic ministry brought repentance to the entire nation of Nineveh, and as a result of his word, Nineveh was able to avert God's judgment for decades (see Jonah 3:10). Malachi was a minor prophet. He was a contemporary to Nehemiah and Ezra. He condemned the people for not tithing (see Mal. 3:8-10), and he addressed serious abuses in Jewish life. During the time of Malachi, the priests were lax and degenerate, receiving defective, inferior sacrifices upon the temple altar. Divorce was common, and God's covenant was ignored. This is a very relevant book for our times.

Micah delivered Messianic prophecy to Israel, and spoke a prophetic judgment. Nahum wrote literary masterpieces as a poetic prophet and predicted the destruction of Nineveh (see Nah. 1:1, 2:8). Noah was divinely warned of the destruction of the world by flood so he built the ark by faith:

> *By faith Noah, being divinely warned of things not yet seen, moved with godly fear, prepared an ark for the saving of his household, by which he condemned the world and became heir of the righteousness which is according to faith* (Heb. 11:7).

Obadiah was a minor prophet who predicted the destruction of Edom (see Obad. 1:1,8). Zechariah had visions with biblical symbolism. He was both a priest and a prophet who prophesied the destruction and restoration of Jerusalem (see Zech. 1:16). Zephaniah was a prophet of royal descent; he held a prominent position within the nation (see Zeph. 1:1).

FORMER PROPHETS

The Former Prophets are Joshua, Elijah, Elisha, Moses, Miriam, Deborah, Samuel.

MAJOR PROPHETS

The four Major Prophets are Isaiah, Daniel, Jeremiah, and Ezekiel. Biblical prophets are only categorized as major or minor prophets due to the length of their writings, not because of the quality of their ministries.

TWELVE MINOR PROPHETS

The twelve Minor Prophets are Amos, Habakkuk, Haggai, Hosea, Joel, Jonah, Malachi, Micah, Nahum, Obadiah, Zechariah, and Zephaniah.

Prophets and seers go through much of the same training process to reach spiritual maturity. Mature, seasoned seers and prophets have teachable spirits. They are humbly submitted to authority. They are loyal and faithful to God. They continually exhibit the fruit of the Spirit (see Gal. 5:22). They are loving, patient, kind, longsuffering, disciplined, cooperative, and respectful toward others. They are accountable for their words and ministry. We must extend grace to those who are learning to operate in their spiritual gifts because no one starts out 100% accurate. Part of the process of learning is making mistakes. In life we often learn more from the mistakes we have made. So if we have zero tolerance for mistakes, we will have a clean manger. But if we desire strong ministers that help build and prosper us in life, we must allow them freedom to experiment and grow in the things of the Lord. We all grow through trial and error. Proverbs 14:4 says, *"Where no oxen are, the manger is clean, but much revenue comes by the strength of the ox."*

If God has a heart to move in a certain way, we should join in His work and embrace the problems and difficulties that may arise. Being a spiritual pioneer and blazing a new trail takes courage. Gamaliel wouldn't take sides, saying, "If this thing is of God it will last, if not it will pass" (Acts 5:34-39). Jesus brought the kingdom of God to earth but He was greatly opposed by the religious system of His day. Prophecy and spiritual gifts were in the Old Testament and they are also in the New Testament. Spiritual gifts are for today; they will not pass away until Jesus, that which is perfect, returns to establish His reign here on earth.

Until then we are called to establish His kingdom here on earth. Are you willing to take a stand and identify yourself with those who embrace spiritual gifts? Jesus and His love is the greatest gift ever given. Joseph of Arimathea took a stand, identifying himself with the Lord by asking for Jesus' dead body while the disciples were hiding in fear and defeat (see John 19:38). They were afraid to be associated with Jesus after His crucifixion. They hid in fear of their lives. Jesus fought every battle with the spirit of love. Jesus' love caused His light to shine in darkness. God's perfect love casts out all fear even fear of failure, rejection, or death.

We all face difficulties, problems, and battles that are part of life's training process to bring us into maturity. The size of our battles determines the size of our character. Little bitty battles bring little bitty victories. Great big battles bring us to our knees in total dependence upon the grace and mercy of God. When God opens a large, effectual door, there is always a large adversary standing there to oppose our success. The outcome of our success or failure is up to us and our correct response in the times of trial. Love is always the correct response because love never fails. When we delight in the Lord, He makes our enemies to be at peace with us.

PROPHETS AND SEERS ARE GOD'S FRIENDS

God shares His heart and His plans with the prophets and seers because they delight in the Lord. They have developed an intimate, committed relationship with God. Their trust is in the Lord and His loving-kindness. He gives them the desires of their heart. Intimacy with God will reveal His ways, and our knowledge and understanding will increase. It takes time and effort to establish intimacy. When that total trust is developed, it removes fear. God always has our best in mind, even when He has to correct or punish us. God's discipline is always for the purpose of promotion, redemption, and increase.

The Holy Spirit enables us to have an intimate relationship with God, who is Spirit. The Bible teaches that our spirits only come alive when they are inhabited by the Holy Spirit (see 1 Pet. 3:18). At the point of salvation, through the acceptance of Jesus as our Savior, the light and the only true way to God, we are saved. After salvation we learn to develop our relationship with God. As we are faithful God gives gifts unto men. When we discover the gifts that God has placed within us, we can develop them to a high level of expertise and spiritual precision.

PROPHETS AND SEERS WERE BEFRIENDED BY KINGS

The Bible states that our gifts will make room for us. Those who are gifted and have an excellent spirit will be brought before kings and influential people. Kings sought out and befriended the prophets and seers because their pure hearts enabled them to stand before God. The godly wisdom and gracious counsel kings received from prophets ensured their kingdoms would prosper. Leaders who seek the advice of prophets will find prosperity; goodness and mercy will follow them through life. If we follow the counsel the prophets receive from God, we will prosper, too. Wise people will place their trust in the Lord. God will establish their way. If we put our trust in the Lord and His prophets, we will succeed (see 2 Chron. 20:20).

TODAY'S PROPHETIC MINISTRY

God is establishing prophetic men and women who will once again find their resting place under the shadow of

God's presence. They are people who, through many dedicated years of prayer and intimate fellowship, have developed a strong relationship with the Lord. These mature prophets have allowed God to tune their ears to hear and their mouths to speak a more sure word of prophecy with godly authority and accuracy. The Lord can trust these prophets with His secrets; He can trust them to carry out His counsel.

These prophets and seers are able to discern between the true and the false, the holy and the profane. They recognize the difference between the voice of their own spirits and that of the Holy Spirit. Their lives have been submitted to and consumed by the fire of God. These holy men and women of God only speak as they are moved by the Holy Spirit. They have been severely tested and tried and have not been found wanting. Mature prophets have beheld the goodness, the kindness, and the severity of the Lord, and they do not speak out of their own understanding.

ENDNOTE

1. For a more in-depth discussion of this topic, see Jack Deere, *Surprised by the Voice of God,* (Grand Rapids: Zondervan, 1998).

Chapter 14

TRANCES

What is a trance? A *trance* is a God-induced condition in which ordinary consciousness and the perception of natural circumstances are withheld, and the soul is susceptible only to the vision imparted by God. The body and its five senses are suspended, causing time to seemingly stand still. Unable to freely move the physical body, the mind is under the control of the Holy Spirit. During a trance you may experience a total inability to function in the natural or experience a partial suspended animation. There is a heightened detachment from one's physical surroundings, as in daydreaming or contemplation. In a dream or vision state, when the soul is momentarily transported out of the body and is preoccupied or distracted from present conditions, it is moved into the unseen world. Trances cause a semi- or half-conscious ecstatic state, as between sleeping and waking. It is a daze characterized by the absence of response to all external stimuli.

A *trance* can be defined as a spiritual condition of "going across; or entering into a hypnotic, cataleptic or ecstatic state; detachment from one's physical surroundings, as in contemplation or daydreaming; a dazed state, as between sleeping and waking, a stupor."

Trances occur during times of fervent prayer, intercession, fasting and meditation, reading of the Bible, and ministry times of impartation when hands are laid on individuals.

Characteristics of a trance include, but are not limited to, falling or experiencing a sensation of falling, having a vision or a visitation, experiencing a loss of strength, and seeing the Lord or an angel of the Lord. While experiencing a trance, a person may receive a vision and/or a visitation from the Lord or from His angels. The presence of the supernatural glory realm causes loss of strength. During trances, one often falls prostrate on his or her face.

Trances position us to receive visions from God the same way that sleep positions us to receive dreams of the night. Daniel fell into a trance before the angel of the Lord. When angelic heavenly beings appear, one often falls into a trance state. This is because the human spirit is not used to the higher levels of glory and power in which heavenly beings dwell. Trances take one into open doors and gates of revelation in the heavenly realms of the Spirit. Here believers receive insight into the powerful manifest presence of God as the Holy Spirit reveals things that will take place in the future.

Cornelius is a New Testament example of a man who fell into a trance. Cornelius, a devout God-fearing man, a centurion of the Italian cohort, lived in Caesarea. He gave numerous alms to the Jewish people and prayed to God continually. About the ninth hour (*nine* means "Holy Spirit-perfect moment of completeness where the fullness of blessing is released)[1] of the day, he saw in a clear vision an angel of God come in. The angel summoned Cornelius, who was greatly alarmed. Cornelius fixed his gaze on the angel and inquired, "What is it, Lord?" The angel exhorted Cornelius, "Your prayers and alms have ascended as a memorial before God. Now dispatch servants to Joppa and send for a man named Simon Peter. He is staying with a tanner also named Simon, whose home is by the sea."

The next day, Peter went up on the housetop at about the sixth hour (*six* means "weakness of man, toil wrestling with carnal and spiritual natures, incompleteness of the physical world, humanity")[2] hour to pray. When he became hungry, his thoughts went to food and he desired to eat. While food preparations were being made, Peter fell into a trance on the ground. In this trance state, Peter had a vision. He saw the heavens opened and something like a great sheet came down, lowered by four corners to the ground (*four* means "weakness, four corners of the earth; world, creation; God's creative works; number of seasons, tides, winds and directions; space; completion").[3] There Peter saw all kinds of four-footed animals and crawling reptile creatures of the earth and birds of the air.

A voice came to him, "Get up, Peter, kill and eat!"

But Peter said, "No way, Lord, I have never eaten anything unholy and unclean."

Again a voice came to him a second time (*two* means "separation division, contrast testimony witness and support, blessing or multiplication"),[4] saying, "What God has cleansed, no longer consider unholy." This happened three times (*three* means "Holy Trinity, perfect witness and testimony, union, approval, completeness, fullness, kindness, entirety, Divine perfection, life Spirit, Godhead's mighty acts"),[5] and immediately the object was taken up into the sky.

The men Cornelius had sent to find Peter arrived while he was still greatly perplexed about what the vision might mean. While Peter reflected on the vision, the Spirit said to him, "I have sent three men for you. Go accompany them." When Peter asked the reason for which they had come, they replied,

> *Cornelius, a centurion, a righteous and God-fearing man well spoken of by the entire nation of the Jews, was divinely directed by a holy angel to send for you to come to his house and hear a message from you* (Acts 10:22).

God prepared Peter to take the message of the gospel to the Gentiles through a vision (see Acts 10:1-33). Cornelius and his household were Peter's converts. The realm of vision has the power to change traditions and negative mindsets and to bring us into the fullness of our destiny. Peter continued to grow in his knowledge and the power of the Lord. Eventually, the supernatural realm was so powerful in Peter's life that people were healed and delivered when Peter walked down the street (see Acts 5:15). God's tangible, manifested presence can rest upon us day and night. We carry God's presence within our beings like Peter did when his shadow healed the sick and set the captives free. We are called to change atmospheres.

WINDS OF THE SPIRIT

The believers in the upper room discerned the Holy Spirit falling. They saw the tongues of fire resting on their heads. They were also able to recognize the sound of the wind of the Spirit blowing. However, they did not leave the upper room just because the fire of God fell. They waited until they heard the voice of the Holy Spirit giving them utterance and direction.

> *When the day of Pentecost had come, they were all together in one place. And suddenly there came from heaven a noise like a violent rushing wind, and it filled the whole house where they were sitting. And there appeared to them tongues as of fire distributing themselves, and they rested on each one of them. And they were all filled with the Holy Spirit and began to speak with other tongues, as the Spirit was giving them utterance* (Acts 2:1-4).

Fire reveals the heart. Sometimes God has to place us in His heavenly pipe and smoke us, reducing us to ashes, before we are willing to submit to His plans and purposes in our lives. But this is a good thing because God is able to give us His beauty for our ashes. He makes all things work together for our good when we totally trust Him and surrender every area of our lives to His loving care. God has the best and the highest plans for us.

Have you ever noticed the beautiful colors that dance around in a fireplace? When the tongues of fire came to rest on people's heads at Pentecost, they displayed all the colors of the Spirit. The fire was sent to burn up their carnal reasoning so they would learn to flow by the promise of the Spirit. Our minds are hostile toward God. They are at enmity with Christ and His divine purposes. The renewed heart needs to lead our lives. As the Spirit of God transforms our minds, then our lives will consistently follow and rely on His direction. Our thinking needs to follow the Spirit's lead so the mind will be made new and be trained and transformed to obey the Spirit's desire.

GOD'S HIGHER THOUGHTS

God's higher thoughts, light, and plans enter our soul to imprint spiritual pictures and blueprints on our image center. God-given strategies are able to make us into world-changers by bringing us revelation knowledge from His heart. Meditating on God's higher thoughts will bring us onto the pathway that leads to the dwelling place of God's light. Meditating upon the Lord and His Word will bring us into His spiritual realm where we can receive revelation. Our dreams are also a gateway for God to visit us in the night season. Through our dreams, God separates and dispels the darkness of sin from us and replaces it with the many colors of His glorious light. He rearranges the chaos in our lives to bring it into perfect order to unlock our destiny by painting a brilliant new life story.

DANIEL

Daniel was known as both a man of prayer and a man with great spiritual understanding. He was able to interpret

GATEWAY *to the* SEER REALM

dreams and all mysteries. When Daniel sought to understand his visions, he saw what appeared to be a man. Daniel heard the voice of the man who called out to him. The archangel Gabriel was sent by God. He gave Daniel skill, understanding of the vision, and the futuristic timing of the event. When Gabriel came near, Daniel fell into a trance on the ground. Daniel remained on the ground until Gabriel touched him to restore his strength.

> When I, Daniel, had seen the vision, I sought to under-
> stand it; and behold, standing before me was one who
> looked like a man. And I heard the voice of a man between
> the banks of Ulai, and he called out and said, "Gabriel,
> give this man an understanding of the vision." So he came
> near to where I was standing, and when he came I was
> frightened and fell on my face; but he said to me, "Son of
> man, understand that the vision pertains to the time of
> the end." Now while he was talking with me, I sank into
> a deep sleep with my face to the ground; but he touched
> me and made me stand upright. He said, "Behold, I am
> going to let you know what will occur at the final period
> of the indignation, for it pertains to the appointed time of
> the end" (Dan. 8:15-19).

Daniel was a man of great, godly wisdom. Through regular times of prayer and meditation, he was able to tap into God's revelatory realm. He gained so much futuristic insight that he was told to seal up the revelation until the times of the end (Dan. 9:20-23 is another good example of this).

We live in the end days where concealed mysteries are being revealed. There is an increase in both natural knowledge and in supernatural knowledge of the ways of God that are being discovered. These are the days when people can travel from one end of the earth to the other. But these are also the days when people are able to ascend and descend heavenly ladders of revelation. We are able to go to and fro into the atmosphere of Heaven and receive knowledge from God's Word about the ways of God.

Daniel was commanded to do two things: *"But as for you, Daniel, conceal these words and seal up the book until the end time; many will go back and forth, and knowledge will increase"* (Dan. 12:4). First, Daniel was told to shut up the words (dabar, which is the Hebrew equivalent to rhema). The spiritual application of *dabar* is "a gateway or portal to the storehouse of God's power"[6] (Daleth, Beth, Resh). *Shut up* is *satham*, which means "to conceal vital information or to keep a witness in protective custody, not allowing them to speak or interact with anyone until it is time to give testimony."[7]

Secondly, Daniel was told to seal the book. The word *seal* is *chatham*, which is similar to *satham*. A royal seal was placed on the book so that only those with full authority could open the book to read. The word *book* is *cepher*, which is also used to express the recording of the verbal words of God.[8] Daniel placed a seal on the words of God so only those who had the proper end-time authority and full understanding could open the book. The *end times* gives the idea of *qets*, when time reaches its full limit or a tipping point and revelation is poured out or released.[9]

> *For it pleased the Father that in Him all the fullness should dwell, and by Him to reconcile all things to Himself, by Him, whether things on earth or things in heaven, having made peace through the blood of His cross* (Col. 1:19-20 NKJV).

Everything in heaven and earth, including the past, present and future dwells within the person of Jesus. All the wonders of God the Father are reserved for certain times. There are mysteries that will be revealed at different seasons to various generations as the end draws near. We live in the time of fullness when the cup of revelation is being poured out on this generation.

THE DISCERNING OF SPIRITS

The discerning of spirits is one of the nine supernatural spiritual gifts mentioned in First Corinthians 12. Phenomena that come from God must be discerned spiritually. Our natural carnal self does not understand the deep things of the spirit of God. They appear foolish to our intellect or natural judgment.

The Bible commands us not to believe every spirit, but to test or judge the spirits to know their origin and purposes (see 1 John 4:1-4). Every spirit that is from God will say that Jesus is the Lord who has come in the flesh! If the spirit doesn't confess that Jesus is God, that spirit is a worldly spirit of antichrist. We need to be able to discern the unlimited movements of the Holy Spirit and heavenly spirits. We must learn to discern the human spirit and the demonic kingdom of darkness as well.

DISCERNING THE SOURCES OF REVELATION

The gift of the discerning of spirits comes from God (see 1 Cor. 12:10). The gift of discerning of spirits is the ability to see in the unseen, invisible realm of the spirit. This gift can be developed through learning to understand the symbolic language of dreams and visions. These gifts are for the purpose of discerning, perceiving, seeing, and revealing to bring godly understanding. God reveals things that have formerly taken place and new things that will come to pass in the future.

It is a supernatural capacity to determine the source of the spirit that is operating in or through a person. The discerning of spirits is a supernatural perception or insight into differentiating between good and evil, between human, demonic or divine spiritual activity. It is a spiritual ability to differentiate between the spirits of angels, cherubim, seraphim, host, living creatures, beast, demonic spirits, human spirits, or the Holy Spirit—as well as anointings, operations of gifts, and mantles.

One can develop a more accurate expression of the spiritual discerning of spirits by spending time in God's presence and in meditating upon His Word. To correctly discern the false, one needs to intimately know the true. The Lord is the one true living God, the everlasting King. All His works are true, and His ways are just. He is the true light that enlightens every person (see John 1:9). Jesus is the true and living vine (see John 15:1). When we are in need of truth and wisdom God tells us to ask and He will give us wisdom liberally (see James 1:5).

> *Whoever is wise, let him understand these things; whoever is discerning, let him know them. For the ways of the Lord are right, and the righteous will walk in them, but transgressors will stumble in them* (Hos. 14:9).

Believers have to develop their spiritual senses to rightly discern what source their revelation is coming from. Mature believers learn to discern spirits by training their five natural and spiritual senses through constant practice. As it says in Hebrews: *"But solid food is for the mature, who because of practice have their senses trained to discern good and evil"* (Heb. 5:14). If we do not practice using the gifts of the Spirit, we will never become proficient or skilled at any level. We will remain at an immature, beginners' level in regards to spiritual acuity.

The Holy Spirit is our lifeline to godly wisdom. He connects us to Heaven. He is the source of revelation that connects us to God. The more time we spend with Jesus and the Holy Spirit the more we will be able to discern the differences between their voices as they guide us through every situation of life. There are saints that have gone before us that now reside in Heaven. They are cheering us on. As we lay down the things that hold us back, we will rise above and run a winning race.

> *Therefore, since we have so great a cloud of witnesses surrounding us, let us also lay aside every encumbrance and the sin which so easily entangles us, and let us run with endurance the race that is set before us, fixing our eyes on Jesus, the author and perfecter of faith...* (Heb. 12:1-2).

The discerning of spirits is a spiritual ability to differentiate between the effecting of miracles, gifts of healing, prophecy, distinguishing of spirits, and various kinds of tongues and the interpretations of tongues—including tongues of angels, demonic spirits, and humans. Certain people learn to specialize in one or more of these spiritual gifts. If you are faithful with the gifts God has given you and you ask for more, the Holy Spirit will add more gifts to you.

> *And to another the effecting of miracles, and to another prophecy, and to another the distinguishing of spirits, to another various kinds of tongues, and to another the interpretation of tongues* (1 Cor.12:10).

The discerning of spirits is a gift that is given by and flows out of the Holy Spirit. It is spiritual wisdom and discernment that goes beyond natural human abilities gained through study. This gift gives insights into the unseen spiritual world. Not only will this gift work to help us discern spiritual beings it will also help us discern the human spirit.

THE HUMAN SPIRIT

Jesus discerned the human spirit. *"Jesus saw Nathanael coming to Him, and said of him, "Behold, an Israelite indeed, in whom there is no deceit"* (John 1:47). Similarly, Paul's spirit was grieved when he discerned that the slave girl was not operating her prophetic gift by the Holy Spirit, but was using the spirit of divination instead (see Acts 16:16-18). Peter and John also discerned the evil within Simon the sorcerer's heart:

> *"Therefore repent of this wickedness of yours, and pray the Lord that, if possible, the intention of your heart may be forgiven you. For I see that you are in the gall of bitterness and in the bondage of iniquity." But Simon answered and said, "Pray to the Lord for me yourselves, so that nothing of what you have said may come upon me"* (Acts 8:22-24).

In Acts 5:1-11, Peter discerned that Ananias and his wife Sapphira had lied to the Holy Spirit. They had determined to sell a piece of property, but kept back a portion of the price while saying they had given the whole, and laid it at the apostle's feet. Peter asked why Ananias had conceived this evil deed in his heart. The Bible tells us that out of the abundance of the heart the mouth speaks (see Matt. 12:34). Ananias did not lie to people, but to the Holy Spirit, who sees all and knows all, even the secrets of our hearts. When Ananias heard Peter's words, he fell down, took his last breath, and died.

Sapphira came in about three hours later, but she was unaware of what had happened to her husband. Peter asked her the selling price of the land, and her figures agreed with those of her husband, Ananias. Peter asked her, "Why have you agreed together to put the Spirit of the Lord to the test? Look! The men who buried your husband are here to bury you as well!" Immediately, her life left her, and she fell dead at Peter's feet. As a result, great fear came over the whole church and over all who heard of these things (see Acts 5:1-11).

Paul also discerned that the lame man from Lystra had the faith to be healed.

> *At Lystra a man was sitting who had no strength in his feet, lame from his mother's womb, who had never walked. This man was listening to Paul as he spoke, who, when he*

had fixed his gaze on him and had seen that he had faith to be made well, said with a loud voice, "Stand upright on your feet." And he leaped up and began to walk (Acts 14:8-10).

Paul also knew that Elymas (Bar-Jesus) the magician was a false prophet who was full of deceit and fraud.

When they had gone through the whole island as far as Paphos, they found a magician, a Jewish false prophet whose name was Bar-Jesus, who was with the proconsul, Sergius Paulus, a man of intelligence. This man summoned Barnabas and Saul and sought to hear the word of God. But Elymas the magician (for so his name is translated) was opposing them, seeking to turn the proconsul away from the faith. But Saul, who was also known as Paul, filled with the Holy Spirit, fixed his gaze on him, and said, "You who are full of all deceit and fraud, you son of the devil, you enemy of all righteousness, will you not cease to make crooked the straight ways of the Lord? Now, behold, the hand of the Lord is upon you, and you will be blind and not see the sun for a time." And immediately a mist and a darkness fell upon him, and he went about seeking those who would lead him by the hand. Then the proconsul believed when he saw what had happened, being amazed at the teaching of the Lord (Acts 13:6-12).

The gift of the discerning of spirits gives us knowledge of what spirit we are dealing with. The discerning of spirits also gives us the needed wisdom and power to overcome evil spirits (see 2 Kings 6:15-17, Acts 9:25-26; 16:16-18). The discerning of spirits can come through our five natural senses of touch, taste, sight, sound, and smell. As we sanctify our senses to God, they become spiritually attuned or "golden." Thus, the ability to discern and perceive by the spirit is heightened. *"O taste and see that the Lord is good; how blessed is the man who takes refuge in Him"* (Ps. 34:8).

As we develop this gift, we can actually begin to see God in a new way and we will also taste His sweetness upon our lips like a honey. When we have our living and being in Him, the gift of the discerning of spirits will work as we tune our spirits into the coexisting spiritual realm to hear, see, and feel spiritual presences by the inspiration of the Holy Spirit.

HOW DOES THIS GIFT OPERATE?

The discerning of spirits will operate differently in each individual who is given the gift. God is not a respecter of persons but He has created each one of us as a unique individual. I can offer you guidelines and personal examples; but we can never place God in a box or bring any type of limitation to His creative abilities. God will express Himself in manifold ways. You may receive a slight impression in your spirit similar to receiving a word of knowledge for healing. You may see lights, feel a slight wind, or sense a change in the spiritual atmosphere. You may be able to hear conversations in a dream, vision, or trance. You may feel a presence through pressure or the sensations of wind, warmth, or oil. Or God may choose to speak to or communicate to you in a different way. The important thing is to get to know Him intimately.

SPIRITUAL TASTE

It is possible to taste the goodness of our God. Have you ever felt as if you have been feasting at His banqueting table on fresh hot bread and butter, wine, succulent fruit, sweet milk, or on a juicy, hot steak? The Bible has several examples of people tasting the revelation of God:

> He said to me, "Son of man, feed your stomach and fill your body with this scroll which I am giving you." Then I ate it, and it was sweet as honey in my mouth (Ezek. 3:3).

So I went to the angel, telling him to give me the little book. And he said to me, "Take it and eat it; it will make your stomach bitter, but in your mouth it will be sweet as honey." I took the little book out of the angel's hand and ate it, and in my mouth it was sweet as honey; and when I had eaten it, my stomach was made bitter (Rev. 10:9-10).

Knowledge is comprised of multiple facts, but discernment deals with spiritual perception in the realm of seeing or feeling.

HOLY SPIRIT DOVE

John the Baptist discerned the Holy Spirit dove descending and remaining upon Jesus at the Jordan River. John said, I have seen the Spirit descending and remaining upon Jesus but I didn't recognize Him.

John testified saying, "I have seen the Spirit descending as a dove out of heaven, and He remained upon Him. I did not recognize Him, but He who sent me to baptize in water said to me, 'He upon whom you see the Spirit descending and remaining upon Him, this is the One who baptizes in the Holy Spirit.' I myself have seen, and have testified that this is the Son of God" (John 1:32-34).

Sometimes the Spirit will come in a way we do not recognize; and then sometimes He will come in a way that is familiar to us. We must always keep our spiritual eyes open and our hearts sensitive so we do not miss Him when He comes.

EVIL SPIRITS

Jesus discerned the evil spirits that caused sickness, disease, and infirmities. Jesus knew the duration of people's crippling afflictions and how to set the captives free.

And there was a woman who for eighteen years had had a sickness caused by a spirit; and she was bent double, and could not straighten up at all. When Jesus saw her, He called her over and said to her, "Woman, you are freed from your sickness" (Luke 13:11-12).

The discerning of spirits is used to minister in the following ways:

1. Deliverance from the legions of evil spirits and demons

2. Uncovers and identifies Satan's servants

3. Breaks the power of word curses and demonic assignments

4. Exposes false doctrine and error that would lead people astray

5. Enables us to follow the moving or era of the Holy Spirit and His anointing

6. Unlocks generational curses in families and individuals

The Scripture tells us to test and try the spirits to discern their source. Is the dream, vision, trance, revelation, insight, impression, or information coming from the flesh, self, or soul; or is it coming from God, from His angels, or even from Satan's demons? There is a dark spiritual realm that attempts to deceive. But, there is also the spiritual realm from the Father of Lights who brings forth good things from His heavenly storehouse.

Beloved, do not believe every spirit, but test the spirits to see whether they are from God, because many false prophets have gone out into the world. By this you know the Spirit of God: every spirit that confesses that Jesus Christ has come in the flesh is from God; and every spirit that does not confess Jesus is not from God; this is the spirit of the antichrist, of which you have heard that it is coming, and now it is already in the world. You are from God, little children, and have overcome them; because greater is He who is in you than he who is in the world. They are from the world; therefore they speak as from the world, and the world listens to them. We are from God; he who knows God listens to us; he who is not from God does not listen to us. By this we know the spirit of truth and the spirit of error (1 John 4:1-6).

Through constant practice and by using the gift of discerning of spirits we will be able to know which spirits come speaking on behalf of God and which ones are from Satan, the father of lies.

DIVINATION

Divination is the art of foretelling or predicting the future or releasing occult knowledge by using occult supernatural spirits of darkness. There are evil angels, spirits, demons, devils, principalities, and powers that rule in darkness. The slave girl operating in a spirit of divination in Acts 16:16 is a good example of the disciples discerning an evil presence. Although she was speaking truth, it was coming from a demonic source that vexed Paul's spirit. He discerned the spirit of divination and cast it out, setting the girl free.

> *It happened that as we were going to the place of prayer, a slave-girl having a spirit of divination met us, who was bringing her masters much profit by fortune-telling. Following after Paul and us, she kept crying out, saying, "These men are bond-servants of the Most High God, who are proclaiming to you the way of salvation." She continued doing this for many days. But Paul was greatly annoyed, and turned and said to the spirit, "I command you in the name of Jesus Christ to come out of her!" And it came out at that very moment* (Acts 16:16-18).

The human soul is being saved and renewed by the Word of God. The soul is made up of our minds, our memories, our will to choose, and our emotions. The soul is capable of developing its own thoughts, opinions, and prejudices. If we determine it is necessary to exercise the gift God gave us of free will, it usually indicates we are choosing to sin by walking away from God's perfect will for our lives. *"But examine everything carefully; hold fast to that which is good; abstain from every form of evil* (1 Thess. 5:21-22). When we examine things with the eyes of God's spirit, we will gain spiritual wisdom and insight. We will be able to remove the false and retain the good.

We are told to test the spirits when they present themselves. It is important to take inventory of the way we feel when we encounter the spirit realm. By asking yourself and the spirit being certain questions, you will gain the needed clarity and be able to discern their source.

SIMPLE PRACTICAL TEST

1. Does the revelation point to Jesus Christ as Lord?

2. Does it agree with Scripture?

3. Does it produce life and freedom?

4. Does it edify, comfort, and exhort people to love God and others?

5. Does the minister have good spiritual fruit? (See Gal. 5:23.)

6. Does the word come to pass, and is it accurate?

7. Does the Holy Spirit in you agree with the revelation?

The conclusion, when all has been heard, is: fear God and keep His commandments, because this applies to every person. For God will bring every act to judgment, everything which is hidden, whether it is good or evil (Eccles.12:13-14).

THE SHIP WRECK SURVIVOR

Sometimes when troubles mount and disappointments seem to bury us, we feel like our ship has wrecked on the sandbar of life never to float again. In our agony and despair we do not discern our situation correctly. Often we only see life from the bottom of the barrel. We are not aware that God is busy working behind the scene to turn everything to our good. An example of this type of failing is presented to us in the story of the man who found himself stranded on a deserted island.

He was the only survivor of a tragic shipwreck. He was washed up on the sandy beach of a small, uninhabited island. He prayed feverishly for God to rescue him. Everyday he scanned the horizon for help, but none seemed forthcoming. Exhausted, he eventually managed to build a little hut out of driftwood to protect himself from the scorching sun and the harsh elements. There he stored his few precious possessions. One day, after scavenging for food and water, he arrived home to find his little hut consumed in flames. Black smoke was billowing up to the sky. He felt the worst had happened, and now everything was lost. He was stunned with disbelief, grief, depression, and anger. He cried out, "Why God? Why? How could you do this to me?"

Early the next morning, he was awakened by the sound of a ship approaching the island! It had come to rescue him! Fatigued from a night of crying, he asked his rescuers, "How did you know I was here?"

They replied, "We saw your smoke signal yesterday, and set our course for your island."

THE MORAL OF THIS STORY

It's easy to get discouraged when things are going badly, but we shouldn't lose heart. We can maintain hope because God is at work in our lives. Even in the midst of our pain and suffering, He is worthy of praise. Remember, the next time your dreams seem to be going up in smoke and your little hut is burning to the ground, that it just may be the smoke signal that is needed to summon the grace of God in your life. God's grace and mercy will lead us to walk in His wisdom if we will only ask.

We need godly wisdom and knowledge in order to build the kingdom of God. Proverbs 24:3-4 says, *"Through wisdom a house is built, and by understanding it is established; by knowledge the rooms are filled with all precious and pleasant riches."* Likewise, God speaks through nature in a revelation of wisdom.

> *Go to the ant, you sluggard! Consider her ways and be wise, which, having no captain, overseer or ruler, provides her supplies in the summer, and gathers her food in the harvest. How long will you slumber, O sluggard? When will you rise from your sleep? A little sleep, a little slumber, a little folding of the hands to sleep—so shall your poverty come on you like a prowler, and your need like an armed man* (Prov. 6:6-11 NKJV).

If we will continue to make a forward motion, taking one step at a time, instead of allowing the painful experiences in life to paralyze us, one day we will find that we have left out troubles far behind. We have walked into a new day. We will find we are happy once again and experiencing life at its fullness. Diligent work will pay off.

KEEP YOUR HEART PURE

The Bible tells us to be diligent in keeping our hearts pure and clean, for out of the heart springs the issues of life (see Prov. 4:23). The spirit or breath of humanity comes from God. He is the giver of life; He is the lamp of the Lord. The Holy Spirit is always searching all the inner depths of peoples' hearts. By completely opening our hearts for the fiery lamp of the Lord to search it, we will be healed of our hurtful past and move on into our destiny with triumph and integrity. Men will always disappoint and hurt us, but we can't quit or give up. If we build walls to protect our wounded hearts, we will not only close ourselves off from the ones who have hurt us, but we will also close ourselves off from God, the very One who can heal and deliver us. God's strong name is our help.

> *When Jesus was in Jerusalem at the Passover, during the feast, many believed in His name, observing His signs which He was doing. But Jesus, on His part, was not entrusting Himself to them, for He knew all men, and because He did not need anyone to testify concerning man, for He Himself knew what was in man* (John 2:23-25).

Jesus did not trust Himself to men and neither should we. Some believers have left the Church due to offenses, wounds of rejection, misunderstanding, envy, misused authority, and control. We may not be able to trust man or his actions completely but we can totally trust God. He only has our best interest at heart.

> *So Jesus said to the twelve, "You do not want to go away also, do you?" Simon Peter answered Him, "Lord, to whom shall we go? You have words of eternal life"* (John 6:67-69).

Peter told the Lord, even if he were offended there was nowhere for him to go. He couldn't go back to living as he used to after tasting of the Lord's goodness.

The Spirit of Holiness draws us back to God, turning our hearts toward repentance and restoration.

> *Just see what this godly sorrow produced in you! Such earnestness, such concern to clear yourselves, such indignation, such alarm, such longing to see me, such zeal, and such a readiness to punish wrong. You showed that you have done everything necessary to make things right* (2 Cor. 7:11 NLT).

God reveals the future so we can prayerfully bring our destiny into our now. God is refining us, not as silver, but in the furnace of affliction for His own sake. This will insure that His name is not profaned and that His glory will rest upon us as we operate by the spirit of holiness. God's ordained works will not burn up, but His fire will reveal His glory. No one wants to live their whole life thinking they are pleasing the Lord only to find they lived a life oriented around works and performance instead of a life of faith. The difficulties of life upset and jar us into turning things around. Distresses and pain turn us back to the way of salvation, so we can gain from coming closer to God. When we overcome trials we have no regrets because the distresses drove us to Him. We become more responsible and reverent, more sensitive and alive, more passionately concerned for His heart desires.

Recently I was awakened to God's voice saying, *"Wood, hay, and stubble..."* The Holy Spirit is showing us weak or habitual areas in our lives that we need to repent of or change. God's fire will consume the works we have done in the flesh that were not inspired by God.

> *Now if any man builds on the foundation with gold, silver, precious stones, wood, hay, straw, each man's work will become evident; for the day will show it because it is to be revealed with fire, and the fire itself will test the quality of each man's work. If any man's work which he has built on it remains, he will receive a reward. If any man's work is burned up, he will suffer loss; but he himself will be saved, yet so as through fire* (1 Cor. 3:12-15).

It's time to set fire to the brush, tares, and weeds and to let our passion for Christ burn bright in our hearts. Seek God until His presence rests upon you.

> *Sow with a view to righteousness, reap in accordance with kindness; break up your fallow ground, for it is time to seek the Lord until He comes to rain righteousness on you* (Hos. 10:12).

The ministry of the seer is going to bring a major shift from just hearing the word of God to seeing the plans of God fulfilled in our lives through dreams, trances, and visions. It is easier to remember something we see than words we hear. We are visual beings. It is important to learn the symbolic, metaphoric language of the Spirit. Napoleon Bonaparte said, "You see, the best things come to one while one is asleep." And, "Finally he says: 'Life is a trivial dream, which fades away....'"[10]

Jesus is our example. He caused the blind to see. Spiritual blindness is just as limiting as physical blindness. If we seek God with our whole heart, He will open our blind eyes to see Him in all of His radiant beauty.

> *As He passed by, He saw a man blind from birth. And His disciples asked Him, "Rabbi, who sinned, this man or his parents, that he would be born blind?"*
>
> *Jesus answered, "It was neither that this man sinned, nor his parents; but it was so that the works of God might be displayed in him. We must work the works of Him who sent Me as long as it is day; night is coming when no one can work. While I am in the world, I am the Light of the world."*
>
> *When He had said this, He spat on the ground, and made clay of the spittle, and applied the clay to his eyes, and said to him, "Go, wash in the pool of Siloam" (which is translated, Sent). So he went away and washed, and came back seeing. Therefore the neighbors, and those who previously saw him as a beggar, were saying, "Is not this the one who used to sit and beg?" Others were saying, "This is he," still others were saying, "No, but he is like him."*
>
> *He kept saying, "I am the one."*
>
> *So they were saying to him, "How then were your eyes opened?"*

He answered, "The man who is called Jesus made clay, and anointed my eyes, and said to me, 'Go to Siloam and wash'; so I went away and washed, and I received sight."

They said to him, "Where is He?"

He said, "I do not know" (John 9:1-12).

Now when John, while imprisoned, heard of the works of Christ, he sent word by his disciples and said to Him, "Are You the Expected One, or shall we look for someone else?"

Jesus answered and said to them, "Go and report to John what you hear and see: the blind receive sight and the lame walk, the lepers are cleansed and the deaf hear, the dead are raised up, and the poor have the gospel preached to them. And blessed is he who does not take offense at Me" (Matt. 11:2-6).

When the Lord anoints our eyes to see and opens our ears to hear we will rise up and walk in a new way.

ENDNOTES

1. Breathitt, *Dream Encounter Symbol Book*, Volume I.

2. Ibid.

3. Ibid.

4. Ibid.

5. Ibid.

6. Strong, *Strong's Exhaustive Concordance*, Hebrew #1697.

7. Ibid., Hebrew #5640.

8. Ibid., Hebrew #5612.

9. Ibid., Hebrew #7093.

10. Emil Ludwig, *Napoleon*, Translated by Eden and Cedar Paul, (New York: Boni and Liveright 1926), 39.

Chapter 15

THE ALL-SEEING HEALER

The seer has the gift of the discerning of spirits, coupled with the word of knowledge. This makes them very powerful in the ministry of physical and emotional healing, miracles, and deliverance. Some sicknesses and diseases have spiritual roots that afflict the person. There are also other aliments that are caused by viruses, germs, generational weaknesses, physical neglect, stress, or abuse of the body.

KINGDOM METHODS

Jesus said, *"But seek first the kingdom of God and His righteousness, and all these things shall be added to you"* (Matt. 6:33). We must seek first the kingdom of God. If we seek the kingdom of God with all of our hearts, our hearts will be enlightened to see. When we see with our hearts, we will enter the kingdom. When we enter the kingdom, we will possess the kingdom. When we possess the kingdom, we will inherit the kingdom. When we inherit the kingdom, we will pass it on to others and advance the kingdom of God, which has no end. It is God's good pleasure to give His children the kingdom.

GOD'S KINGDOM MANIFESTS HEALING

God's kingdom is demonstrated through His love, power, rule, character, righteousness, peace, and joy manifested in the Holy Spirit. The kingdom of God does not come through observation, but through spiritual perception with eyes of faith beholding. The kingdom of God is within believers. It is manifested when we move in healing power. The result of the kingdom coming is seen through signs, wonders, and miracles. We can't see the face of an invisible God, but we can see the effects of the unseen realm of the Spirit when it manifests in salvation, healing, and deliverance. Revival comes when we establish God's kingdom in a geographic area. The kingdom of God within us is bigger than the physical world that surrounds us. Change comes from within. If we release the kingdom from within us, the world will be changed.

Jesus used numerous healing methods, depending on what He saw the Father doing and on the person's individual needs. The late healer, John G. Lake said, "Science is the discovery of how God does things." Scientists are now beginning to understand that knowledge and seeing into time—past, present, and future—are only limited by our belief that we cannot. If we are able to exercise faith to see the future, God will reveal it to us.

What do you see in the future? What do you look like in the future? Are you healed and whole? Or do you see yourself sick? If we can believe that we are healed, we will be. We must see ourselves healed in order to be healed. We can perceive the unperceivable, know the unknown, and see the unseen realm of truth. There is a time to "heal" and a time to be healed. As Solomon wrote, *"To everything there is a season, a time for every purpose under heaven"* (Eccles. 3:1 NKJV).

God's Word is spirit and truth. The methods of healing Jesus demonstrated for us can be used in any culture and with all age groups. We must face every giant, any obstacles, and the horrid things we fear, and we must overcome them with faith and truth. God's truth enables us to gain insights into root causes and foresight into seeing, receiving, being, or ministering divine healing. God speaks to and sees us as healed, complete in Him.

Jesus laid hands upon the sick in obedience to the law of contact and transmission. The power of God is resident within the believer. To increase this power, spend time with God. He is the source of all power. To release that power to someone else, simply speak the word. When we speak healing or creative faith-filled words and contact a person with the touch of our hands, the person permits the power of the Holy Spirit to be transmitted. When the Holy Spirit touches someone, they are healed. Handkerchiefs, clothes, and aprons that are prayed over or worn when a person is under a powerful anointing can also receive an anointing. They can act as storage batteries for the Holy Spirit's power to be released when the cloth comes in contact with a person who needs healing.

God did special miracles at the hands of Paul: *"So that even handkerchiefs or aprons were brought from his body to the sick, and the diseases left them and the evil spirits went out of them"* (Acts 19:12). As a result, the Word of God grew mightily and all of Asia came to know God. The Holy Spirit is tangible and transferable, and He will displace sickness and disease, as well as refresh, save, deliver, and heal the mind, will, and emotions. We need to take the shackles off of God. Let Him have a chance to bless humankind without limitations.

ARE ALL HEALED INSTANTLY?

Why aren't all people healed instantly? When the healing virtue is administered through declarative prayer or prophecy, the healing process begins and may only become evident to the person later. There is a process of believing, standing, and fighting for our healing. This process strengthens our faith and spiritual muscles so that the enemy cannot steal the healing.

In Mark 8:23-25, Jesus took a blind man by the hand and led him out of the town because there was so much unbelief in town. When He had spit on his eyes and put His hands upon him, the man saw men as trees walking. It was only after Jesus had laid hands upon him the second time that his sight was fully restored. Healing is by degree and based on two conditions: the degree of healing virtue administered, and the amount or degree of faith that gives action and power to the virtue administered. Faith is the conduit that causes the Word of God to connect and prosper. When the gospel is preached, people reach out and receive the message by faith. They benefit from what they believe as truth in their heart. They receive what they believe and enter into God's rest having received the manifestation of His promises.

> For indeed the gospel was preached to us as well as to them; but the word which they heard did not profit them, not being mixed with faith in those who heard it. For we who have believed do enter that rest, as He has said: "So I swore in My wrath, 'They shall not enter My rest,'" although the works were finished from the foundation of the world (Heb.4:2-3 NKJV).

THE MIRACLE REALM

Healing takes place gradually like a seed that grows when it is planted. Where miracles are instantaneous, they come suddenly, defying the natural realm. Miracles pop into being like a kernel of popcorn. Although when miracles take place we are often surprised; they should be an everyday occurrence when we walk by faith and not by sight. The "miracle realm" should be our natural realm where we live and exist. The spiritual realm places us where communion with God is a normal experience. Miracles are God's native breath. When our minds are renewed by God's Spirit, we are empowered to develop vision far beyond anything we have ever imagined. Oftentimes, we are slow to emphasize the spiritual nature of humanity. People have lost their sense of relationship and responsibility toward God and other people. This has made people self-centered and lawless.

However, we cannot ignore the spiritual side of humanity without magnifying the intellectual and the physical. There must be an expectation of normalizing miracles and developing the spiritual nature of people to a point where we can enjoy fellowship with the Father. We must become "above-minded." Our human intellect is ever conscious of supernatural forces that we cannot understand without the help of the Holy Spirit. We sense the spirit realm and long for its freedom and creative power. Yet we cannot enter into spiritual freedom until we are no longer ruled by self and sin. This is why people must learn to surrender to the Spirit. The Spirit must be enthroned, active, and in control rather than the intellect; the Spirit must rule above both mind and matter.

The object of healing is the abiding health of body, soul, and spirit. The healing of the spirit unites the spirits of people to God forever. The healing of the soul corrects psychic disorder and brings the soul processes into harmony with the mind of God. And the healing of the body completes the union of people with God when the Holy Spirit possesses all.

When God walked with Adam and Eve in the Garden, they communed through the realm of the Spirit. It wasn't until the fall that God had to use His audible voice to communicate with Adam and Eve. Before the fall, God spoke to them spirit to spirit. After the fall, they heard a new sound when God's presence entered the garden. Here's how the Bible records it:

> *They heard the sound of the Lord God walking in the garden in the cool of the day, and the man and his wife hid themselves from the presence of the Lord God among the trees of the garden. Then the Lord God called to the man, and said to him, "Where are you?"*

He said, "I heard the sound of You in the garden, and I was afraid because I was naked; so I hid myself."

And He said, "Who told you that you were naked? Have you eaten from the tree of which I commanded you not to eat?" (Gen. 3:8-11)

Sin causes us to shrink back from God, instead of approaching Him with bold confidence when He comes to commune with us. We see our nakedness instead of His great grace that covers us. Instead of His still small voice bringing comfort, we withdraw in fear. Repentance releases us from the bondage of sin and restores the sound of heaven back to us.

WALKING OUT OUR COMMISSION

God sent Jesus to teach us the ways of the kingdom of God. Each one of us is called to be like Jesus. We can do the same and greater works as Jesus, if we ask in His name.

Truly, truly, I say to you, he who believes in Me, the works that I do, he will do also; and greater works than these he will do; because I go to the Father. "Whatever you ask in My name, that will I do, so that the Father may be glorified in the Son. If you ask Me anything in My name, I will do it" (John 14:12-14).

Binding and loosing the kingdom of God in people's lives is our right because He said in Matthew 16:19,

I will give you the keys of the kingdom of heaven; and whatever you bind on earth shall have been bound in heaven, and whatever you loose on earth shall have been loosed in heaven.

We were born to rule over the world and the kingdom of darkness (*kingdom* means "the King's domain"). Our purpose is to destroy the works of the evil one and execute God's justice through being in Christ and ruling in righteousness. For thousands of years, the Church has been praying the "Lord's Prayer," which expresses this mandate perfectly:

> *In this manner, therefore, pray: Our Father in heaven, hallowed be Your name. Your kingdom come. Your will be done on earth as it is in heaven. Give us this day our daily bread. And forgive us our debts, as we forgive our debtors. And do not lead us into temptation, but deliver us from the evil one. For Yours is the kingdom and the power and the glory forever. Amen* (Matt. 6:9-13 NKJV).

Where there is death, we bring life. Where there is sickness, we release the healing power of the kingdom of light. Light will always dispel darkness. Evil consists of pain, poverty, sickness, brokenness, and failure. We receive the power to overcome evil when we are born again.

> *Now to Him who is able to do far more abundantly beyond all that we ask or think, according to the power that works within us* (Eph. 3:20).

Every person on earth has been given a measure of faith and a measure of God's light. If we ask, God will increase that measure of faith and our light will shine brighter than the noonday sun. God answers our prayers and works through us according to the amount of His power we have received. God is all powerful; but so often we only ask or receive a small portion of His power when He wants to bless us beyond our wildest imaginations. When we are born again the kingdom of God begins to grow in us and it continues to expand throughout all eternity.

> *Jesus answered him, "I assure you, most solemnly I tell you, that unless a person is born again (anew, from above), he cannot ever see (know, be acquainted with, and experience) the kingdom of God"* (John 3:3 AMP).

In First Thessalonians 5:23-24, we see that Jesus died on the cross to give us total life through triune salvation. This means that when the trinity—God the Father, God the Son, and God the Holy Spirit—sent Jesus, the only begotten son, to die for our sins, His death gave us eternal life. We are created in the image of God. Jesus' death saved our whole being. At salvation our spirit is awakened, our soul is renewed or born again, and our body is made whole through His death, burial, and resurrection. Jesus paid the full price so we can have a salvation that is full and complete, lacking nothing.

> *Now may the God of peace Himself sanctify you completely; and may your whole spirit, soul, and body be preserved blameless at the coming of our Lord Jesus Christ* (1 Thess. 5:23 NKJV).

Further, in Matthew 4:17, the Bible says, *"Jesus began to preach and to say, 'Repent, for the kingdom of heaven is at hand.'"* *Repentance* means "to change one's mind, to turn completely around, to do an about-face (i.e., to walk in a new direction and to change the way we think)." Stop thinking and responding in the natural realm, which is temporal and only brings temporary change. We must deal with our hidden sins and our mental strongholds that hold us back from experiencing the power of God working through us.

The abundance of God's kingdom, which He has chosen for us to walk in, is hidden in the glory realm of the supernatural and invisible. To connect with God and receive His provision, we must tap into the spirit realm through faith. He does not hide things from us but He has hidden them for us to find. It is His desire for us to seek to know Him with our whole heart. When we search for God we will find Him.

> *It is the glory of God to conceal a matter, but the glory of kings is to search out a matter. As the heavens for height and the earth for depth, so the heart of kings is unsearchable* (Prov. 25:2-3).

We can know this invisible God who dwells in Heaven and in the heart of man. The unseen world is eternal and is able to change the realm of the natural where we live. How can we be like Jesus? By faith! Our faith in God releases us to transcend the natural and enter into the supernatural realm of God's existence. Faith-filled prayers release God to build His heavenly kingdom in our world.

The Beatitudes tell us how we can see and experience the kingdom of God:

> *Blessed* [happy] *are the poor in spirit, for theirs is the kingdom of heaven. Blessed are those who mourn, for they shall be comforted. Blessed are the meek, for they shall inherit the earth. Blessed are those who hunger and thirst for righteousness, for they shall be filled. Blessed are the merciful, for they shall obtain mercy. Blessed are the pure in heart,* [comes through repentance] *for they shall see God. Blessed are the peacemakers, for they shall be called sons of God. Blessed are those who are persecuted for righteousness' sake, for theirs is the kingdom of heaven* (Matt. 5:3-10 NKJV).

How do we tap into the realm of faith? We believe in the unseen. *"Now faith is the substance of things hoped for, the evidence of things not seen"* (Heb. 11:1 NKJV). Faith thrives in the unseen realm. Faith helps us navigate the corridors and gateways of the supernatural. Through faith, the eyes of our hearts are opened to witness the spectacular visions and beauty of the glory realm. This is what Paul prayed for the believers at Ephesus:

> *That the God of our Lord Jesus Christ, the Father of glory, may give to you the spirit of wisdom and revelation in the knowledge of Him, the eyes of your understanding being enlightened; that you may know what is the hope of His calling, what are the riches of the glory of His inheritance in the saints, and what is the exceeding greatness of His*

power toward us who believe, according to the working of
His mighty power (Eph. 1:17-19 NKJV).

Jesus paid the ultimate price for our salvation at Calvary so every believer would have the ability to see into the invisible through the eyes of our hearts. If we don't see, it's because, due to the teaching of people's traditions, our hearts have been hardened by our sin, doubt, or unbelief. We are in need of His cleansing power once again through repentance. Faith enables us to enter into the storage rooms of Heaven and appropriate the treasures and riches of His knowledge, wisdom, health, and wealth. We are admonished to seek first the kingdom of heaven and His righteousness and all these things shall be added unto us (see Matt. 6:33). If we focus on heavenly things we will draw those things into our life. We have been hidden in God before time began. When Jesus is the focus of our life and our heart's desire, when He comes in His glory to minister, we will also be covered in His glory.

> *Set your mind on things above, not on things on the earth.*
> *For you died, and your life is hidden with Christ in God.*
> *When Christ who is our life appears, then you also will*
> *appear with Him in glory* (Col. 3:2-4 NKJV).

As we learn to worship God in spirit and in truth, the eyes of our hearts will be opened to see what He is doing in the realms of the Spirit. We can hide ourselves in Him, totally surrendered, so that Christ in us may manifest in all His glory. The eyes of the Lord are seeking those who love Him with their whole being. He is seeking those who will worship Him in spirit and in truth. When God finds a true worshipper, He lends His strength to them and shares His secrets.

> *"But the hour is coming, and now is, when the true wor-*
> *shipers will worship the Father in spirit and truth; for the*
> *Father is seeking such to worship Him. God is Spirit, and*
> *those who worship Him must worship in spirit and truth."*

> *The woman said to Him, "I know that Messiah is com-*
> *ing" (who is called Christ). When He comes, He will tell*
> *us all things"* (John 4:23-25 NKJV).

Every time the Christ in us, the hope of glory, comes to the forefront in our lives, He leads us in the realm of the Spirit (see Col. 1:27). David was a man after God's own heart and he declared in Psalm 16:7-8,

> *I will bless the Lord who has given me counsel; My heart*
> *also instructs me in the night seasons. I have set the Lord*
> *always before me; because He is at my right hand I shall*
> *not be moved* (NKJV).

Interestingly, this verse reminds me of the ministry of William Branham. He is considered by many to be the initiator of the healing and charismatic revival that began in 1947. William had an angelic encounter when he was fasting. This same angel would come and stand at his right side to give William specific words of knowledge when he was ministering. William was unique because he knew how to partner with the Lord and with His angels to release healing in a spectacular way. William was a man of great faith.

Faith enables us to operate in the revealed will of God. Faith flows from the hearts of those who know God experientially, not just intellectually, and have seen Him do great exploits through them. The covenant of God empowers us to move in the same anointing and power that Jesus did when He walked the earth. For us to be satisfied with less is to walk in wickedness. Daniel made this clear when he wrote, *"Those who do wickedly against the covenant he shall corrupt with flattery; but the people who know their God shall be strong, and carry out great exploits"* (Dan. 11:32 NKJV).

In this passage, the phrase "know their God" comes from the Hebrew word *yada,* which means "to know (properly, to ascertain by seeing); a variety of senses, (including observation, care, recognition; and causatively, instruction, designation, punishment, etc.).” (Strong's #3045) The opposite of *yada* is unbelief. Unbelief is placing our faith in something other than God. Unbelief takes stock in the inferior natural realms of reality. People of faith are realists who have their beliefs rooted in a superior heavenly reality. The spiritual realm is the real realm of the eternal. The natural realm is the temporal realm that is passing away. Earthly reality does not rule over the unseen spiritual dimension of God.

Sickness weakens the body as sin cripples the soul; it brings death and separation. Satan rules in and through people. We allow him access by giving him permission or by coming into agreement with his lies and plans, thereby empowering him. God does not place sickness on people for the purpose of teaching them a lesson or to help build godly character. Heaven is perfect in every way; there is no sickness or disease in Heaven. God's desire is for it to be *“On earth, as it is in heaven…”* (Matt. 6:10).

We access the glory realm through turning our heart towards God in love. We can also release our faith, worship, prayer, declarations, prophesy, and fasting as an offering to God. We can bring perfection and wholeness into this earthly realm as we demonstrate His powerful kingdom. We move all of Heaven and earth by our faith. Don't allow the soul (comprised of our mind, will, and emotions) to oppose the things of the spirit. The soul does not understand how the spirit works, so the spirit must be dominant when it comes to issues of faith.

Hebrews 11:2-34 describes what people in the Bible obtained by faith:

- By faith, the elders obtained a testimony.

- We understand Enoch walked with God. He was translated, taken away having pleased God.

- Noah became an heir.

- Abraham obeyed and dwelled in a land of promise.

- Sarah received holy laughter and the strength to conceive; she judged God as faithful.

- By faith, Abraham received his covenant promises.

- Isaac blessed his son.

- Joseph gave a prophecy of what would follow his death.

- By faith, Moses' parents preserved him, seeing he was special.

- Moses refused to be aligned with the whole Egyptian system and chose instead to be rejected by people.

- By faith, the walls of Jericho fell.

- Rahab the harlot and her family did not perish.

- By faith, they subdued kingdoms, worked righteousness, obtained promises, shut the mouths of lions, quenched the violence of fire, escaped the edge of the sword, and were made strong and valiant in battle as they turned to fight their enemies.

What is the source of our faith? The Bible tells us in Romans 10:17 that *"faith comes by hearing, and hearing by the word of God"* (NKJV). We need the Holy Spirit to help us interpret Scripture for a "now application" in our lives. What is the opposite of faith? Fear: *F*uture *E*vents *A*ppearing *R*eal. Fear is a substance that draws the realms of darkness to us through the stench of rotten flesh. Fear hardens our hearts, blinds our eyes, and deafens our ears to the voice of Holy Spirit. Fear causes our bodies to react in the same way as if a doctor would inject alcohol into our systems to induce a medical heart attack by paralyzing the muscles. Intimidation and fear rule our hearts when we come into agreement with the enemy's plans of destruction, sickness, and defeat.

God is calling us to reject fear and to live by faith:

I tell you that He will avenge them speedily. Nevertheless, when the Son of Man comes, will He really find faith on the earth? (Luke 18:8 NKJV).

We are told throughout the Bible, "Do not fear!" God wants to give us the kingdom of God while we are still living here on earth. Some say we have to take and advance the kingdom of God by force. But as heirs of God, I believe it is the Father's good pleasure to give us the kingdom. Only those who are thieves break in. Those who are not of God's kingdom or His nature have to fight or force their way into something that does not belong to them. God has given us the keys to the kingdom. As Jesus said, *"Do not fear, little flock, for it is your Father's good pleasure to give you the kingdom"* (Luke 12:32 NKJV).

We must have great faith! Smith Wigglesworth exercised great faith as a lifestyle. He was born in 1859 in Menston, Yorkshire, England and died in 1947 at the age of eighty-seven. He was converted to Christ in a Wesleyan Methodist church at the age of eight. When he received the baptism of the Holy Spirit it radically transformed his life. Although he was a humble, rough plumber, he moved in an evangelistic and the healing anointing with signs wonders and miracles. He even raised several people from the dead including his own wife several times. He was called a twentieth century apostle. Smith was used by God to dramatically shape the early Pentecostal and Holiness movements and brought revival to his generation. People who exercise this type of great faith make us feel inferior or uncomfortable by their supernatural thinking, bold statements, and faith-filled conduct. But their anointing should draw us to them by their light, causing us to want to emulate their kingdom actions.

Conversely, unbelief feels safe because we remove the element of risk and we always get what we expect—nothing! Faith—though unseen—must be assertive, active, and progressively focused on establishing Heaven's kingdom by destroying the works of darkness. Through faith, the eternal realm of God's glorious light collides with the temporal, inferior, natural realm, bringing changes that reflect God's divine plans for individual lives.

Tangible faith that brings God's anointing is not the absence of doubt, but the presence of a belief in a higher, all-knowing power that is able to do the impossible through a simple, ordinary man or woman. To see into the realms of the unseen, we must move in faith, which is connected to love and spiritual authority that is given to us by God. Entering into His rest and submitting our lives through surrendering our will to God enables us to walk in the peace of God that passes our earthly understanding. This peace will enable us to hear and see God, who empowers us to cast out devils and heal the sick.

We tap into faith through abandoning ourselves to total trust in His ways. When we adhere to the Living Word, He moves us into the ability to surrender to Him. Once we have surrendered to the moving of His spirit, we can demonstrate His kingdom. To please God, we must allow the Holy Spirit to train us to move in greater measures of faith. When our faith is truly active and aggressive, we will loudly proclaim our desperate need for experiencing His healing touch, even when others selfishly try to restrain us. Jesus didn't see people by their race, gender, social standing, or wealth. Jesus saw all people through sincere eyes of love.

> *And behold, two blind men sitting by the road, when they heard that Jesus was passing by, cried out, saying, "Have mercy on us, O Lord, Son of David!" Then the multitude warned them that they should be quiet; but they cried out all the more, saying, "Have mercy on us, O Lord, Son of David!" So Jesus stood still and called them, and said, "What do you want Me to do for you?" They said to Him,*

"Lord, that our eyes may be opened." So Jesus had compassion and touched their eyes. And immediately their eyes received sight, and they followed Him (Matt. 20:30-34 NKJV).

Jesus is love. He loves everyone and desires that we are made whole in Him. Just one touch from the Master's hand and we will see Him for the compassionate healer he is.

Aggressive faith is demonstrated in pushing through the crowds unnoticed, believing that if we can just enter His presence, His healing virtue will bring wholeness. The woman with the issue of blood modeled this for us:

Now a certain woman had a flow of blood for twelve years, and had suffered many things from many physicians. She had spent all that she had and was no better, but rather grew worse. When she heard about Jesus, she came behind Him in the crowd and touched His garment. For she said, "If only I may touch His clothes, I shall be made well." Immediately the fountain of her blood was dried up, and she felt in her body that she was healed of the affliction (Mark 5:25-30 NKJV).

Whether faith is demonstrated through bold, aggressive acts or quiet, reflective reverence, it is still violent in the spiritual realms. Faith enters into the unseen world to connect the seen world with the power and presence of God that is available for us to access. Our spiritual eyes of faith see what our Heavenly Father is doing in Heaven, which enables us to release it in the natural realm and establish Heaven on earth.

Prayer releases the reality of Heaven in our lives so we can transform those we touch. His spirit rests upon us in seasons of prayer and thanksgiving, which releases renewal in our spirits so we can be facilitators of revival. Jesus taught us to imitate His intimate relationship with His Father through prayer, fasting, and worship. Intimate sessions of prayer equip us to be stewards of the heavenly treasures placed in us as we abide in Christ here on earth.

Faith that overcomes obstacles breaks through the barriers of doubt and unbelief. God's presence and His healing power increase in an atmosphere of corporate faith, expectancy, and belief. Faith activates the presence of God's peace to rest upon us. God grants us quiet spiritual authority to cast out devils and to heal the sick. God-granted authority is not in the volume of our voices while we preach, heal the sick, or cast out devils, but in the measure of the volume of intimate time we spend gazing into His beautiful face. Bold faith causes blind people to receive heavenly sight as they cry out for justice when the angry crowds tell them their cries are futile. Strong faith causes obscure, isolated, desperate people who have suffered under years of shame to press through multitudes of people, assured that only one touch of His hem will transmit healing and restoration.

We must become violent with our pursuit for healing. The kingdom suffers violence from outside forces when we are sick. The violent take their promises back from the enemy by force (see Matt. 11:12). Grab on and hold onto God's promises. Ground must be taken while we are conquering strongholds of thought from within and vain imaginations that are hurled at us from our accusers. Heaven watches and waits as our prayers of faith enable the release of powerful miracles of healing. How do we access the power that is available in the heavenly realms? How do we cast out fear? We cast out fear by walking in love. Only God's perfect love can remove fear. Remember, God is love, and it's because of His love that Jesus was sent to the world.

> *There is no fear in love; but perfect love casts out fear, because fear involves torment. But he who fears has not been made perfect in love. We love Him because He first loved us* (1 John 4:18-19 NKJV).

He who does not love does not know God, for God is love (1 John 4:8 NKJV).

For God so loved the world that He gave His only begotten Son, that whoever believes in Him should not perish but have everlasting life. For God did not send His Son into the world to condemn the world, but that the world through Him might be saved (John 3:16-17 NKJV).

Jesus' life taught His disciples to experience intimacy with the Father through prayer and worship and to establish His kingdom on the earth. We hold God-given authority as Heaven's ambassadors here on earth (see 2 Cor. 5:20). We serve in kingly and priestly positions (see Rev. 1:6; 5:10). As our heavenly Father reveals His heart to us, the path of our destiny call unfolds before us. Embracing God's will for our lives and His total acceptance of our imperfections enables us to extend love and grace to the unlovable. As God's chosen ambassadors, we must understand the protocol of Heaven to exhibit God's love during our earthly existence.

God exists outside the confines of time and our earthly understanding. Yet He desires for us to bring the knowledge of Him and His heavenly kingdom into this temporal realm. God-given faith enables us to realize the eternal possibilities that Heaven has granted to us.

For as the body without the spirit is dead, so faith without works is dead also (James 2:26 NKJV).

May Christ through your faith [actually] dwell (settle down, abide, make His permanent home) in your hearts! May you be rooted deep in love and founded securely on love... (Eph. 3:17 AMP).

God's desire is for us to live in prosperity. He wants us to enjoy the fulfillment of our hopes and dreams, and to experience the abundance that comes from Him and flows into every expression of our lives. Jesus spent intimate quality time with the Father. Jesus knew His Father's presence, His will, His ways, and His voice. Jesus often withdrew from the multitude of people that would throng around Him just to obtain a glimpse of Father God and receive His loving touch. Jesus knew the importance of being alone basking in His Father's presence.

Let's develop our own intimate relationships with the Father and be filled with the Spirit because faith works by love. It is Jesus' love that caused His compassion.

And now abide faith, hope, love, these three; but the greatest of these is love (1 Cor. 13:13 NKJV).

For [if we are] in Christ Jesus, neither circumcision nor uncircumcision counts for anything, but only faith activated and energized and expressed and working through love (Gal. 5:6 AMP).

Possessing the faith to do a service for someone or believing something but never taking action on that faith means that goal will never happen. We have faith without moving into works, so the faith remains dead. We must have faith that is actively serving others so we can do the same works that Jesus did here on earth. According to Hebrews 11:6, it is impossible to please God without faith. If we develop our faith we should also believe that He will reward us for seeking Him, loving Him, and serving Him.

Recalling unceasingly before our God and Father your work energized by faith and service motivated by love and unwavering hope in [the return of] our Lord Jesus Christ (the Messiah) (1 Thess. 1:3 AMP).

Jesus said to him, "You shall love the Lord your God with all your heart, with all your soul, and with all your mind.' This is the first and great commandment. And the second is like it: 'You shall love your neighbor as yourself.'

On these two commandments hang all the Law and the Prophets" (Matt. 22:37-40 NKJV).

The more we love God the more we will love our neighbor as ourselves. We must learn to walk in love with every part of our being because it is a commandment. Love opens our eyes to see beyond someone's rough exterior. Eyes of love gaze into the inner person to discern that they need a kind word or a smile to encourage them that they can make it one more day.

SEERS' WORD OF KNOWLEDGE GALLERY

Seers' spiritual eyes have been developed to look again and gaze beyond the limitations of the natural realms. Through prayer, their spiritual ears can tune in to hear angelic conversations and the voice of the Holy Spirit as He leads them in the spirit realm. To be successful, like seers, we must develop our skills in ministering in the gifts of the Spirit and in the discerning of spirits. Through constant use and practice, seers are able to discern what spirit is motivating a person's actions or responses.

Our bodies are fearfully and wonderfully made. Since we are made in the image of the Father of Light, our bodies respond to different colors of light. Each of our internal organs is a different color. When we are healthy, they have a bright, beautiful color. When we are sick, even our skin, the body's largest organ, takes on a yellow, toxic, dull color. Doctors recommend getting some fresh air and sunlight when people are depressed. The rays of colored light bring healing. The various internal organs respond favorably and are restored by different colors of light and bright-colored vegetables, fruits, and vitamins.

Open my eyes, that I may see wondrous things *from Your law* (Ps.119:18 NKJV).

*And seeing the multitudes, **He felt compassion for them,** because they were distressed and dispirited like sheep without a shepherd* (Matt. 9:36).

*For we have not an high priest which cannot be **touched with the feeling of our infirmities;** but was in all points tempted like as we are, yet without sin* (Heb. 4:15 KJV).

Every good and perfect gift is from above, coming down from the Father of the heavenly lights, who does not change like shifting shadows (James 1:17 NIV).

See it! Feel it! Hear it! Say it! Smell it! Taste it! Heal it! Do it!

Body: chronic illness; sickness; or disease: *(yellow)*; all sexual sins or abuses; immorality; sensual: *(pink)*; addictions: drugs; sex; food; all excesses: *(red)*.

Soul: resentment; anger; hatred; lust; murder; trauma; death: *(red)*; rebellion: *(orange)*; fear; coward; timid; intellectual pride; deceitful: *(yellow)*; criticism; gossip; envy; greed; pride; arrogance; jealousy; unforgiveness; bitterness; vengeance: *(green)*; rejection; loneliness; isolation; despair; hopelessness; sorrow; grief; depression: *(blue)*; stress; mental disorders: *(indigo)*; emotional disorders: *(violet)*.

Spirit: occult involvement: *(orange)*; witchcraft; curses; inner vows; control; manipulation; Satanism; Freemasonry.

Ankles: *(red)* walk of faith; weak faith made strong; God's power is needed to heal a poor self image.

Arms: *(green)* don't rely on your own might, power and strength but on the help of our Savior and Deliverer; striker; God's eternal, victorious, protecting, ruling, holy; glorious; redeeming; evil arms will be broken.

Back: *(indigo)* past situation; *top of spine:* consistent resistance; pressing; spirit of stubbornness; stress; *spine:* human efforts; relying on one's own strength instead of God; *middle:*

bearing false burdens; tension; *lower back:* anxiety; depression and fear; financial difficulties.

Breast: (indigo) nurture, Shekinah glory; abiding; dwelling; comfort; fruitfulness; fertility; birth; new life; nourish; sustainer; El Shaddai, the Many Breasted One; Almighty God; *sore or painful:* false elementary "milk" teaching; *top:* heartache; disappointment; pain; hurts or wounds.

Buttocks: (yellow; orange) God's goodness; leaving sin behind; procrastination; "sitting on things"; sciatic nerve problems; difficulty in their spiritual walk; past situation that is behind or over; going backwards; backsliding; to place, conceal, or keep out of view.

Calves: spiritual walk; *if painful: (red)* straining, striving, or running in your own strength.

Cheeks: (red) triumph; patience; beauty; embarrassed, shame, or shy; turn the other cheek; trial; personal assault on character; abuse "taking a hit."

Chest: upper: (indigo) fear; timidity; shy; causes thyroid to malfunction; restriction or band indicates: rebellion; heart conditions; spirit of heaviness; respiratory conditions; infirmed spirit.

Collarbone: left: (indigo) lesbian spirit; perversion; unclean; *right:* homosexual spirit; perversion; unclean; deceptive, lying spirit.

Ears: (yellow) heat: ears to hear; ability to intently listen to God's voice; spiritual wisdom; tests the words; spirit of truth; instruction; understanding; deaf and dumb spirit; confusion; *ringing or buzzing:* like a mosquito indicates witchcraft; wrong teaching, *negative words or curses spoken:* off balance; puss; infection; doubt and unbelief.

Elbows: (orange) intercessors on their face before the Lord; humility; relationship; prostrate; out of joint; improper position or alignment in workplace or service.

Eyes: (indigo) spiritual vision, depth or maturity; seers' anointing; heavenly perspective; window to the soul; gate

for light or darkness; sight; insight; foresight; enlightenment of revelation with revealed knowledge, understanding
and nobility; illumination; victorious; spiritually dim; unfit;
unclean; lust; grief; resentment; envy; desire for revenge:
"an eye for an eye"; spirit of stupor; blindness; doubt and
unbelief; willful ignorance; *third eye:* occult involvement; free
masonry; false or eastern religions.

Feet: (red) natural or spiritually humble walk; messenger
of God's gospel; behavior; offense; tread on serpents and
scorpions; ones' heart attitude; immoveable; stubborn; *Pain
in sole:* hindering, crippling spirit; *heat:* preparation to travel
with the gospel of peace.

Fingers: look for or sense a buzzing; pulse; color change;
manifestation of oil; temperature increase or decrease; slight
wind; vibration; or pressure. *Thumb:* apostolic; govern; pray
for those close to you; entrepreneur; touches all five fold
ministries; administrative; delegate; sees the big picture.
Forefinger: prophet; wisdom to point the way; gives godly
direction; encouragement; instruction; conviction; vision;
speaks destiny; guide; pray for those who teach, instruct,
and heal. *Middle finger:* evangelist; reaches out; gathers; pray
for the President, leaders, and administrators. *Ring Finger:*
pastor; guard; married to the body of Christ; manage people; love; compassion; mercy gifts; nurtures; feelings. *Pinky:*
teacher; grounds; relationships with God and others; pray
for yourself; gets in the ear gate; lays foundation line upon
line; detailed; breaks difficult things down into simplicity.

Hands: palms become red, hot, and covered with oil
means healing anointing or gifts of miracles; relationship;
agreement; link; deeds; strength; powerful connection;
action; work both natural or spiritual; possession; labor;
service; idolatry spiritual warfare; pleading; prayer shield;
appraisal; correct; provision; destiny; castigate; correct; *Right
hand:* faith released to move in or develop your God-given
gifts and abilities; promise of allegiance; strength; adoration;

loyal; love; honor; fellowship; resistance. *Left hand:* gifts; talents; anointing or abilities we were born with or received but not mature or activated; judgment. *Palms:* hot; oil; gifts of healing. *(Indigo) fingers or palm:* intercessor with authority. *Base or heel of hand hot:* indicates gifts of help or support ministry. *His brightness was like the light; He had rays flashing from His hand, and there His power was hidden* (Hab. 3:4 NKJV).

Head: *(violet)* process of thinking; contemplation; thoughts; authority; head of an organization; President; Pastor; God's ruler-ship or Christ's headship; employee; power; Lordship; husband; protection; blessing or anointing; prosperity; exaltation; promotion; judgment; trust; band of pressure around *forehead or temple:* mind control, idolatry; witchcraft, oppression, manipulation, *(orange)* a *hooded feeling* or *downcast indicates:* shame; insanity; grief; depression; confusion; mind blinding spirits; vulnerable to attacks; needs to be renewed from carnal reasoning; double-minded; unstable; pride; pornography distorting correct view; intellectual ascent; high-minded.

Heart: *(green)* God's promises written on the tablets of our heart; emotional pain or heartache; stabbing pain indicates witchcraft; or physical condition; enlargement; curse; freemasonry.

Heel: *(red)* God of peace; power to crush or bruise serpent; betrayed by a friend.

Hips: *(orange)* reproduction; fertility; fruitful; loins of truth; mind; support; joint; walking into the deep things; right: false gospel or light; left: false messiah or Jesus.

Kidney: *(orange)* spirit of truth; lack of vitamin C; dehydration; witchcraft curses; not properly discerning spirits or filtering wrong teachings.

Knee: *(orange)* prayerful; humility; service; honor; reverence; obedience; *if painful:* spirit of poverty; faith being attacked; needs spiritual strengthening and encouragement;

idolatry; compliance or conformity; submitting to cruel or wrong words.

Legs: (red) a person's natural or spiritual walk; strength; pillar; support of the body; lame legs: foolish decisions causing destruction.

Mouth: (violet) knowledge and understanding; singing praises; speaking truth; anointed words of deliverance and salvation; holy kiss; evil curses; angry words; gossip; back biting; slander; accusation; homosexual spirit; *Jaw:* rebellion; set in their ways; religious traditions; repetitive prayers; TMJ needs healing.

Neck: (yellow) strength; authority; command; decisive; self-determination or strong will; hardness of heart; *back of neck:* stiff necked; rebellious; stubborn; rigid; domineering; unyielding; tenacious; controlling.

Nose: (indigo) smelling the fragrance of the Lord; lilacs; honey; roses; bread; rain; or demonic presence; if clogged: interference with ability to properly discern spirits, people, or situations; sticking their nose where it doesn't belong; intruding; strife; busybody; nosebleed: conflict; disagreement; confrontation; trouble; clash; spiritual or physical attack; *sinuses:* religious spirit; doubt and unbelief.

Ribs: (blue; indigo) stabbing pains or strain may indicate spirit of grief or word curses; difficulty in relationships or marriage; lack of unity.

Shins: (red) if painful: running or striving in your own strength; harassing spirit; kicked or wounded by a close friend or associate.

Shoulders: (green) government; ruler; strength to carry weight; decisive; bear up; authority; dependable; beauty; temptation; witchcraft; stubborn; rebellious; religious spirit wants to rule; falsely yoked to mans' purposes and not building the kingdom; mantle needs to increase.

Stomach: (yellow) hunger for spiritual things: humility; prostrate intercessor; *sick feeling or nausea:* witchcraft; infirmed or unclean spirit.

Thigh: (red) faith; promise of kindness, loyalty, and faithfulness; strength; the carnal person; flesh; lust; seduction; reproduction; self-will needs to submit to God.

Toes: (red) balanced or in need of balance in life, teachings, or relationships.

Womb: (violet) fruitfulness; multiplication; barrenness; issues of un-forgiveness; bitterness; religious unfruitful spirit.

Wrist: (orange) relationships being blocked by religious or lying spirit of accusation and bitterness; maintaining things in your own strength.

MINISTRY MODEL

When you are ministering healing to someone, use this simple list as a guideline to help you achieve the desired results.

- Ask the person's name and whether the person is born again with Jesus Christ as Savior. Pray for salvation and healing accordingly.

- Speak in love; bring hope, truth, and assurance through Holy Spirit.

- Determine the spiritual door or entry point (fear, rejection, rebellion, or trauma).

- Lead the person in a prayer of repentance; remove unforgiveness and bitterness; renounce and break any sins, occult spirits, curses, or inner vows.

- Use the name of Jesus, His blood, and Scriptures; the Holy Spirit will lead.

- Offer a prayer of thanksgiving; invite Holy Spirit to fill and make the person whole.

The most important thing to remember is: do not get stuck in following some type of set formula. Guidelines are there to help guide, not to form a legalistic boundary. Be sensitive to always submit to and follow the leading of the Holy Spirit. He always knows exactly what each person needs to heal and set them free. Listen, Look, and Learn from Holy Spirit.

The more we practice moving in the healing anointing the more proficient we will become. Jesus knew the thoughts of the scribes when they spoke critical evil words about Jesus within their hearts. Jesus was able to see the faith of those who brought the paralytic to Him lying on a bed. They knew if they could get their friend into the presence of Jesus he would be healed. We are the Jesus the world sees now. If they can get into our presence are they healed? If you said no then keep practicing, and some day that no will be a resounding yes!

> *Seeing their faith, Jesus said to the paralytic, "Take courage, son; your sins are forgiven." And some of the scribes said to themselves, "This fellow blasphemes." And Jesus knowing their thoughts said, "Why are you thinking evil in your hearts? Which is easier, to say, 'Your sins are forgiven,' or to say, 'Get up, and walk'? But so that you may know that the Son of Man has authority on earth to forgive sins"—then He said to the paralytic, "Get up, pick up your bed and go home." And he got up and went home. But when the crowds saw this, they were awestruck, and glorified God, who had given such authority to men* (Matt. 9:2-8).

The presence of God is made known to seers through the spiritual realm of revelation knowledge. Through the constant use of their spiritual senses, seers are able to perceive the manifestation of the spiritual realm in various forms. The giftings of seers allow them to transcend physical boundaries and natural limitations. Their hearts are open to feel the slightest spiritual breath, glance, or touch of the Holy Spirit.

Seers can see visions with their physical eyes opened or closed; it does not matter whether they are awake or asleep. Their eyes can peer into the invisible realms to see with clarity. Seers can discern the presence of beings that are concealed behind the cloak of nothingness. To seers, the invisible spiritual realm is just as tangible and real as the natural physical realm we exist in every day. They are able to coexist in both the natural and spiritual realms. Seers flow back and forth between the two worlds of the natural and the supernatural to bring forth and reveal that which is sealed or concealed in God.

IT IS TIME TO SEE

We need to develop our ability to see eye to eye with God as never before. To achieve our destiny, we need to see it. Part of seeing our future is forgiving, releasing, and forgetting the past offenses so reconciliation can come. *"For the eyes of the Lord move to and fro throughout the earth that He may strongly support those whose heart is completely His"* (2 Chron. 16:9).

When our heart beats with compassion as God's heart for the souls of all men, our eyes will be opened to see God's vision. God will lend His strength to help us accomplish His eternal plan on earth. God is releasing a clear vision so we can carry out His heavenly strategies here on earth.

Seers, prophets, and the watchmen of God are also coming into a new realm of vision and spiritual understanding. God is orchestrating divine encounters. The Almighty is pouring out dreams and visions in an increased measure upon all flesh.

> *And it shall come to pass in the last days, says God, That I will pour out of My Spirit on all flesh; Your sons and*

your daughters shall prophesy, your young men shall see visions, your old men shall dream dreams. And on My menservants and on My maidservants I will pour out My Spirit in those days; and they shall prophesy (Acts 2:17-18 NKJV).

We live in the time when the visitations of angelic messengers of fire are increasing dramatically. Father is lifting us out of the old and transforming us into the supernatural realm of the impossible, into the unfathomable, immeasurable spiritual "breakout." God has released the river of anointing to spring up within our spirits to water the dry and thirsty (see John 7:38).

He [God] has made everything suited to its time; also, He has given human beings an awareness of eternity; but in such a way that they can't fully comprehend, from beginning to end, the things God does (Eccles. 3:11 CJB).

God is eternal, but He created time for us to exist in. Einstein taught that time is relative. Time, like a corkscrew, starts wide at the top and narrows toward the bottom. During the days of Noah, people lived to be hundreds of years old; today the life expectancy has decreased to fewer than one hundred years. During Noah's time, a 650-year-old person would be like a sixty-five-year-old person today. As the corkscrew of time tapers, events and knowledge get closer together until they reach the point where they align or almost become parallel to each other.

When time aligns we can run to and fro or from the starting point to the end point very quickly and with little effort. Events that occur in the timeline of life, such as wars and their rumors, earthquakes, and natural calamity, are all recurring more frequently as they bounce off the point, causing a chain reaction and coming together again through the corridor of time. These are natural signs of time narrowing; and that time is about to reach its zenith or end.

As time draws to an end, knowledge increases. The word for knowledge, *yada*, represents knowledge of God and His ways. Scriptural study allows each generation to build upon the knowledge of God they gleaned from the previous generation. When we reach the tipping point or the fullness of time, the level of godly knowledge and understanding of that which has been "shut up" (*satham*) will be revealed. What an amazing time!

Often seers and prophets enter into the realms of the Spirit where angels present them sacred scrolls to eat and books to read. These sacred heavenly manuscripts represent prophetic promises. When the words on these instruments are consumed, the person who assimilated them becomes the living message. This person is able to move in the power and demonstrate the anointing contained in the promise.

Seers begin to shine with God's glory (see Isa. 60). The scrolls and divine books give seers the key of David that opens doors that no person can shut. There are heavenly revelatory doors (see Rev. 4:1-2) of authority and geographic doors (see Rev. 3:7-8) of opportunity that are now standing open. We are in the time of the double doors. The two-leaved gates have opened and they will not shut (see Isa.45:1 KJV) Mysteries that have been concealed in the heart of God from the beginning of time are revealed. Some revelation the prophets entertain and assimilate is to be shared with others, while God instructs that some details that seers perceive are not to be made common knowledge.

Revelation is birthed to be nurtured and prayed over, so it can come into existence at the fullness of time. The voice of Heaven is speaking a second time for us to prophesy again concerning many peoples and nations and tongues and kings.

Ezekiel is an example of an Old Testament prophet who was given a scroll to eat that contained lamentations, mourning, and woe. Ancient scrolls are also being handed out to the modern-day seers of our time. They will see it, read it, feed on it, and become the message to be distributed to the multitudes.

> *"Now you, son of man, listen to what I am speaking to you; do not be rebellious like that rebellious house. Open your mouth and eat what I am giving you." Then I looked, and behold, a hand was extended to me; and lo, a scroll was in it. When He spread it out before me, it was written on the front and back, and written on it were lamentations, mourning and woe.*
>
> *Then He said to me, "Son of man, eat what you find; eat this scroll, and go, speak to the house of Israel." So I opened my mouth, and He fed me this scroll. He said to me, "Son of man, feed your stomach and fill your body with this scroll which I am giving you." Then I ate it, and it was sweet as honey in my mouth* (Ezek. 2:8–3:3).

Seers are able to observe numerous years and sometimes decades into the future. In Daniel's case, he saw thousands of years into the future to our time and dispensation. We live in the times when the wise will understand the end times.

> *"But you, Daniel, shut up the words, and seal the book until the time of the end; many shall run to and fro, and knowledge shall increase." Then I, Daniel, looked; and there stood two others, one on this riverbank and the other on that riverbank. And one said to the man clothed in linen, who was above the waters of the river, "How long shall the fulfillment of these wonders be?"* (Dan. 12:4-6 NKJV)
>
> *And he said, "Go your way, Daniel, for the words are closed up and sealed till the time of the end. Many shall be purified, made white, and refined, but the wicked shall do wickedly; and none of the wicked shall understand, but the wise shall understand"* (Dan. 12:9-10 NKJV).

SEE, OBEY, SAY, AND PRAY

Daniel knew how to decree, declare, and repent of sin to open spiritual gates into the natural realms. Daniel prayed until he experienced breakthrough empowerment and he was released into the spiritual realms of angels, revelation, wisdom, and knowledge.

> *Now while I was speaking, praying, and confessing my sin and the sin of my people Israel, and presenting my supplication before the Lord my God for the holy mountain of my God, yes, while I was speaking in prayer, the man Gabriel, whom I had seen in the vision at the beginning, being caused to fly swiftly, reached me about the time of the evening offering. And he informed me, and talked with me, and said, "O Daniel, I have now come forth to give you skill to understand"* (Dan. 9:20-22 NKJV).

Prayer is the gateway to the spiritual realm of vision and revelation. Daniel was visited by the angel Gabriel in the vision realm. Gabriel, the archangel over dreams and visions, gave Daniel skill with spiritual understanding. We are learning how to cooperate with the angelic host, who will enable the spiritual eyes of our hearts to be enlightened to see.

> *...While making mention of you in my prayers; that the God of our Lord Jesus Christ, the Father of glory, may give to you a spirit of wisdom and of revelation in the knowledge of Him. I pray that the eyes of your heart may be enlightened, so that you will know what is the hope of His calling, what are the riches of the glory of His inheritance in the saints, and what is the surpassing greatness of His power toward us who believe* (Eph. 1:16-19).

Jesus is the door. Without developing an intimate relationship with Jesus we will not reach the heavenly door (see Rev. 4:1) that is standing open waiting for us. Obedience to God and dying to our own selfish ways will cause us to gain a greater understanding. Living holy lives that are surrendered to the kingdom of God is essential to walk in God's authority and power. We need to press into His presence and pray like never before.

Prayer is simply talking to God and sharing your hopes, dreams, and desires. But prayer is a two-way street. Remain in prayer waiting in His presence to hear Him share His heart, too. God is about relationship, not performance. We need to picture our hands reaching up to God for help. Sometimes my prayer is as simple as "Help me, Lord!" or "Mercy." Without His help, we can do nothing. Sometimes when our hand reaches up to heaven God places a sword in it.

God's Word is like a sword. The Word of God will vindicate us and avenge us of our enemies and those who have falsely accused, hurt, or used us. God has the power to protect us or to bring restoration of everything that has been stolen from us.

Daniel is an example of a godly person who was persecuted by those who were jealous of him. Yet at the end of his trial everything was restored. Daniel found himself in a den of lions. The lions were not able to devour him because God had sent an angelic host to shut the mouths of the lions. Let's learn to bless our enemies with love, grace, and mercy. The angelic host that is with us is more than those who are surrounding us with the intent for malice.

Almost half of the Bible contains recorded examples of angelic visitations, supernatural visionary or dream experiences, rapturous spiritual encounters, and prophetic adventures. The Bible is a book about the supernatural power of God. Over one-third of the Bible deals with dreams, visions, and their interpretations. The amazing gifts God has given seers make them great interpreters of mysteries, dreams, and visions. Daniel and Joseph were brought before the great and mighty kings of their day because they were gifted as dream seers. Seers view the things that transpire in this realm as spiritual reality. Those who are not gifted as seers intently listen to their amazing stories, spiritual wisdom, and explanations.

CLEAR VISION, NEW ORDER

Samuel Saw the Lord

Desperate prayer caused the Lord to remember Hannah as He turned His eyes toward her. His glance healed her barrenness. The Lord gave her more than a son in Samuel; He gave her a prophet and seer for a nation. When the seer Samuel was being trained to minister to the Lord by the priest Eli, the word of the Lord and visions were infrequent. Eli was not only losing his natural eyesight, but he was also spiritually dull. Eli was asleep on his watch and in his place of service.

However, one night all of that changed. The boy Samuel had lain down in the temple near the ark of God's presence, but he was still very aware. While the boy Samuel rested under God's shadow by the ark, the Lord called him by name. Samuel jumped up and ran to Eli saying, "Here I am, you called?" Eli stirred and replied, "I did not call you, go back to sleep." Slumber seemed to be Eli's answer to everything. When Samuel was resting by the ark, again the Lord called him, "Samuel!" The little boy responded to the voice and ran to Eli saying, "Here I am, for you called me." Again Eli responded, "I did not call you, my son, lie down again." At this point in Samuel's training, he had never heard the voice of the Lord nor had the Lord's image been revealed to him. So for a third time the Lord called to Samuel. And Samuel arose a third time and ran to Eli, who finally caught on. The almost blind priest finally discerned that the Lord was calling Samuel unto Himself. Samuel's training process as a seer had begun (see 1 Sam. 3:2-14).

Samuel told Eli, "Here I am!" but when the Lord appeared he said, "Speak Lord, your servant listens." Other great men of God have said those same words to the Lord. Abraham, Moses, Jacob, Samuel, and Ananias all said to God, "Here I am!" I believe it is time for each one of us to cry out to God, "Here I am! Prepare and purify me. Open my eyes to see and my ears to hear the still small voice, and then send me to the nations."

When Samuel came onto the scene, the old priestly order's sight had grown dull in the natural and in the spiritual. Eli was fat and lazy from all his slumbering, and hearing the word of the Lord was rare. The people lacked vision. It was time for God to awaken a new order. God chose to call, visit, and train Samuel in the new way. God gives a clear vision when He releases a new order. The older generation, though passing away, is able to pass on their keys of wisdom to the next generation. Eli instructed Samuel to lie down in his place of rest while he waited for the coming of the Lord. Samuel acknowledged the visible presence of the Lord when He came and declared, "I have ears to hear His voice."

When the Church learns to acknowledge the presence of the Lord when He comes and to yield to the moving of His Spirit, Christ will once again open the doors of Heaven and come visit us. For so long, Jesus has been outside the majority of His Church, knocking on the door and waiting for us to hear Him and give Him an invitation to come in. When we repent for closing Him out with our programs and learn to hear the call of His voice and see Him in the realm of vision, we will be able to follow His lead.

The Lord said to Samuel, "Behold, I am about to do a thing in Israel at which both ears of everyone who hears it will tingle. In that day I will carry out against Eli all that I have spoken concerning his house, from beginning to end. For I have told him that I am about to judge his house forever for the iniquity which he knew, because his sons brought a curse on themselves and he did not rebuke them. Therefore I have sworn to the house of Eli that the iniquity of Eli's house shall not be atoned for by sacrifice or offering forever" (1 Sam. 3:11-14).

Eli knew his sons were doing evil, yet he refused to correct them. Samuel was afraid to tell Eli the vision, so he stayed in bed until morning. But Eli found Samuel carrying out his temple duties and asked him, "What did the Lord say to you last night? Tell me everything! Do not suppress or soften one word! Tell me exactly what the Lord said to you!" So Samuel recited the Lord's words and explained the vision he saw to Eli. Samuel held nothing back from him. Eli said, "The Lord is God. Let him do whatever He thinks is the best." (See 1 Samuel 3:15-18).

God told Eli that he was going to judge his house for the iniquity, but he still didn't repent or correct his sons. But in the new order, Samuel both heard and saw the plans of God, and his ears tingled as God brought balance and clarity to His temple. Samuel grew up in the presence of the Lord. The Lord enabled Samuel to maintain a flawless prophetic record. None of the words Samuel received from God failed. Everyone in Israel, from Dan in the north to Beersheba in the south, recognized that Samuel was a seer—a true prophet of God. God continued to show up and reveal Himself to Samuel through word and vision at Shiloh.

We must have a fresh seal of the Holy Spirit resting upon us, with Jesus as the center of our lives. We must give God first place in our lives by honoring Him with our time. As we wait on the Lord, we become strong and our hearts take courage. Intercession and prayer enable Christ to be formed within us. *"My children, with whom I am again in labor until Christ is formed in you"* (Gal. 4:19). Intercession will release revelation and prophetic insights on how and what to pray to get answers.

> *"While You extend Your hand to heal, and signs and wonders take place through the name of Your holy servant Jesus." And when they had prayed, the place where they had gathered together was shaken, and they were all filled with the Holy Spirit and began to speak the word of God with boldness* (Acts 4:30-31).

God wants us to lie down and get into our places of rest so He can visit us in the realm of the Spirit. It is time to wait in God's presence until we are filled with His power. We are always trying to be human *doings* when God has called us to be human *beings*. God wants us to rest under the shadow of the ark of His presence so we can hear His voice, experience His intimate love, and see a vision of our future. As we enter into rest, He will find His resting place in us. God inhabits the praises of His people. We need to connect to and release the kingdom of God that is within each of us. Love for God and humankind will demonstrate the reality of His glorious presence and the truth of the gospel of the kingdom.

Following the death of Samuel, the company of prophets seemed to disappear until the times of Elijah and Elisha, when they reappeared with the title, "sons of the prophets." Gifts and callings can be passed down the bloodline. It is part of our godly heritage. The prophetic and seer gifts take the longest time to train because they are so specialized and must be precisely accurate. It takes all five of the ministry gifts in operation to develop a well-rounded person.

The New Testament engages the fivefold ministry gifts to equip the body of Christ for spiritual service.

> *And He gave some as apostles, and some as prophets [seers], and some as evangelists, and some as pastors and teachers, for the equipping of the saints for the work*

of service, to the building up of the body of Christ (Eph. 4:11-12).

The restoration of the seer's ministry is so important to the success of the church. The seer is the one who brings the vision of what God desires to the body of Christ. The original Hebrew of Proverbs 29:18 says that "Where there is no one that sees as God sees, the people perish. Where there is no revelation, the people cast off restraint; but happy is he who keeps the law."

PRAYER OF THE SEER

My prayer for you, dear one, is that after reading 'Gateway to the Seers Realm,' your eyes will be open to see Jesus, the most Beautiful One! I pray that you will constantly commune with Jesus, Holy Spirit, and heavenly Father in prayer. That your prayers will bring you into the vision realm, to see the answers to your prayers materializing before they physically manifest. Believe and know you are able to open a spiritual gateway for the answers to your prayers to come into existence.

Let's pray:

> *Dear Lord, please remove the veils that blind the eyes and give us insight with understanding and the Spirit of wisdom with revelation knowledge. Let us become seers of Your glory. Anoint our eyes to see and ears to hear what the Holy Spirit is saying. Through the Spirit of revelation, give us access to the heart, mind, and words of Christ where all the mysteries of the kingdom of Heaven are hidden. Immerse us in the Spirit of love.*

I pray that a hunger will develop in your spirit to look beyond the natural barriers of time, space, and seasons into the endless expanse of eternity. That your spiritual eyes will see things ahead of time through visitations and angelic messengers and in dreams, visions, and trances. See into the depths of the Spirit and gaze beyond "nothingness" to give evidence of God.

I pray that you will gaze into the ancient books of mysteries and read heavenly scrolls to receive strong visual revelation and physical impressions and see prophetic words. I pray that you will become accustomed to hearing both the audible and the internal voice of the Lord. I pray that you become the history maker God has called you to be as He reveals His story through you.

I pray your heart will record the eternal pictures of Heaven issued by the Father—His wisdom, counsel, and actions so that Christ is openly revealed, for you to see Him—and in seeing Him, you'll become like Him, manifesting the power and glory of His divine reality. Then demonstrate God's presence in your everyday life so that people can see His loving-kindness manifested through the miraculous touch that heals and delivers.

May God's will bring a heightened sensitivity to your spiritual perceptions by aligning them with your natural senses so you may carry a double portion of the essential silence of God's perspective into spiritual perception.

I pray God will mirror Himself in and through you as He steps into your reality, out of the invisible realm and into the natural realm, transforming you into a supernatural person who reflects His revelation to the outside world from the dimensions of God Himself. May you see Him, perceive Him, and know what He is doing so that you can release His will to the world.

Take a small sliver of His magnificence and begin to demonstrate God's presence and reveal the greatness of God. Prepare a holy place of spiritual authority for God to rest His head. The Christ within you will rise up in powerful demonstration, and then just follow His lead. Mirror God's actions to give them entrance or manifestation; to establish God's presence on earth. Communicate the extensions of God's limitlessness and His expansion. You are called to bring into existence what God brings out, displays, or reveals through the breathing ebb and flow of the Spirit's creativity.

Remember the three things that will lead you toward spiritual maturity, completeness, and consummation: steady trust in God, an unswerving hope, and an extravagant love—but most of all love!

May God richly bless you on your journey of spiritual discovery.

Love, Barbie

CONCLUDING CHALLENGE

There are those in the world who are searching for more than what they see with their natural eyes. Many in the church are also endeavoring to establish the kingdom of God on earth. People who feel deeply about the natural and supernatural realm are seeking more. The common everyday experience of sleep, work, eat, sleep repetitive routine has become unbearable. God did not mean for us to travel through this experience called life without a viable companion to accompany us along our way.

To those who have established their faith in Jesus and accepted the doctrines and teaching of the church, salvation has come. Jesus is the cornerstone on which the kingdom of God has been established. To turn your heart and life over to Jesus is the single most important step toward establishing your eternal security in what is a sure and imminent future. To refuse to turn to Christ is to banish yourself from the only possible hope you have in accomplishing anything significant with your actions and routine.

If you are one of those who endeavor to accomplish something of lasting value, then you feel the unction inside to make things happen. You are not satisfied with the status quo. The outcome of one day must exceed that of previous days, and this axiom is not related to output of a factory or the bottom line of a company. To see past the normal experience of wind, rain, earth, and sky and to pierce the veil which clouds our eyes and keeps us satiated with the atoms and string particles holding life together becomes mundane. God has more for your life. The experience of His presence and power lingers just beyond the veil for those who are open and seeking this experience.

Prophets of old experienced the heightened awareness of God's Spirit resting on their spirit. The eyes of the spirit opened to the glory of God's understanding and the moments of normalcy passed into supernatural phenomena to establish God's Word in this earth. Scripture was birthed and the natural ears of man heard the voice of God on the vocal cords of mere man as the ecstatic prophet proclaimed the future.

God called all of Israel to ascend the mountain with Moses. Israel chose to let Moses go alone as a representative. Moses wished that all would prophecy. God is once again speaking into the common ordinary lives of men and women to establish His kingdom in a greater capacity, in a firmer manner. Be moved by His wish for man to step up to the next level. Do not be satisfied with letting another take your place with God. Build and cultivate your personal relationship with God. Allow the Spirit to speak to your heart and to show you His plan for your life and those who do not see. Become what God intended from the beginning. Allow your spirit to be awakened to the wind of the Spirit. Take to your breast the firm ground of the spirit realm, the one in which we will live after this life is over. Breach the veil and peer into the things God will show you.

Bring back to this side the things of God. Reveal His character and love for man. Tell of His goodness and mercy. Expose the exploits of our God to a world that is seeking more than the mundane existence of a life filled with time constraints and busyness. Become busy with the things of the seer realm. See the spirit realm and understand that the other side is closer and more obtainable than previously believed. Allow your spirit man to believe. Allow the Spirit of God to dwell in you and to call you to the next level. Be satisfied with the relationship Creator God intended for you from the beginning and look upon the things He extends to you to see.

Steven A. Breathitt, M.Div.
www.BreathoftheSpiritMinistries.com
www.MyOnar.com
www.DreamsDecoder.com

ABOUT BARBIE BREATHITT

Barbie Breathitt is an author, ordained minister, dedicated educator, and respected teacher of the supernatural manifestations of God. Barbie's dynamic teaching skills, intelligence, and quick wit make her a favorite with audiences everywhere. Through prayer, intense study, and years of research, Barbie has become a recognized leader in dream interpretation and has equipped people in more than forty nations around the globe. Her prophetic gifting and deep spiritual insights have helped thousands of people understand the supernatural ways in which God speaks to us today.

Barbie has degrees from Abraham Baldwin Agricultural College and Southeastern University. Barbie earned her Ph.D. from Tabernacle Bible College and Seminary.

Through her tangible faith and motivating life stories, Barbie challenges her audience to dive into the deeper mysteries of God with the anticipation of hearing His voice more clearly. Her desire is to span denominational boundaries with a clear message of hope, signs, and wonders, and the demonstration of the power of God.

Her passion in life is to help individuals pursue their understanding of a loving God and to find their highest purpose and destiny in Him.

Barbie's latest literary work is *Dream Encounters: Seeing Your Destiny from God's Perspective.* Barbie's other writings include *Dream Encounters Manual,* with accompanying CD set; *Revelatory Encounters Manual,* with accompanying CD set; *Healing Encounters Manual,* with CD set; and *Angelic Encounters Manual,* with CD set. These are part of a vast library of over one hundred messages recorded on CD and in MP3 digital format. She considers her greatest writing achievement to be the *Dream Encounter Symbols* booklets: Volume One, Volume Two, and Volume Three. These writings, as well as Barbie's *Dream Sexology* book, contain thousands of dream symbols garnered from the Bible and ancient Hebrew interpretations. These resources and other products are available from any of her Websites:

www.BarbieBreathitt.com

www.BarbieBreathittEnterprises.com

www.MyOnar.com

OTHER PRODUCTS FROM BARBIE BREATHITT

BOOKS

Action Symbols Vol. IV

Dream Encounters – Seeing your DESTINY from GOD'S Perspective

Dream Sexology

Dream Encounters Symbols Vol. I

Dream Encounters Symbols Vol. II

Dream Encounters Symbols Vol. III

When Will My Dreams Come True?

Hearing and Understanding the Voice of God

So You Want to Change the World

Dream Encounters Anointing Oil

DVDs

Colorado Dream Encounters

NJ Dream Encounters Workshop DVD

CD SETS AND MANUALS

Revelatory Encounters

Dream Encounters

Angelic Encounters

Healing Encounters

IN THE RIGHT HANDS, THIS BOOK WILL CHANGE LIVES!

Most of the people who need this message will not be looking for this book. To change their lives, you need to put a copy of this book in their hands.

> *But others (seeds) fell into good ground, and brought forth fruit, some a hundred-fold, some sixty-fold, some thirty-fold* (Matthew 13:8).

Our ministry is constantly seeking methods to find the good ground, the people who need this anointed message to change their lives. Will you help us reach these people?

> *Remember this—a farmer who plants only a few seeds will get a small crop. But the one who plants generously will get a generous crop* (2 Corinthians 9:6).

EXTEND THIS MINISTRY BY SOWING
3 BOOKS, 5 BOOKS, 10 BOOKS, OR MORE TODAY,
AND BECOME A LIFE CHANGER!

Thank you,

Don Nori Sr., Founder
Destiny Image
Since 1982